CHICAGO LECTURES
IN LAW
AND ECONOMICS

General Editor

ERIC A. POSNER

Professor of Law
University of Chicago

New York, New York
FOUNDATION PRESS
2000

Cover photo: Michelle Litvin, 1999

COPYRIGHT © 2000 By FOUNDATION PRESS
11 Penn Plaza, Tenth Floor
New York, NY 10001
Phone Toll Free 1–877–888–1330
Fax (212) 760–8705
fdpress.com

Printed in the United States of America

ISBN 1–56662–972–1

 TEXT IS PRINTED ON 10% POST
CONSUMER RECYCLED PAPER

PREFACE

These essays are based on the Coase Lectures presented by faculty of the University of Chicago Law School. The lectures, named for Nobel Laureate and emeritus Chicago faculty member Ronald Coase, are designed to introduce law students, and especially first-year law students, to the economic analysis of law. The lectures thus assume no prior knowledge of economics, and only the most minimal knowledge of the law. The essays collected in this book are for the most part faithful reproductions of the lectures, with citations added for the purpose of guiding the reader to the relevant literature.

Readers should feel free to pick and choose among the essays; they are in no particular order. A first-year student might want to read the essays on contracts (Baird, Craswell, and (partly) Eric Posner); torts (Levmore); and property (Epstein). But the essays that are nominally connected to second- and third-year courses—corporations and financial regulation (Miller), intellectual property (Dam) —are also accessible. The other essays are more generally methodological. Richard Posner's essay is a general introduction to law and economics. Sykes' is on the use of statistical studies in law. Picker's is about game theory. Ramseyer's is about public choice; or, the relationship, one might say, between the economic analysis of politics and the economic analysis of law. Sunstein's essay takes a critical approach to law and economics, highlights the anomalies of rational choice theory, and suggests that much behavior is better explained using psychology and sociology. Eric Posner's essay looks at one popular model used in law and economics—the agency model —and shows how it can be applied to many different areas of the law.

The reader should keep in mind a number of limitations. The essays are informal rather than rigorous, suggestive rather than definitive, general rather than narrow. They are meant to get minds thinking about the law in new ways, not to provide answers. Readers who want to know more should consult the articles and books that are cited in the notes.

*

TABLE OF CONTENTS

                                                                    Page

PREFACE iii

1. Alan O. Sykes, An Introduction to Regression Analysis 1

2. Randal C. Picker, An Introduction to Game Theory and the
    Law.. 29

3. Douglas G. Baird, The Law and Economics of Contract
    Damages... 49

4. Geoffrey P. Miller, Das Kapital: Solvency Regulation of the
    American Business Enterprise 65

5. Richard Craswell, Freedom of Contract 82

6. J. Mark Ramseyer, Public Choice 101

7. Kenneth W. Dam, Intellectual Property in an Age of Soft-
    ware and Biotechnology.. 113

8. Cass R. Sunstein, Social Norms and Social Roles 135

9. Richard A. Epstein, Transaction Costs and Property Rights:
    Or Do Good Fences Make Good Neighbors?.......................... 175

10. Richard A. Posner, Values and Consequences: An Introduc-
    tion to Economic Analysis of Law 189

11. Saul Levmore, Carrots and Torts.. 203

12. Eric A. Posner, Agency Models in Law and Economics 225

Index 245

*

CHICAGO LECTURES
IN LAW
AND ECONOMICS

*

1. An Introduction to Regression Analysis

Alan O. Sykes*

Regression analysis is a statistical tool for the investigation of relationships between variables. Usually, the investigator seeks to ascertain the causal effect of one variable upon another—the effect of a price increase upon demand, for example, or the effect of changes in the money supply upon the inflation rate. To explore such issues, the investigator assembles data on the underlying variables of interest and employs regression to estimate the quantitative effect of the causal variables upon the variable that they influence. The investigator also typically assesses the "statistical significance" of the estimated relationships, that is, the degree of confidence that the true relationship is close to the estimated relationship.

Regression techniques have long been central to the field of economic statistics ("econometrics"). Increasingly, they have become important to lawyers and legal policy makers as well. Regression has been offered as evidence of liability under Title VII of the Civil Rights Act of 1964,[1] as evidence of racial bias in death penalty litigation,[2] as evidence of damages in contract actions,[3] as evidence of violations under the Voting Rights Act,[4] and as evidence of damages in antitrust litigation,[5] among other things.

In this lecture, I will provide an overview of the most basic techniques of regression analysis—how they work, what they assume, and how they may go awry when key assumptions do not hold. To make the discussion concrete, I will employ a series of illustrations involving a hypothetical analysis of the factors that determine individual earnings in the labor market. The illustrations will have a legal flavor in the latter part of the lecture, where they will incorporate the possibility that earnings are impermissibly

* Frank and Bernice Greenberg Professor of Law, University of Chicago, The Law School. I thank Donna Cote for helpful research assistance. This lecture was delivered in October 1993.

1. See, e.g, Bazemore v. Friday, 478 U.S. 385, 400 (1986).

2. See, e.g., McCleskey v. Kemp, 481 U.S. 279 (1987).

3. See, e.g., Cotton Brothers Baking Co. v. Industrial Risk Insurers, 941 F.2d 380 (5th Cir.1991).

4. See, e.g., Thornburgh v. Gingles, 478 U.S. 30 (1986).

5. See, e.g., Spray–Rite Service Corp. v. Monsanto Co., 684 F.2d 1226 (7th Cir.1982).

influenced by gender in violation of the Federal Civil Rights laws.[6] I wish to emphasize that this lecture is *not* a comprehensive treatment of the statistical issues that arise in Title VII litigation, and that the discussion of gender discrimination is simply a vehicle for expositing certain aspects of regression technique.[7] Also, of necessity, there are many important topics that I omit, including simultaneous equation models and generalized least squares. The lecture is limited to the assumptions, mechanics, and common difficulties with single equation, ordinary least squares regression.

I. What is Regression?

For purposes of illustration, suppose that we wish to identify and quantify the factors that determine earnings in the labor market. A moment's reflection suggests a myriad of factors that are associated with variations in earnings across individuals—occupation, age, experience, educational attainment, motivation, and innate ability come to mind, perhaps along with factors such as race and gender that can be of particular concern to lawyers. For the time being, let us restrict attention to a single factor—call it education. Regression analysis with a single explanatory variable is termed "simple regression."

A. Simple Regression

In reality, any effort to quantify the effects of education upon earnings without careful attention to the other factors that affect earnings could create serious statistical difficulties (termed "omitted variables bias"), which I will discuss later. But for now let us assume away this problem. We also assume, again quite unrealistically, that "education" can be measured by a single attribute—years of schooling. We thus suppress the fact that a given number of years in school may represent widely varying academic programs.

At the outset of any regression study, one formulates some hypothesis about the relationship between the variables of interest, here, education and earnings. Common experience suggests that better educated people tend to make more money. It further suggests that the causal relation likely runs from education to earnings rather than the other way around. Thus, the tentative hypothesis is

6. See 42 U.S.C. § 2000e–2 (1988), as amended.

7. Readers with a particular interest in the use of regression analysis under Title VII may wish to consult the following references: Campbell, Regression Analysis in Title VII Cases—Minimum Standards, Comparable Worth, and Other Issues Where Law and Statistics Meet, 36 Stan. L. Rev. 1299 (1984); Connolly, The Use of Multiple Regression Analysis in Employment Discrimination Cases, 10 Population Res. & Pol. Rev. 117 (1991); Finkelstein, The Judicial Reception of Multiple Regression Studies in Race and Sex Discrimination Cases, 80 Colum. L. Rev. 737 (1980); Fisher, Multiple Regression in Legal Proceedings, 80 Colum. L. Rev. 702 (1980), at 721–25.

that higher levels of education cause higher levels of earnings, other things being equal.

To investigate this hypothesis, imagine that we gather data on education and earnings for various individuals. Let E denote education in years of schooling for each individual, and let I denote that individual's earnings in dollars per year. We can plot this information for all of the individuals in the sample using a two-dimensional diagram, conventionally termed a "scatter" diagram. Each point in the diagram represents an individual in the sample.

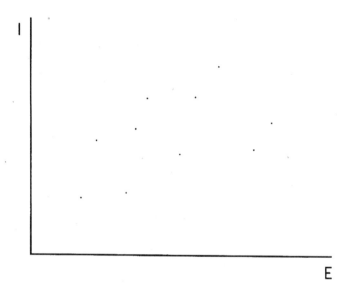

The diagram indeed suggests that higher values of E tend to yield higher values of I, but the relationship is not perfect—it seems that knowledge of E does not suffice for an entirely accurate prediction about I.[8] We can then deduce either that the effect of education upon earnings differs across individuals, or that factors other than education influence earnings. Regression analysis ordinarily embraces the latter explanation.[9] Thus, pending discussion below of omitted variables bias, we now hypothesize that earnings

---

8. More accurately, what one can infer from the diagram is that if knowledge of E suffices to predict I perfectly, then the relationship between them is a complex, non-linear one. Because we have no reason to suspect that the true relationship between education and earnings is of that form, we are more likely to conclude that knowledge of E is not sufficient to predict I perfectly.

9. The alternative possibility—that the relationship between two variables is unstable—is termed the problem of "random" or "time varying" coefficients and raises somewhat different statistical problems. See, e.g., H. Theil, Principles of Econometrics 622–27 (1971); G. Chow, Econometrics 320–47 (1983).

for each individual are determined by education and by an aggregation of omitted factors that we term "noise."

To refine the hypothesis further, it is natural to suppose that people in the labor force with no education nevertheless make some positive amount of money, and that education increases earnings above this baseline. We might also suppose that education affects income in a "linear" fashion—that is, each additional year of schooling adds the same amount to income. This linearity assumption is common in regression studies but is by no means essential to the application of the technique, and can be relaxed where the investigator has reason to suppose a priori that the relationship in question is nonlinear.[10]

Then, the hypothesized relationship between education and earnings may be written:

$$I = \alpha + \beta E + \epsilon$$

where:

α = a constant amount (what one earns with zero education)

β = the effect in dollars of an additional year of schooling on income, hypothesized to be positive

ϵ = the "noise" term reflecting other factors that influence earnings

The variable I is termed the "dependent" or "endogenous" variable, E is termed the "independent," "explanatory" or "exogenous" variable, α is the "constant term," and β the "coefficient" of the variable E.

Remember what is observable and what is not. The data set contains observations for I and E. The noise component ϵ is comprised of factors that are unobservable, or at least unobserved. The parameters α and β are also unobservable. The task of regression analysis is to produce an *estimate* of these two parameters, based upon the information contained in the data set and, as shall be seen, upon some assumptions about the characteristics of ϵ.

To understand how the parameter estimates are generated, note that if we *ignore* the noise term ϵ, the equation above for the relationship between I and E is the equation for a line—a line with an "intercept" of α on the vertical axis and a "slope" of β.

---

10. When nonlinear relationships are thought to be present, investigators typically seek to model them in a manner that permits them to be transformed into linear relationships. For example, the relationship $y = cx^a$ can be transformed into the linear relationship $\log y = \log c + \alpha * \log x$. The reason for modeling nonlinear relationships in this fashion is that the estimation of linear regressions is much simpler, and their statistical properties are better known. Where this approach is infeasible, however, techniques for the estimation of nonlinear regressions have been developed. See, e.g., G. Chow, supra note 9, at 220–51.

Returning to the scatter diagram, the hypothesized relationship thus implies that somewhere on the diagram may be found a line with the equation $I = \alpha + \beta E$. The task of estimating α and β is equivalent to the task of estimating where this line is located.

What is the best estimate regarding the location of this line? The answer depends in part upon what we think about the nature of the noise term ϵ. If we believed that ϵ was usually a large negative number, for example, we would want to pick a line lying above most or all of our data points—the logic is that if ϵ is negative, the true value of I (which we observe), given by $I = \alpha + \beta E + \epsilon$, will be less than the value of I on the line $I = \alpha + \beta E$. Likewise, if we believed that ϵ was systematically positive, a line lying below the majority of data points would be appropriate. Regression analysis assumes, however, that the noise term has no such systematic property, but is on average equal to zero—I will make the assumptions about the noise term more precise in a moment. The assumption that the noise term is usually zero suggests an estimate of the line that lies roughly in the midst of the data, some observations below and some observations above.

But there are many such lines, and it remains to pick one line in particular. Regression analysis does so by embracing a criterion that relates to the *estimated* noise term or "error" for each observation. To be precise, define the "estimated error" for each observation as the vertical distance between the value of I along the estimated line $I = \alpha + \beta E$ (generated by plugging the actual value of E into this equation) and the true value of I for the same observation. Superimposing a candidate line on the scatter diagram, the estimated errors for each observation may be seen as follows:

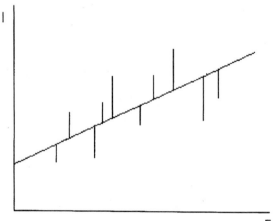

With each possible line that might be superimposed upon the data, a different set of estimated errors will result. Regression analysis then chooses among all possible lines by selecting the one for which the sum of the squares of the estimated errors is at a minimum. This is termed the minimum sum of squared errors (minimum SSE) criterion The intercept of the line chosen by this criterion provides the estimate of α, and its slope provides the estimate of β.

It is hardly obvious why we should choose our line using the minimum SSE criterion. We can readily imagine other criteria that might be utilized (minimizing the sum of errors in absolute value,[11] for example). One virtue of the SSE criterion is that it is very easy to employ computationally. When one expresses the sum of squared errors mathematically and employs calculus techniques to ascertain the values of α and β that minimize it, one obtains expressions for α and β that are easy to evaluate with a computer using only the observed values of E and I in the data sample.[12] But computational convenience is not the only virtue of the minimum SSE criterion—it also has some attractive statistical properties under plausible assumptions about the noise term. These properties will be discussed in a moment, after we introduce the concept of multiple regression.

B.   Multiple Regression

Plainly, earnings are affected by a variety of factors in addition to years of schooling, factors that were aggregated into the noise term in the simple regression model above. "Multiple regression" is a technique that allows additional factors to enter the analysis separately so that the effect of each can be estimated. It is valuable for quantifying the impact of various simultaneous influences upon a single dependent variable. Further, because of omitted variables bias with simple regression, multiple regression is often essential even when the investigator is only interested in the effects of one of the independent variables.

---

11. It should be obvious why simply minimizing the sum of errors is not an attractive criterion—large negative errors and large positive errors would cancel out, so that this sum could be at a minimum even though the line selected fitted the data very poorly.

12. The derivation is so simple in the case of one explanatory variable that it is worth including here: Continuing with the example in the text, we imagine that we have data on education and earnings for a number of individuals, let them be indexed by j. The actual value of earnings for the jth individual is I_j, and its estimated value on any line with intercept α and slope β will be $\alpha + \beta E_j$. The estimated error is thus $I_j - \alpha - \beta E_j$. The sum of squared errors is then $\Sigma_j(I_j - \alpha - \beta E_j)^2$. Minimizing this sum with respect to α requires that its derivative with respect to α be set to zero, or $-2\Sigma_j(I_j - \alpha - \beta E_j) = 0$. Minimizing with respect to β likewise requires $-2\Sigma_j E_j(I_j - \yen - \beta E_j) = 0$. We now have two equations

For purposes of illustration, consider the introduction into the earnings analysis of a second independent variable called "experience." Holding constant the level of education, we would expect someone who has been working for a longer time to earn more. Let X denote years of experience in the labor force and, as in the case of education, we will assume that it has a linear effect upon earnings that is stable across individuals. The modified model may be written:

$$I = \alpha + \beta E + \gamma X + \epsilon$$

where γ is expected to be positive.

The task of estimating the parameters α, β and γ is conceptually identical to the earlier task of estimating only α and β. The difference is that we can no longer think of regression as choosing a line in a two-dimensional diagram—with two explanatory variables we need three dimensions, and instead of estimating a line we are estimating a plane. Multiple regression analysis will select a plane so that the sum of squared errors—the error here being the vertical distance between the actual value of I and the estimated plane—is at a minimum. The intercept of that plane with the I-axis (where E and X are zero) implies the constant term α, its slope in the education dimension implies the coefficient β, and its slope in the experience dimension implies the coefficient γ.

Multiple regression analysis is in fact capable of dealing with an arbitrarily large number of explanatory variables. Though people lack the capacity to visualize in more than three dimensions, mathematics does not. With n explanatory variables, multiple regression analysis will estimate the equation of a "hyperplane" in n-space such that the sum of squared errors has been minimized. Its intercept implies the constant term, and its slope in each dimension implies one of the regression coefficients. As in the case of simple regression, the SSE criterion is quite convenient computationally. Formulae for the parameters α, β, γ ... can be derived readily and evaluated easily on a computer, again using only the observed values of the dependent and independent variables.[13]

The interpretation of the coefficient estimates in a multiple regression warrants brief comment. In the model $I = \alpha + \beta E + \gamma X + \epsilon$, α captures what an individual earns with no education or experience, β captures the effect on income of a year of education, and captures the effect on income of a year of experience. To put it slightly differently, β is an estimate of the effect of a year of education on income, holding experience constant. Likewise, γ is

in two unknowns that can be solved for α and β.

13. The derivation may be found in any standard econometrics text. See, e.g., E. Hanushek & J. Jackson, Statistical Methods for Social Scientists 110–116 (1977); J. Johnston, Econometric Methods 122–32 (2d ed. 1972).

the estimated effect of a year of experience on income, holding education constant.

II.   Essential Assumptions and Statistical Properties of Regression

As noted, the use of the minimum SSE criterion may be defended on two grounds: its computational convenience, and its desirable statistical properties. We now consider these properties and the assumptions that are necessary to ensure them.[14]

Continuing with our illustration, the hypothesis is that earnings in the "real world" are determined in accordance with the equation $I = \alpha + \beta E + \gamma X + \epsilon$—true values of α, β and γ exist, and we desire to ascertain what they are. Because of the noise term ϵ, however, we can only estimate these parameters.

We can think of the noise term ϵ as a random variable, drawn by nature from some probability distribution—people obtain an education and accumulate work experience, then nature generates a random number for each individual, called ϵ, which increases or decreases income accordingly. Once we think of the noise term as a random variable, it becomes clear that the *estimates* of α, β, and γ (as distinguished from their true values) will also be random variables, because the estimates generated by the SSE criterion will depend upon the particular value of ϵ drawn by nature for each individual in the data set. Likewise, because there exists a probability distribution from which each ϵ is drawn, there must also exist a probability distribution from which each parameter estimate is drawn, the latter distribution a function of the former distributions. The attractive statistical properties of regression all concern the relationship between the probability distribution of the parameter estimates and the true values of those parameters.

We begin with some definitions. The minimum SSE criterion is termed an *estimator*. Alternative criteria for generating parameter estimates (such as minimizing the sum of errors in absolute value) are also estimators.

Each parameter estimate that an estimator produces, as noted, can be viewed as a random variable drawn from some probability distribution. If the mean of that probability distribution is equal to the true value of the parameter that we are trying to estimate, then the estimator is *unbiased*. In other words, to return to our illustration, imagine creating a sequence of data sets each containing the same individuals with the same values of education and experience, differing only in that nature draws a different ϵ for each individual for each data set. Imagine further that we recompute our parameter estimates for each data set, thus generating a range of estimates

---

14. An accessible and more extensive discussion of the key assumptions of re-   gression may be found in Fisher, supra note 7.

for each parameter α, β and γ if the estimator is unbiased, we would find that on average we recovered the true value of each parameter.

An estimator is termed *consistent* if it takes advantage of additional data to generate more accurate estimates. More precisely, a consistent estimator yields estimates that converge on the true value of the underlying parameter as the sample size gets larger and larger. Thus, the probability distribution of the estimate for any parameter has lower variance[15] as the sample size increases, and in the limit (infinite sample size) the estimate will equal the true value.

The variance of an estimator for a *given* sample size is also of interest. In particular, let us restrict attention to estimators that are unbiased. Then, lower variance in the probability distribution of the estimator is clearly desirable[16]—it reduces the probability of an estimate that differs greatly from the true value of the underlying parameter. In comparing different unbiased estimators, the one with the lowest variance is termed *efficient* or *best*.

Under certain assumptions, the minimum SSE criterion has the characteristics of unbiasedness, consistency and efficiency—these assumptions and their consequences follow:

(1) If the noise term for each observation, ϵ, is drawn from a distribution that has a mean of zero, then the sum of squared errors criterion generates estimates that are unbiased and consistent.

That is, we can imagine that for each observation in the sample, nature draws a noise term from a different probability distribution. As long as each of these distributions has a mean of zero (even if the distributions are not the same), the minimum SSE criterion is unbiased and consistent.[17] This assumption is logically sufficient to ensure that one other condition holds—namely, that each of the explanatory variables in the model is uncorrelated with the expected value of the noise term.[18] This will prove important later.

---

15. "Variance" is a measure of the dispersion of the probability distribution of a random variable. Consider two random variables with the same mean (same average value). If one of them has a distribution with greater variance, then, roughly speaking, the probability that the variable will take on a value far from the mean is greater.

16. Lower variance by itself is not necessarily an attractive property for an estimator. For example, we could employ an estimator for β of the form "$\beta=17$"

irrespective of the information in the data set. This estimator has zero variance.

17. See, e.g, P. Kennedy, A Guide to Econometrics 42–44 (2d ed. 1985).

18. If the expected value of the noise term is always zero irrespective of the values of the explanatory variables for the observation with which the noise term is associated, then by definition the noise term cannot be correlated with any explanatory variable.

(2) If the distributions from which the noise terms are drawn for each observation have the same variance, and the noise terms are statistically independent of each other (so that if there is a positive noise term for one observation, for example, there is no reason to expect a positive or negative noise term for any other observation), then the sum of squared errors criterion gives us the best or most efficient estimates available from any *linear* estimator (defined as an estimator that computes the parameter estimates as a linear function of the noise term, which the SSE criterion does).[19]

If assumption (2) is violated, the SSE criterion remains unbiased and consistent but it is possible to reduce the variance of the estimator by taking account of what we know about the noise term. For example, if we know that the variance of the distribution from which the noise term is drawn is bigger for certain observations, then the size of the noise term for those observations is *likely* to be larger. And, because the noise is larger, we will want to give those observations less weight in our analysis. The statistical procedure for dealing with this sort of problem is termed "generalized least squares," which is beyond the scope of this lecture.[20]

III.   An Illustration—Discrimination on the Basis of Gender

To illustrate the ideas to this point as well as to suggest how regression may have useful applications in a legal proceeding, imagine a hypothetical firm that has been sued for wage discrimination on the basis of gender. To investigate these allegations, data have been gathered for all of the firm's employees. The questions to be answered are (a) whether discrimination is occurring (liability); and (b) what its consequences are (damages). We will address them using a modified version of the earnings model developed in Section I.

The usefulness of *multiple* regression here should be intuitively apparent. Suppose, for example, that according to the data, women at the firm on average make less than men. Is this fact sufficient to establish actionable discrimination? The answer is no if the difference arises because women at this firm are less well-educated, for example (and thus by inference less productive), or because they are less experienced.[21] In short, the legal question is whether women earn less after all of the factors that the firm may permissibly consider in setting wages have been taken into account.

To generate the data for this illustration, I assume a hypothetical "real world" in which earnings are determined by equation (1):

19. E.g., id. at 44; J. Johnston, supra note 13, at 126–27.

20. See, e.g., id. at 208–66.

21. See, e.g., Miller v. Kansas Electric Power Cooperative, Inc., 1990 WL 120935 (D.Kan.).

(1) Earnings = 5000 + 1000*School + 50*Aptitude + 300*Experience – 2000 *Gendum + Noise

where "School" is years of schooling; "Aptitude" is a score on an 04 aptitude test between 100 and 240; "Experience" is years of experience in the work force; and "Gendum" is a variable that equals 1 for women and zero for men (more about this variable in a moment). To produce the artificial data set, I made up 50 observations (corresponding to 50 fictitious individuals) for each of the explanatory variables, half men and half women. In making up the data, I deliberately tried to introduce some positive correlation between the schooling and aptitude variables, for reasons that will become clear later. I then employed a random number generator to produce a noise term drawn from a normal distribution with a standard deviation (the square root of the variance) equal to 3000 and a mean of zero. This standard deviation was chosen more or less arbitrarily to introduce a considerable but not overwhelming amount of noise in proportion to the total variation in earnings. The right hand side variables were then used to generate the "actual value" of earnings for each of the 50 "individuals."

The effect of gender on earnings in this hypothetical firm enters through the variable Gendum. Gendum is a "dummy" variable in econometric parlance because its numerical value is arbitrary, and it simply captures some non-numerical attribute of the sample population. By construction here, men and women both earn the same returns to education, experience and aptitude, but holding these factors constant the earnings of women are $2000 lower (the variable Gendum equals 1 for women and zero for men). In effect, the constant term (baseline earnings) is lower for women, but otherwise women are treated equally. In reality, of course, gender discrimination could arise in other ways (such as lower returns to education and experience for women, for example), and I assume that it takes this form only for purposes of illustration.

Note that the random number generator that I employed here generates noise terms with an expected value of zero, each drawn from a distribution with the same variance. Further, the noise terms for the various observations are statistically independent (the realized value of the noise term for each observation has no influence on the noise term drawn for any other observation). Hence, the noise terms satisfy the assumptions necessary to ensure that the minimum SSE criterion yields unbiased, consistent and efficient estimates. The expected value of the estimate for each parameter is equal to the true value, therefore, and no other linear estimator will do a better job at recovering the true parameters than the minimum SSE criterion. It is nevertheless interesting to see just *how* well regression analysis performs. I used a standard computer package to estimate the constant term and the coefficients of the four independent variables from the "observed" values of Earnings, School, Aptitude, Experience, and Gendum for each of the 50 hypothetical individuals. The results are reproduced in Table 1, under the column labeled "Estimated Value." (We will discuss the last three columns and the R^2 statistic in the next section.)

Table 1
(Noise term with Standard Deviation of 3000)

Variable	"True Value"	Estimated Value	Std Error	t-statistic	Prob (2 Tail)
Constant	5000.0	4136.7	3781.8	1.094	.280
School	1000.0	1584.6	288.1	5.500	.000
Aptitude	50.0	6.4	27.3	0.236	.814
Experience	300.0	241.7	80.8	2.992	.004
Gendum	−2000.0	−1470.4	1402.2	−1.049	.300

R^2 = .646

Note that all of the estimated parameters have the right sign. Just by chance, it turns out that the regression overestimates the returns to schooling, and underestimates the other parameters. The estimated coefficient for Aptitude is off by a great deal in proportion to its true value, and in a later section I will offer an hypothesis as to what the problem is. The other parameter estimates, though obviously different from the true value of the underlying parameter, are much closer to the mark. With particular reference to the coefficient of Gendum, the regression results correctly suggest the presence of gender discrimination, though its magnitude is underestimated by about 25% (remember that an overestimate of the same magnitude was just as likely ex ante, that is, before the actual values for the noise terms were generated).

The source of the error in the coefficient estimates, of course, is the presence of noise. If the noise term were equal to zero for every observation, the true values of the underlying parameters could be recovered in this illustration with perfect accuracy from the data for only five hypothetical individuals—it would be a simple matter of solving five equations in five unknowns. And, if noise is the source of error in the parameter estimates, intuition suggests that the magnitude of the noise will affect the accuracy of the regression estimates, with more noise leading to less accuracy on average. We will make this intuition precise in the next section, but before proceeding it is perhaps useful to repeat the parameter estimation experiment for a hypothetical firm in which the data contain less noise. To do so, I took the "data" for the independent variables used in the experiment above and again generated values for earnings for the 50 hypothetical individuals using equation (1), changing only the noise terms. This time, the noise terms were drawn by the random number generator from a normal distribution with standard deviation of 1000 rather than 3000 (a significant reduction in the amount of noise). Reestimating the regression parameters from this modified data set produced the results in Table 2:

Table 2
(Noise term with Standard Deviation of 1000)

Variable	"True Value"	Estimated Value	Std Error	t-statistic	Prob (2 Tail)
Constant	5000.0	4784.2	945.4	5.060	.000
School	1000.0	1146.2	72.0	15.913	.000
Aptitude	50.0	39.1	6.8	5.741	.000
Experience	300.0	285.4	20.2	14.131	.000
Gendum	−2000.0	−1867.6	350.5	−5.328	.000

$R^2 = .964$

Not surprisingly, the estimated parameters here are considerably closer to their true values. It was not certain that they would be, because after all their expected values are equal to their true values regardless of the amount of noise (the estimator is unbiased). But on average we would expect greater accuracy, and greater accuracy indeed emerges here. Put more formally, the probability distributions of the parameter estimates have greater variance, the greater the variance of the noise term. The variance of the noise term thus affects the degree of confidence that we have in the accuracy of regression estimates.

In real applications, of course, the noise term is unobservable as is the distribution from which it is drawn. The variance of the noise term is thus unknown. It can, however, be estimated using the difference between the predicted values of the dependent variable for each observation and the actual value (the "estimated errors" defined earlier). This estimate in turn allows the investigator to assess the explanatory power of the regression analysis and the "statistical significance" of its parameter estimates.

IV. Statistical Inference and Goodness of Fit

Recall that the parameter estimates are themselves random variables, dependent upon the random variables ϵ. Thus, each estimate can be thought of as a draw from some underlying probability distribution, the nature of that distribution as yet unspecified. With a further assumption, however, we can compute the probability distribution of the estimates, and use it to test hypotheses about them.

A. Statistical Inference

Most readers are familiar, at least in passing, with a probability distribution called the "normal." Its shape is that of a "bell curve," indicating among other things that if a sample is drawn from the distribution, the most likely values for the observations in the sample are those close to the mean and least likely values are those farthest from the mean. *If we assume that the noise terms* ϵ *are all drawn from the same normal distribution,* it is possible to show that the parameter estimates have a normal distribution as well.[22]

The variance of this normal distribution, however, depends upon the variance of the distribution from which the noise terms are drawn. This variance is unknown in practice, and can only be estimated using the estimated errors from the regression to obtain an estimate of the variance of the noise term. The estimated variance of the noise term in turn can be used to construct an estimate of the variance of the normal distribution for each coefficient. The square root of this estimate is called the "standard error" of the coefficient—call this measure "s".

It is also possible to show[23] that if the parameter estimate, call it π, is normally distributed with a mean of μ, then $(\pi - \mu)/s$ has a "Student's t" distribution. The t-distribution looks very much like the normal, only it has "fatter" tails and its mean is zero. Using this result, suppose we hypothesize that the true value of a parameter in our regression model is μ. Call this the "null hypothesis." Because the minimum SSE criterion is an unbiased estimator, we can deduce that our parameter estimate is drawn from a normal distribution with a mean of μ if the null hypothesis is true. If we then subtract μ from our actual parameter estimate and divide by its standard error, we obtain a number called the *t-statistic* which is drawn from a t-distribution if the null hypothesis is true. This statistic can be positive or negative as the parameter estimate from which it is derived is greater or less than the hypothesized true value of the parameter. Recalling that the t-distribution is much like a normal with mean of zero, we know that large values of the t-statistic (in absolute value) will be drawn considerably less fre-

---

22. See, e.g., E. Hanushek & J. Jackson, supra note 13, at 66–68; J. Johnston, supra note 13, at 135–38. The supposition that the noise terms are normally distributed is often intuitively plausible, and may be loosely justified by appeal to "central limit theorems" which hold that the average of a large number of random variables tends toward a normal distribution even if the individual random variables that enter into the average are not normally distributed. See, e.g., R. Hogg & A. Craig, Introduction to Mathematical Statistics 192–95 (4th ed. 1978); W. Feller, An Introduction to Probability Theory and Its Applications, Volume I 243–48 (3d ed. 1968). Thus, if we think of the noise term as the sum of a large number of independent, small disturbances, theory affords considerable basis for the supposition that its distribution is approximately normal.

23. See sources cited note 22 supra.

quently than small values of the t-statistic. And, from the construction of the t-statistic, large values for that statistic arise (in absolute value), other things being equal, when the parameter estimate on which it is based differs from its true (hypothesized) value by a great deal.

This insight is turned on its head for hypothesis testing. We have just argued that a large t-statistic (in absolute value) will arise fairly infrequently if the null hypothesis is correct. Hence, when a large t-statistic *does* arise, it will be tempting to conclude that the null hypothesis is false. The essence of hypothesis testing with a regression coefficient, then, is to formulate a null hypothesis as to its true value, and then to decide whether to accept or reject it according to whether the t-statistic associated with that null hypothesis is large enough that the plausibility of the null hypothesis is sufficiently in doubt.[24]

One can be somewhat more precise. We might resolve that the null hypothesis is implausible if the t-statistic associated with our regression estimate lies so far out in one tail of its t-distribution that such a value, or one even larger in absolute value, would arise less than, say, 5% of the time if the null hypothesis is correct. Put differently, we will reject the null hypothesis if the t-statistic falls either in the uppermost tail of the t-distribution, containing 2.5% of the draws representing the largest positive values, or in the lowermost tail, containing 2.5% of the draws representing the largest negative values. This is called a "two-tailed test."

Alternatively, we might have a strong prior belief about the true value of a parameter that would lead us to accept the null hypothesis even if the t-statistic lies far out in *one* of the tails of the distribution. Consider the coefficient of the gender dummy in Table 1 as an illustration. Suppose the null hypothesis is that the true value of this coefficient is zero. Under what circumstances would we reject it? We might find it implausible that the true value of the coefficient would be positive, reflecting discrimination *against* men. Then, even if the estimated coefficient for the gender dummy is positive with a large positive t-statistic, we would still accept the null hypothesis that its true value is zero. Only a negative coefficient estimate with a large negative t-statistic would lead us to conclude that the null hypothesis was false. Where we reject the null hypothesis only if a t-statistic that is large in absolute value has a particular sign, we are employing a "one-tailed test."

---

24. I limit the discussion here to hypothesis testing regarding the value of a particular parameter. In fact, other sorts of hypotheses may readily be tested, such as the hypothesis that all parameters in the model are zero, the hypothesis that some subset of the parameters are zero, and so on.

To operationalize either a one-or two-tailed test, it is necessary to compute the exact probability of a t-statistic as large or larger in absolute value as the one associated with the parameter estimate at issue. In turn, it is necessary to know exactly how "spread out" is the t-distribution from which the estimate has been drawn. A further parameter that we need to pin down the shape of the t-distribution in this respect is called the "degrees of freedom," defined as the number of observations in the sample less the number of parameters to be estimated. In the illustrations of tables 1 and 2, we have 50 observations in the sample, and we are estimating 5 parameters, so the t-distribution for any of the parameter estimates has 45 degrees of freedom. The fewer the degrees of freedom, the more "spread out" is the t-distribution and thus the greater is the probability of drawing large t-statistics. The intuition is that the larger the sample, the more collapsed is the distribution of any parameter estimate (recall the concept of consistency above). By contrast, the more parameters we seek to estimate from a sample of given size, the more information we are trying to extract from the data and the less confident we can be in the estimate of each parameter—hence, the associated t-distribution is more "spread out."[25]

Knowing the degrees of freedom for the t-distribution allows an investigator to compute the probability of drawing the t-statistic in question, or one larger in absolute value, assuming the truth of the null hypothesis. Using the appropriate one-or two-tailed test (the former necessary only when the t-statistic is of the right sign), the investigator then rejects the null hypothesis if this probability is sufficiently small.

But what do we mean by "sufficiently small?" The answer is by no means obvious, and depends upon the circumstances. It has become convention in social scientific research to test one particular null hypothesis—namely, the hypothesis that the true value of a coefficient is zero. Under this hypothesis, μ in our notation above is equal to zero, and hence the t-statistic is simply π/s, the coefficient estimate divided by its standard error. It is also convention to embrace a "significance level" of .10, .05 or .01—that is, to inquire whether the t-statistic that the investigator has obtained, or one even larger in absolute value, would arise more than 10%, 5% or 1% of the time when the null hypothesis is correct. Where the answer to this question is no, the null hypothesis is rejected and the coefficient in question is said to be "statistically significant." For example, if the parameter estimate that was obtained is far enough from zero that an estimate of that magnitude, or one even farther

---

25. See sources cited note 13 supra.

from zero, would arise less than 5% of the time, then the coefficient is said to be significant at the .05 level.

The question whether the conventional social scientific significance tests are appropriate when regression analysis is used for legal applications, particularly in litigation, is a difficult one that I will defer to the concluding section of this lecture. I will simply assume for now that we are interested in the general problem of testing some null hypothesis, and that we will reject it if the parameter estimate obtained lies far enough out in one of the tails of the distribution from which the estimate has been drawn. We leave open the question of what constitutes "far enough," and simply seek to compute the probability under a one- or two-tailed test of obtaining an estimate as far from the mean of the distribution as that generated by the regression if the null hypothesis is true.

Most computerized regression packages report not only the parameter estimate itself (π in our notation), but also the standard error of each parameter estimate ("s" in our notation). This value, coupled with the hypothesized true parameter value (μ in our notation), can then be employed to generate the appropriate t-statistic for any null hypothesis. Many regression packages also report a number called the "t-statistic," which is invariably based upon the conventional social scientific null hypothesis that the true parameter value is zero. Finally, some packages report the probability that the t-statistic at issue could have been generated from a t-distribution with the appropriate degrees of freedom under a one-or two-tailed test.[26]

Returning to Tables 1 and 2, all of this information is reported for each of the five parameter estimates—the standard error, the value of the t-statistic for the null hypothesis that the true parameter value is zero, and the probability of getting a t-statistic that large or larger in absolute value under a two-tailed test with 45 degrees of freedom. To interpret this information, consider the estimated coefficient for the gender dummy in Table 1. The estimated coefficient of –1470.4 has standard error of 1402.2 and thus a t-statistic of –1470.4/1402.2 = –1.049. The associated probability under a two-tailed test is reported as .30. This means that if the

---

26. If the regression package does not report these probabilities, they can readily be found elsewhere. It has become common practice to include in statistics and econometrics books tables of probabilities for a t-distributions with varying degrees of freedom. Knowing the degrees of freedom associated with a t-statistic, therefore, one can consult such a table to ascertain the probability of obtaining a t-statistic as far from zero or farther as the one generated by the regression (the concept "far from zero" again defined by either a one- or two-tailed test). As a point of reference, when the degrees of freedom are large (say, 50 or more), then the .05 significance level for a two-tailed test requires a t-statistic approximately equal to 2.0.

true value of the coefficient for the gender dummy were zero, a coefficient greater than or equal to 1470.4 in absolute value would nevertheless arise 30% of the time given the degrees of freedom of the t-distribution from which the coefficient estimate is drawn. A rejection of the null hypothesis on the basis of a parameter estimate equal to 1470.4 or greater in absolute value, therefore, will be erroneous three times out of ten when the null hypothesis is true. By conventional social science standards, therefore, the significance level here is too low to reject the null hypothesis, and the coefficient of the gender dummy is not statistically significant. It is noteworthy that in this instance (in contrast to any real world application), we know the true parameter value, namely –2000.0. Hence, if we employ a conventional two-tailed significance test, we are led erroneously to reject the hypothesis that gender discrimination is present.

As noted, we may regard the two-tailed test as inappropriate for the coefficient of the gender dummy because we find the possibility of discrimination against men to be implausible. It is a simple matter to construct an alternative one-tailed test: Table 1 indicates that a coefficient estimate of 1470.4 or greater in absolute value will occur 30% of the time if the true value of the coefficient is zero. Put differently, an estimate of the gender dummy coefficient greater than or equal to 1470.4 will arise 15% of the time, and an estimate less than or equal to –1470.4 will arise 15% of the time. It follows that if we are only interested in the lower tail of the t-distribution, rejection of the null hypothesis (when it is true) will be erroneous only 15% of the time if we require a parameter estimate of –1470.4 or smaller. The one-tailed significance level is thus .15, still below the conventional thresholds for statistical significance.[27] Using such significance levels, therefore, we again are led to accept the null hypothesis, in this case erroneously.

I offer this illustration not to suggest that there is anything wrong with conventional significance tests, but simply to indicate how one reduces the chance of erroneously rejecting the null hypothesis (call this a "Type I" error) only by increasing the chance of erroneously accepting it (call this a "Type II" error). The conventional significance tests implicitly give great weight to the importance of avoiding Type I errors, and less weight to the avoidance of Type II errors, by requiring a high degree of confidence in the falsity of the null hypothesis before rejecting it. This seems perfectly appropriate for most scientific applications, in which the researcher is justifiably asked to bear a considerable burden of proof before the scientific community will accept that the

27. The result in this illustration is general—for any t-statistic, the probability of rejecting the null hypothesis erroneously under a one-tailed test will be exactly half that probability under a two-tailed test.

data establish an asserted causal relation. Whether the proponent of regression evidence in a legal proceeding should bear that same burden of proof is a more subtle issue.

B.   Goodness of Fit

Another common statistic associated with regression analysis is the R^2. This has a simple definition—it is equal to one minus the ratio of the sum of squared *estimated* errors (the deviation of the actual value of the dependent variable from the regression line) to the sum of squared deviations about the mean of the dependent variable. Intuitively, the sum of squared deviations about its mean is a measure of the total variation of the dependent variable. The sum of squared deviations about the regression line is a measure of the extent to which the regression fails to explain the dependent variable (a measure of the noise). Hence, the R^2 statistic is a measure of the extent to which the total variation of the dependent variable *is* explained by the regression. It is not difficult to show that the R^2 statistic necessarily takes on a value between zero and one.[28]

A high value of R^2, suggesting that the regression model explains the variation in the dependent variable well, is obviously important if one wishes to use the model for predictive or forecasting purposes. It is considerably less important if one is simply interested in particular parameter estimates (as, for example, if one is searching for evidence of discrimination as in our illustration, and thus focused on the coefficient of the gender dummy). To be sure, a large unexplained variation in the dependent variable will increase the standard error of the coefficients in the model (which are a function of the estimated variance of the noise term), and hence regressions with low values of R^2 will often (but by no means always) yield parameter estimates with small t-statistics for any null hypothesis. Because this consequence of a low R^2 will be reflected in the t-statistics, however, it does not afford any reason to be concerned about a low R^2 per se.

As a quick illustration, turn back to Tables 1 and 2. Recall that the noise terms for the data set from which the estimates in Table 1 were generated were drawn from a distribution with a standard deviation of 3000, while for Table 2 the noise terms were drawn from a distribution with a standard deviation of 1000. The unexplained variation in the earnings variable is likely to be greater in the first data set, therefore, and indeed the R^2 statistics confirm that it is (.646 for Table 1 and .964 for Table 2). Likewise, because the estimated variance of the noise term is greater for the estimates in Table 1, we expect the coefficient estimates to have larger

28.   See, e.g., E. Hanushek & J. Jackson, supra note 13, at 57–58.

standard errors and smaller t-statistics. This expectation is also borne out on inspection of the two Tables. Variables with coefficients that are statistically significant by conventional tests in Table 2, therefore, such as the gender dummy, are not statistically significant in Table 1.

In these illustrations, the value of R^2 simply reflects the amount of noise in the data, and a low R^2 is not inconsistent with the minimum SSE criterion serving as an unbiased, consistent and efficient estimator because we know that the noise terms were all independent draws from the same distribution with a zero mean. In practice, however, a low value of R^2 *may* indicate that important and systematic factors have been omitted from the regression model. This possibility raises again the concern about omitted variables bias.

V. Two Common Statistical Problems in Regression Analysis

Much of the typical econometrics course is devoted to what happens when the assumptions that are necessary to make the minimum SSE criterion unbiased, consistent and efficient do not hold. I cannot begin to provide a full sense of these issues in such a brief lecture, and will simply illustrate two of the many complications that may arise, chosen because they are both common and quite important.

A. Omitted Variables

As noted, the omission from a regression of some variables that affect the dependent variable may cause an "omitted variables bias." The problem arises because any omitted variable becomes part of the noise term, and the result may be a violation of the assumption necessary for the minimum SSE criterion to be an unbiased estimator.

Recall that assumption—that each noise term is drawn from a distribution with a mean of zero. We noted that this assumption logically implies the absence of correlation between the explanatory variables included in the regression and the expected value of the noise term (because whatever the value of any explanatory variable, the expected value of the noise term is always zero). Thus, suppose we start with a properly specified model in which the noise term for every observation has an expected value of zero. Now, omit one of the independent variables. If the effect of this variable upon the dependent variable is not zero for each observation, the new noise terms now come from distributions with non-zero means. One consequence is that the estimate of the constant term will be biased (part of the estimated value for the constant term is actually the mean effect of the omitted variable). Further, unless the omitted variable is uncorrelated with the included ones, the coefficients of the included ones will be biased because they now reflect not only an estimate of the effect of the variable with which they are associated, but also partly the effects of the omitted variable.[29]

To illustrate the omitted variables problem, I took the data on which the estimates reported in Table 1 are based, and reran the regression after omitting the schooling variable. The results are in Table 3:

Table 3
Omitted Variable Illustration

Variable	"True Value"	Estimated Value	Std Error	t-statistic	Prob (2 Tail)
Constant	5000.0	9806.5	4653.8	2.107	.041
School	1000.0	omitted			
Aptitude	50.0	107.5	25.6	4.173	.000
Experience	300.0	256.9	103.3	2.487	.017
Gendum	−2000.0	−2445.5	1779.0	−1.375	.176

$R^2 = .408$

You will note that the omission of the schooling variable lowers the R^2 of the regression, which is not surprising given the original importance of the variable. It also alters the coefficient estimates. The estimate for the constant term rises considerably, because the mean effect of schooling on income is positive. It is not surprising that the constant term is thus estimated to be greater than its true value. An even more significant effect of the omission of schooling is on the coefficient estimate for the aptitude variable, which increases dramatically from below its true value to well above its true value and becomes highly significant. The reason is that the schooling variable is highly correlated (positively) with aptitude in the data set—the correlation is .69—and because schooling has a positive effect on earnings. Hence, with the schooling variable omitted, the aptitude coefficient is erroneously capturing some of the (positive) returns to education as well as the returns to "aptitude." The consequence is that the minimum SSE criterion yields an upward biased estimate of the coefficient for aptitude, and in this case the actual estimate is indeed above the true value of that coefficient.

The effect on the other coefficients is more modest, though non-trivial. Notice, for example, that the coefficient of Gendum increases (in absolute value) significantly. This is because schooling happens to be positively correlated with being male in my fictitious

---

29. See J. Johnston, supra note 13, at 168–69; E. Hanushek & J. Jackson, supra note 13, at 81–82. The bias is a function of two things—the true coefficients of the excluded variables, and the correlation within the data set between the included and the excluded variables.

data set—without controlling for schooling, the apparent effect of gender is exaggerated because females are somewhat less well educated on average.

The omitted variables problem is troublesome to investigators not simply because it requires them to collect data on more variables to avoid it, but because the omitted variables are often unobservable. Real world studies of gender discrimination are perhaps a case in point. One can readily imagine that earnings depend on such factors as innate ability and motivation, both of which may be unobservable to an investigator. Omitted variables bias may then become something that the investigator cannot avoid, and an understanding of its consequences then becomes doubly important. For an investigator concerned primarily with the coefficient of the gender dummy, it might be argued, the omitted variables bias caused by the exclusion of innate ability and motivation should be modest because the correlation in the sample between gender and those omitted variables might plausibly be assumed to be small. Where the problem appears likely to be serious, by contrast, the utility of conventional regression as an investigative tool diminishes considerably.[30]

I note in passing that the problem of including extraneous or irrelevant variables is less serious. Their expected coefficient is zero and the estimates of the other coefficients are not biased, although the efficiency of the minimum SSE criterion is lessened.[31]

I also note in passing a problem that is closely related to the omitted variables problem, termed "errors in variables." In many regression studies, it is inevitable that some explanatory variables will be measured with error. Such errors become part of the noise term. Let us assume that in the absence of measurement error, the noise terms obey the assumption needed for unbiasedness and consistency—they are all drawn from a distribution with zero mean, and are thus uncorrelated with the explanatory variables. With measurement error, however, this assumption will no longer hold.

Imagine, for concreteness, that earnings depend on education, experience and so on, as hypothesized earlier, and on innate ability as suggested above. Instead of supposing that innate ability is an omitted variable, however, suppose that the aptitude test score included in the regression is a "proxy" for innate ability. That is,

---

30. Econometricians have developed some more sophisticated regression techniques to deal with the problem of unobservable variables, but these are not always satisfactory because of certain restrictive assumptions that an investigator must make in using them. See, e.g., Griliches, Errors in Variables and Other Unobservables, 42 Econometrica 971 (1974). An accessible discussion of the omitted variables problem and related issues may be found in P. Kennedy, supra note 17, at 69–72.

31. Id.

we regard it as an imperfect measure of ability, correlated with it but not perfectly. When the test score underestimates ability, the noise term rises, and when the aptitude score overestimates ability the noise term falls. The result is a negative correlation between the noise term and the aptitude/ability variable. Put differently, if the noise term without measurement error is drawn from a distribution with zero mean, then the noise term including the measurement error is drawn from a distribution with a mean equal to the magnitude of that error. The consequence once again is bias in the estimated coefficients of the model.[32]

B.   Multicollinearity

The multicollinearity problem does not result in biased coefficient estimates, but does increase the standard error of the estimates and thus reduce the degree of confidence that one can place in them. The difficulty arises when two independent variables are closely correlated, creating a situation in which their effects are difficult to separate.

The following illustration will convey the essential intuition: Suppose that two Law School faculty members (call them Baird and Picker) regularly address alumni luncheons, held partly for the purpose of stimulating alumni contributions. Assume that each time one gives a luncheon speech, the other does too, and that the only available datum on alumni contributions is aggregate monthly giving. We somehow know that each time both give a speech in a month, alumni contributions rise by $10,000. When they each give two speeches in a month, contributions rise by $20,000, and so on.

Thus, by hypothesis, we know the *joint* effect of a speech by both Baird and Picker ($10,000), but nothing in the data permit us to ascertain their individual effects. Perhaps each speech increases contributions by $5,000, but it might be that one speaker induces an extra $10,000 in giving and the other none, or that one speaker induces an extra $30,000 in giving and the other reduces giving by $20,000. In econometric parlance, the data on speeches given by Baird and Picker are perfectly collinear—the correlation between the number of speeches per month by Baird and the number per

---

32. One standard technique for addressing this problem is termed "instrumental variables," which replaces the tainted variable with another variable that is thought to be closely associated with it but also thought uncorrelated with the disturbance term. For a variety of reasons, however, the instrumental variables technique is not satisfactory in many cases, and the errors in variables problem is consequently one of the most serious difficulties in the use of regression techniques. A discussion of the instrumental variables technique, and of other possible response to the errors in variables problem may be found in P. Kennedy, supra note 17, at 113–16; J. Johnston, supra note 13, at 281–91.

month by Picker is 1.0. An attempt to estimate the effect of the number of speeches given by each upon contributions would fail and result in an error message from the computer (for reasons that we need not detail, it would find itself trying to divide by zero).

The term "multicollinearity" usually refers to a problem in the data short of the perfect collinearity in our illustration, but where changes in two variables are nevertheless highly correlated to the point that it is difficult to separate their effects. Because multicollinearity does not go to any property of the noise term, the minimum SSE criterion can still be unbiased, consistent and efficient. But the difficulty in separating the effects of the two variables introduces greater uncertainty into the estimator, manifest as an increase in the standard errors of the coefficients and a reduction in their t-statistics.

One illustration of the effects of multicollinearity may already have been provided. In our discussion of Table 1, we noted that the coefficient estimate for the aptitude variable was far below its true value. As it turns out, aptitude and schooling are highly correlated in the data set, and this affords a plausible conjecture as to why the coefficient for the schooling variable is too high and that for aptitude insignificantly small (some of the effects of aptitude in the sample are captured by the schooling coefficient).

To give another illustration, which incidentally allows us to introduce another use of "dummy" variables, suppose that gender discrimination at our hypothetical firm affects the earnings of women in two ways—through an effect on the baseline earnings of women as before, and through an effect on the returns to education for women. In particular, recall that in equation (1) both sexes earned $1,000 per year of schooling. Suppose now that males earn $1000, but females earn only $800. This effect can be captured mathematically by an "interaction term" incorporating the gender dummy, so that earnings are now determined in accordance with equation (2):

(2) Earnings = 5000 + 1000*School + 50*Aptitude + 300*Experience – 2000*Gendum – 200*Gendum*School

Using the same hypothetical data for the explanatory variables as before, I produced new values of earnings using equation (2) and (just for variety's sake) noise terms drawn from a distribution with standard deviation of 2000. I then estimated a regression from the new data set, including the variable Gendum*School as an additional explanatory variable. The results are in Table 4, where the variable "Interact" is simply Gendum*School.

Table 4
Multicollinearity Illustration

Variable	"True Value"	Estimated Value	Std Error	t-statistic	Prob (2 Tail)
Constant	5000.0	3500.2	2130.6	1.643	.108
School	1000.0	962.3	144.0	6.679	.000
Aptitude	50.0	61.2	12.3	4.966	.000
Experience	300.0	288.3	36.7	7.861	.000
Gendum	−2000.0	−4243.7	2916.5	−1.455	.153
Interact	−200.0	14.8	198.2	.075	.941

$R^2 = .909$

Observe that, in contrast to Table 1, the coefficient for the gender dummy is now higher than the real value by more than a factor of two. The coefficient for the interaction term, by contrast, has the wrong sign and is close to zero. The other parameter estimates are not too far off the mark.

The poor results for the coefficients of Gendum and Interact are almost certainly a result of a severe multicollinearity problem. Note that whenever Gendum = 0, Interact = 0 as well. Gendum is positive only when Interact is positive. We would expect a high correlation between them, and indeed the correlation coefficient is 0.96. Under these circumstances, it is no surprise that the regression cannot separate the effects of the two variables with any accuracy. The estimated coefficient for Interact is insignificant by any plausible test, and the coefficient for Gendum also has a large standard error that produces a rather poor t-statistic despite the high absolute value of the coefficient estimate.

Notwithstanding the considerable uncertainty introduced into the coefficient estimates, however, it is plausible that the multicollinearity problem here is not disastrous for an investigator interested in identifying the extent of gender discrimination. The reason is that the estimate of the *joint* effects of the Gendum and Interact may not be too far afield—one is inflated and one is understated, with the errors to a great extent canceling each other—and as a legal matter an estimate of the joint effect may be all that is needed. The caveat is that multicollinearity reduces the t-statistics for both variables, and might thereby lead the investigator to reject the hypothesis that discrimination is present at all. To deal with the effects of multicollinearity here, therefore, the investigator might simply wish to discount the low t-statistics, or else to omit one of the two variables and recognize that the coefficient estimate for the included variable will be biased and will include the effect of the omitted variable.[33]

---

33. It is important to recollect that this approach raises the problem of omitted variables bias for the other variables as well.

In many instances, however, the investigator will not be satisfied with an estimate of the joint effect of two variables, but needs to separate them. Here, multicollinearity can become highly problematic. There is no simple, acceptable solution for all cases, though various options warrant consideration, all beyond the scope of this lecture.[34]

VI.   A Final Note on the Law: Regression Analysis and the Burden of Proof

A key issue that one must confront whenever a regression study is introduced into litigation is the question of how much weight to give it. I hope that the illustrations in this lecture afford some basis for optimism that such studies can be helpful, while also suggesting considerable basis for caution in their use.

I return now to an issue deferred earlier in the discussion of hypothesis testing—the relationship between the statistical significance test and the burden of proof. Suppose, for example, that to establish *liability* for wage discrimination on the basis of gender under Title VII, a plaintiff need simply show by a preponderance of the evidence that women employed by the defendant suffer some measure of discrimination.[35] With reference to our first illustration, we might say that the required showing on liability is that, by a preponderance of the evidence, the coefficient of the gender dummy is negative.

Unfortunately, there is no simple relationship between this burden of proof and the statistical significance test. At one extreme, if we imagine that the parameter estimate in the regression study is the *only* information we have about the presence or absence of discrimination, one might argue that liability is established by a preponderance of the evidence if the estimated coefficient for the gender dummy is negative regardless of its statistical significance or standard error. The rationale would be that the negative estimate, however subject to uncertainty, is unbiased and is the best evidence we have.

But this is much too simplistic. Very rarely is the regression estimate the only information available, and when the standard errors are high the estimate may be among the least reliable information available. Further, regression analysis is subject to considerable manipulation. It is not obvious precisely which variables should be included in a model, or what proxies to use for included variables that cannot be measured precisely. There is

---

34. See P. Kennedy, supra note 17, at 146–56.

35. See, e.g., Texas Department of Community Affairs v. Burdine, 450 U.S. 248 (1981).

considerable room for experimentation, and this experimentation can become "data mining" whereby an investigator tries numerous regression specifications until the desired result appears. An advocate quite naturally may have a tendency to present only those estimates that support the client's position. Hence, if the best result that an advocate can present contains high standard errors and low statistical significance, it is often plausible to suppose that numerous even less impressive results remain hidden, and conceivably shielded from discovery by the work product doctrine.[36]

For these reasons, those who use regression analysis in litigation tend to report results that satisfy the conventional significance tests—often the 5% significance level—and to suppose that less significant results are not terribly interesting.[37] Before most experts would feel comfortable asserting that gender discrimination has been established by a study such as that in our illustration, therefore, they likely would require that the coefficient estimate for the gender dummy be negative and statistically significant. Even then, they would anticipate a vigorous cross-examination based on a number of matters, many suggested by the discussion above.

Still more difficult issues arise when an exact parameter estimate is needed for some purpose, such as for computing damages. The fact that the parameter is "statistically significant" simply means that by conventional tests, one can reject the hypothesis that its true value is zero. But there are surely many other hypotheses about the parameter value that cannot be rejected, and indeed the likelihood that regression will produce a perfectly accurate estimate of any parameter is negligible. About the only guidance that can be given from a statistical standpoint is the obvious—parameter estimates with proportionally low standard errors are less likely to be wide of the mark than others.

Ultimately, therefore, statistics itself does not say how much weight a regression study ought be given, or whether it is reasonable to use a particular parameter estimate for some legal purpose or other. These assessments are inevitably entrusted to triers of fact, whose judgments on the matter if well informed are likely as good as those of anyone else.

---

36. I will not digress on the rules of discovery here. In practice, the raw data may be discoverable, for example, while the expert's undisclosed analysis of the data may not be.

37. See the discussion in Fisher, Statisticians, Econometricians and Adversary Proceedings, 81 J. Am. Stat. Assn. 277 (1986).

Study Questions:

1. In order to show that its black employees have not been harmed by workplace discrimination, a large corporate defendant in a civil rights lawsuit produces a statistical study that shows that black employees earn more on average than white employees. The dependent variable is salary; the independent variable is a dummy variable for race. Is the study persuasive? How could it be improved?

2. An automobile manufacturer invents and produces a very safe car and markets it to very risk-averse people. After several years, a consumer watchdog group discovers that the car is involved in more accidents than most other cars of comparable cost. Does it follow that the new car is in fact unsafe or poorly designed? How might a statistical study be designed in order to answer this question?

3. Suppose that residents of a certain neighborhood suffer from respiratory disease at a much higher rate than the national average. The rate of disease in the neighborhood rises and falls with the amount of pollution emitted by two nearby factories. One factory emits pollutant X; another factory emits pollutant Y; and both factories emit the same amount of pollutant. Does it make sense to shut both factories down? How should the problem be investigated?

2. An Introduction to Game Theory and the Law

Randal C. Picker[1]

I am pleased to have the opportunity to give the third of the three lectures in the Law School's inaugural Coase Lecture Series. I have to confess I am still at a stage in life when I think about how things will look on my resume, and to put down the Coase Lecture, I suspect, adds real luster to it. Nonetheless, we might want to call these lectures something else. My suggestion is "The Bar Stool Lecture Series." That wouldn't sound as distinguished and hence wouldn't do much for my resume, but it more accurately captures what the mission of the talk is. Here is the test for this talk: Given two bar stools and a stack of cocktail napkins, could the ideas in this talk be explained to an intelligent person in a crowded bar with a bank of TVs showing the Bulls and the Blackhawks? If this talk succeeds at that level, I will have accomplished my mission; if it does not, then I will have to consult with the Dean to get a larger budget for field research for my next big talk.

The bar stool test is a test of simplicity, of making an idea accessible to someone who is not a specialist in an area. It is a test that all of Ronald Coase's work that I know passes quite easily. It is the remarkable combination of simplicity and depth, which I guess travel together if you are smart enough, that defines Coase's work. The material that I will discuss today is, I think, fairly simple, though some of it is relatively new. And to give credit where credit is due, some of the work I will describe today is part of a joint effort with Doug Baird and Rob Gertner.

This will be an eight-cocktail-napkin talk: I want to talk about two basic forms for games, the normal form and the extensive form;

1. Paul H. Leffman Professor of Commercial Law, University of Chicago Law School. I have benefited from extensive discussions with Douglas G. Baird and Robert H. Gertner. I thank the Sarah Scaife Foundation and the Lynde and Harry Bradley Foundation for their generous research support. This lecture was delivered in June 1993.

Some of the material in part 2b of this essay has been published before in the Law School Alumni Magazine of the University of Chicago. See Randal C. Picker, "Law and Economics II: The Sequel," 39 U. Chi. L. School Record 10 (Spring 1993). Much of the analysis contained herein is taken from selected chapters of Douglas G. Baird, Robert H. Gertner, and Randal C. Picker, Game Theory and the Law (Harvard Univ. Press, 1994). A version almost identical to this essay appeared as the law and economics selection for a symposium on interdisciplinary approaches to the law in 27 Loyola (Los Angeles) University Law Review 127 (1993).

four ways of predicting the outcomes of games, through dominance arguments, Nash arguments, backwards induction, and forward induction; and two interesting ideas about game theory and the law.

1.   Game Theory and Strategic Behavior

As a discipline, law and economics advanced on the strong back of classical microeconomics. Individual decisionmakers maximized utility or profits subject to constraints. These individuals were treated either as pricetakers in competitive settings or pricesetters in monopolies. They were also perfectly informed. A sizable and largely successful academic legal literature grew out of taking first derivatives and ruthlessly applying the discipline of the microeconomist's marginal analysis to a vast array of legal problems.[2]

The last twenty years have seen a major shift in the fundamental methodological tools used by microeconomic theorists. Game theory has emerged to augment the standard, polar approaches of pure competition and monopoly. In a competitive setting, individuals or firms are seen as having no real decisions to make. Prices are given, and individuals and firms are pricetakers. The other production paradigm, monopoly, treats the monopolist as a pricesetter for a given demand curve. In a game-theoretic setting, rational actors need worry about the actions of others—this is the fundamental strategic interdependence that game theory addresses. Other settings lack the back-and-forth quality that characterizes strategic settings.

Game theory sounds like fun—visions of the gamut from Candyland to Monopoly spring to mind. A definition might be useful; as a rough cut, try: *game theory is a set of tools and a language for describing and predicting strategic behavior.* I will discuss in a bit what these tools are and how to apply them, but I want to focus first on the core concept in the definition, strategic behavior. Strategic settings are situations in which one person would like to take into account how a second person will behave in making a decision, and the second person would like to do likewise. Strategic settings typically involve two or more decisionmakers, and the possibility of linking one decision to a second decision, and vice versa.

Consider the airlines industry. Whether Northwest will cut fares may depend on how American and United will respond, and the same, of course, is true for them. Indeed, Northwest recently

---

2.   A sample of well-known textbooks and research monographs makes the point. Look at Mitch Polinsky's *Introduction to Law and Economics*, which is now in its second edition; Cooter and Ulen's *Law and Economics* textbook, which came out in 1988; and two torts monographs, Landes and Posner's *The Economic Structure of Tort Law* and Steven Shavell's *Economic Analysis of Accident Law*, both of which were published in 1987.

filed suit against American, claiming that American's introduction of a new pricing schedule was part of a scheme of predatory pricing designed to put Northwest out of business.[3] Oligopolistic industries—airlines, computer microprocessors or operating systems, for example—are natural settings for strategic interactions.

But so is a country road. I have risen for an early-morning walk. I would like to enjoy the view, take in the scenery, and generally ignore the cars going by me. You unfortunately are driving your new Mazda Miata. You want to see how the car handles, to test how it drives through turns and its acceleration. If I knew that you were driving like a maniac, I would want to take that into account in deciding whether to pay much attention to the road. If you knew that I was soaking in the countryside and ignoring the road, you would want to take that into account as well. Our behavioral decisions are intertwined, and we need to take that fact into account when we seek to predict likely outcomes. The legal system should take this into account as well when it establishes antitrust laws for oligopolistic industries or a torts scheme for ordinary accidents.

2. Normal Form Games, Dominant Strategies, and the Hidden Role of Law

a. The Prisoner's Dilemma

The best known bit of game theory is the Prisoner's Dilemma. I will go through the analysis to make clear how much game theory has already crossed over and to establish some terminology, and will then move on to more natural settings. So consider the following "game":

| | | Prisoner 2 | |
		Silent	Confess
Prisoner 1	Silent	-2, -2	-10, 0
	Confess	0, -10	-6, -6

Payoffs: (Prisoner 1, Prisoner 2)

Figure 1: Prisoner's Dilemma

Here is the story that this game is trying to capture. We have two prisoners, or, more generally, two players. They both have

---

3. See Bridget O'Brian, *"Predatory Pricing Issue is Due to be Taken Up in* *American Air's Trial,"* Wall Street Journal, July 12, 1993, a1.

committed a serious crime, but the district attorney cannot convict either one of them of this crime without extracting at least one confession. The district attorney can, however, convict them both on a lesser offense without the cooperation of either. The district attorney tells each prisoner that if neither confesses, they will both be convicted for the lesser offense. Each will go to prison for two years. This outcome is represented in the upper left cell.

If, however, one of the prisoners confesses and the other does not, the prisoner who confesses will go free and the other will be tried for the serious crime and given the maximum penalty of ten years in prison. This applies to both prisoners and is represented in the off-diagonal cells. Finally, if both confess, the district attorney will prosecute both for the serious crime, but not ask for the maximum penalty. They will both go to prison for six years. This is the final cell, the lower right cell.

This is a *normal form game*. We have identified the players, our two prisoners; the choices, or strategies, available to them (here, to be silent or confess); and the outcomes associated with the four different strategy pairs. The layout here in the bimatrix is the standard way of representing this normal form game.

Now the solution of the game. Each prisoner wants to minimize time spent behind bars and has no other goal. Moreover, each is indifferent to how much time the other spends in prison. I ignore the possibility of altruism or spite. I also ignore the reputational issues that might arise from being known as a snitch or fear of reprisal for confessing. Finally, the two prisoners have no way of communicating with each other. Each must decide without knowing what the other will do.

This is a game in which each prisoner has a *strictly dominant strategy*. Each is better off confessing regardless of what the other does. One can solve the game by recognizing that each prisoner is likely to reason in the following way: "If the other prisoner has decided to keep silent, I am better off confessing. That way I spend no time behind bars at all, rather than two years. What about the other possibility? If the other prisoner confesses, I am also better off confessing. As bad as serving a six-year sentence might be, serving a ten-year sentence is worse. No matter what the other person does, I am better off confessing. No prison is better than two years and six years is better than ten years." Because both prisoners will likely engage in this reasoning, both are likely to confess.

The outcome—both prisoners confess—seems counterintuitive at first because the prisoners would have been better off if both had remained silent. But this result follows once we assume that we have structured the payoffs correctly. Even if each prisoner erroneously believed that the other was altruistic and would confess, we would still have the same outcome, *given our assumption that the prisoners care only for themselves.* If a prisoner believes (for whatever reason) the other will remain silent, confessing is a way of avoiding prison altogether, the best outcome of all. (Again, if the prisoners care about something in addition to the length of time spent in jail, we have specified the payoffs incorrectly. The premise of the game is that the players are both selfish.) The result is not at all odd once one recognizes that the prisoners lack a means of committing themselves to remaining silent. As long as the two prisoners cannot reach any agreement with each other and as long as their only concern is time spent in prison (and not, let us say, their reputations as finks), their individual interest will lead them to confess, even though they are jointly better off remaining silent.

The power of the Prisoner's Dilemma comes from the incongruence between private benefit and the collective good. Individually rational decisionmaking leads to collective disaster. The Prisoner's Dilemma is thus often seen as one of the main theoretical justifications for government intrusion into private decisionmaking.[4] Legislation almost appears attractive given the collective disaster that results from individual decisionmaking in the dilemma.

I say "almost" for two reasons. First, the existence of private failure tells us nothing about whether government decisionmaking enjoys a comparative advantage over private decisionmaking. The Churchill line about democracy—"democracy is the worst form of Government except all those other forms that have been tried from time to time"—may apply here as well. We need to know much about the quality of government decisionmaking before we can summarily abandon private decisionmaking. The second reason for being cautious about relying on a simple game-theoretic model such as the Prisoner's Dilemma to justify legal intervention will require more hardware, so I will return to it at the end of this talk.

b.   An Example from the Law of Torts

Many legal settings can be represented as normal form games and solved by identifying dominant strategies. Consider an accident on a country road involving a motorist and a pedestrian. The likelihood of an accident turns both on how much care the motorist uses in driving and how much care the pedestrian uses in crossing the street. We do not expect the motorist to drive so slowly that there is never any possibility of hitting a pedestrian. Nor do we insist that the pedestrian cross only when there is no car in sight. We want them both to take sensible precautions. If both act reasonably, the chances of an accident as well as the inconvenience to both parties are minimized. If they could bargain with each

4. See, e.g., Cass R. Sunstein, *After the Rights Revolution: Reconceiving the* *Regulatory State* 49–51 (Harvard Univ. Press, 1990).

other, we would expect that each would agree to act in this way. The problem arises, of course, because the two are strangers and they cannot communicate with each other. The motorist and the pedestrian both recognize that the actions of the other influence what will happen, and that basic fact must be recognized if we are to have a sensible analysis of the situation. Game theory is the right tool for this problem.

To jump right in, consider the following "game":

	Motorist	
Pedestrian	No Care	Due Care
No Care	*-100, 0*	-100, -10
Due Care	-110, 0	-20, -10

Payoffs: (Pedestrian, Motorist)

Figure 2: No Reallocation Law

Here are the stylized facts that this game is seeking to represent. If an accident takes place between the motorist and the pedestrian, the motorist and her car will not be hurt, but the pedestrian will of course suffer harm. Assume that we can represent the harm to the pedestrian as a dollar amount and set that amount at $100. Both the motorist and the pedestrian decide on how much care to take. Assume that they each choose between taking "no care" and "due care." Representing the decision of how much care to take as a binary choice oversimplifies greatly, but it is the natural place to start. Assume that it costs nothing to exercise "no care" but costs $10 to exercise "due care." "Due care" is really a legal term for a physical level of care. Consistent with the convention, "due care" is the level of care that minimizes the total expected costs of the accident. We also need to know how the care choices relate to the probability of an accident occurring. Assume that the accident is certain to happen unless both the motorist and the pedestrian exercise "due care," but that there is still a one in ten chance of an accident occurring even if both exercise "due care."

So far, we have set out the brute facts of nature: the choices available to our players (the motorist and the pedestrian), or what a game theorist would call the strategies of the players, and the physical consequences associated with those strategies (whether an accident takes place and the resulting harm). To fully specify this game, we need one more item, and it is this item that determines the precise structure of the game set forth above. We need to know the legal rule for allocating the harms of an accident. The problem of strategic behavior that the legal analyst faces is a simple problem of simultaneous decisionmaking. The amount of care that the motorist and pedestrian each take would turn on the amount of care each expects the other to take. The amount of care that each takes will turn in some measure on the legal rule that is in place— when and to what extent the motorist will have to pay damages to the pedestrian in the event of an accident. The first question for the legal analyst concerns the effect of changes in the legal rule on the behavior of the parties. Start with a rule of no liability, or of letting the parties bear their own losses. In this case, if an accident occurs, the motorist is not harmed and the pedestrian is harmed, and the legal rule of no liability does not reallocate any of the harm by having the motorist pay damages.

We can now explain the game in figure 2 and determine how to solve it. In a legal regime of no liability, a regime in which the motorist was never liable for the accident, the motorist would enjoy a payoff of $0 and the pedestrian a payoff of –$100 if neither exercised care. The cost of "no care" is zero, an accident is certain to happen, and the accident harms the pedestrian to the tune of $100. If both exercised care, the motorist would receive a payoff of –$10 and the pedestrian a payoff of –$20. (The pedestrian invests $10 in care and, assuming the pedestrian is risk neutral, still faces $10 in expected accident costs, a one in ten chance of a $100 accident.) If the motorist exercises care and the pedestrian does not, the motorist receives a payoff of –$10 (the cost of taking care) and the pedestrian a payoff of –$100 (the cost of the accident, which by assumption is certain to arise unless both take care). Finally, if the motorist does not take care and the pedestrian does, the motorist has a payoff of $0 and the pedestrian a payoff of –$110 (the pedestrian invests $10 in taking care and still suffers a $100 injury).

What is the likely outcome of this game? In this model, taking care costs the motorist $10 and provides no benefit to the motorist in return. The motorist always does better by not taking care than by taking care. We can predict the motorist's likely choice of strategy because there is a single strategy ("no care") that, in the context of this model, is better for the motorist no matter what choice the pedestrian makes. In the language of game theory, this is a *dominant strategy* (really a *strictly* dominant strategy). In corresponding fashion, a strategy which is always worse than another strategy, again regardless of what the other player does, is a *dominated* strategy. In figure 2, "due care" is a dominated strategy for the motorist. We should predict—as we did in analyzing the

Prisoner's Dilemma—that a player will embrace a dominant strategy wherever possible and will not embrace any strategy that is dominated by another.

This idea by itself, however, tells us only what the motorist is likely to do in this model. We cannot use this concept to predict the pedestrian's behavior. Neither of the strategies available to the pedestrian is dominated by the other. It makes sense for the pedestrian not to take care when the motorist does not, but to take care when the motorist does. The pedestrian lacks a dominant strategy because either course of action could be better or worse than the other depending upon what the motorist does. Note that this game differs from the Prisoner's Dilemma in this regard, as in that game, both players had a dominant strategy. To predict the pedestrian's behavior, we need to take the idea that players play dominant strategies one step further. Not only will a player likely adopt a strictly dominant strategy, but a player will predict that the other player is likely to adopt such a strategy and will act accordingly. We can predict, in other words, that the pedestrian will choose a strategy based on the idea that the motorist will not choose a strategy that is strictly dominated by another. This idea travels under the name of *iterated dominance* and allows us to solve this game. The pedestrian should understand that the motorist has a dominant strategy—play "no care"—and therefore the pedestrian should play "no care" as well. Given that the motorist plays "no care," the payoff to the pedestrian from playing "due care" is –$110 and that from playing "no care" is –$100. (Recall that the accident is certain to happen unless both players play "due care"; once the motorist will not, the pedestrian is better off by not wasting any money on care.) The pedestrian should play "no care" as well. Neither player exercises care. Note that to reach this solution, we proceeded iteratively: we first identified the strategy that the motorist would play using dominance arguments—this is the first iteration—and we next identified the pedestrian's strategy *given* the motorist's strategy as determined in the first stage of the argument—this is the second iteration. This is the logic of iterated dominance.

This extension of the idea that dominated strategies are not played requires us to make a further assumption about the rationality of the players. Players not only act rationally and do the best they can given their preferences, but they also believe that others act rationally and do the best they can given their preferences. This solution concept seems plausible if the number of iterations is small. After all, most people act rationally most of the time and we can choose our own actions in anticipation that they will act this way. If we accept this solution concept, we can solve the game in figure 2. The pedestrian will not exercise care because the pedestrian will believe that the motorist will not exercise care and, in that event, the pedestrian, under our assumptions, is better off not exercising care either. We cannot, however, make this prediction as confidently as we can predict the motorist's behavior. The solution to the game turns not only on the motorist acting in a way that advances her self-interest, but also on the pedestrian anticipating that the motorist will in fact act in this way.

You might think that these results are specific to the particular numbers set forth in figure 2. The specific result is, though the result that matters is not. In the example in figure 2, the pedestrian chooses to exercise no care when the motorist exercises no care. That outcome is tied directly to the particular probability function for accidents, which makes it worthless for one player to exercise any care if the other player is exercising no care. In general— meaning for different probability functions for accidents—the pedestrian might choose more or less than "due care." The general result is the result that matters: under a rule of no reallocation of losses and where any harm from the accident will be borne by the pedestrian, the motorist lacks an appropriate incentive to take care. Indeed, as shown above—and this is a general result—exercising "no care" is a dominant strategy.

Thus, play under a rule of no liability puts us far from the social goal of having both players exercise due care. This result in itself is hardly startling. To say that the strategy of taking due care is dominated by another strategy of taking less than due care restates in the language of game theory a familiar insight from law and economics, the insight that in a world without tort law, parties tend to take less than due care because they do not fully internalize the costs of their actions.[5] The motorist enjoys all the benefits of driving fast, but does not bear all the costs (the danger of injuring the pedestrian). By capturing the problem of the pedestrian and the motorist in the form of a two-by-two game, however, not only are the incentives of the motorist made manifest, but we can readily understand how a change in the legal rules alters the incentives of the motorist and the pedestrian at the same time.

To see this, consider the legal regime of negligence coupled with contributory negligence. This is the regime that Anglo–American law has embraced for a long time. Under this regime, the pedestrian can recover only if the motorist is negligent and if the pedestrian is not. This rule of law leads to the normal form game set out in figure 3:

5. See, e.g., W. Landes and R. Posner, *The Economic Structure of Tort* *Law* 62 (Cambridge, Harvard Univ. Press, 1987).

Motorist

	No Care	Due Care
No Care	-100, 0	-100, -10
Due Care	-10, -100	-20, -10

Pedestrian

Payoffs: (Pedestrian, Motorist)

Figure 3: Negligence With Contributory Negligence

Compare figure 3 with figure 2. The two figures are identical except in the box in which the pedestrian exercises due care and the motorist fails to do so. In this event, the motorist rather than the pedestrian bears the cost of the accident. The pedestrian bears the cost of the accident whenever the pedestrian fails to exercise care and in the case in which both players exercise care. The legal rule does not change the strategies available to the players or the sum of the payoffs in each box. All that changes is the allocation of the cost of the accident between the parties.

In this game, unlike the game in figure 2, the pedestrian has a dominant strategy. The pedestrian is always better off taking care. The motorist no longer has a dominant strategy. Whether the motorist is better off taking care turns on whether the pedestrian also takes care. If we accept the idea of iterated dominance, however, we can predict the strategy that the motorist will choose. The motorist will recognize that the pedestrian will play "due care" and then decide to play "due care." Hence, under this legal regime, both pedestrian and motorist will take due care.

A comparison between the two models focuses our attention on the way in which this legal rule works and reveals a counterintuitive insight about the role of law. The only difference between figure 2 and figure 3 is in the box representing the strategy combination in which the pedestrian exercises "due care" and the motorist does not. In figure 2, the payoffs were –$110 and $0 for the pedestrian and the motorist respectively. In figure 3, they are –$10 and –$100. This strategy combination is not the solution to either game: in figure 2, neither player exercises care, while in figure 3 both players exercise care. Yet it is how the negligence/contributory negligence regime reallocates the harm when the pedestrian takes care and the motorist does not—an outcome that is not reached in either game—that completely alters the expected play of the game. Under either liability rule, we would never expect to observe the pedestrian exercising due care and the motorist exercising no care, but it is precisely how the law treats the outcome that will not happen that determines whether the efficient due care–due care outcome occurs. *A legal rule brings about changes through the consequences it attaches to behavior that never happens either when the legal rule is in place or when it is not.*

This model also focuses on a central assumption underlying the Anglo–American rule. To believe that this rule works, we must believe both that the motorist acts rationally and that the motorist believes that the pedestrian acts rationally as well. The motorist will take care in order to avoid liability only if the motorist believes that the pedestrian is similarly motivated to act in a way that tries to avoid bearing the cost of accidents and will take care as well. If the motorist believed that the pedestrian would not take care, the motorist would not take care either. This liability rule turns crucially on the assumption that the motorist believes that the pedestrian will exercise due care.

This explicit game-theoretic approach isolates two features of the law in a useful way. First, it makes clear the rationality assumptions required. We must assume not only that individuals behave rationally, but that individuals expect others to behave rationally as well. Second, this way of looking at the problem reveals one of the important but subtle ways in which a legal rule works. A change in a legal rule can alter the behavior of both parties even by changing outcomes that are never seen under either the new or the old regime.[6]

3. Extensive Form Games and Backwards Induction

Not all games or legal situations can be resolved using dominance arguments. For example, consider the problem of choosing on which side of the road to drive. In this country, we drive on the right hand side, in England, on the left. Think of two players faced with that choice in the absence of a governmental setting:

6. For additional analysis of torts issues from the perspective of dominant and dominated strategies, see Daniel Orr, "*The Superiority of Comparative Negligence: Another Vote,*" 20 J. Legal Stud. 119 (1991); Tai–Yeong Chung, *Efficiency of Comparative Negligence: A Game Theoretic Analysis*, Mimeo, Department of Economics, Social Science Center, Univ. of Western Ontario, London, Ontario (1992).

	Player 2	
	Left	Right
Left	4, 3	0, 0
Right	0, 0	3, 4

Player 1

Payoffs: (Player 1, Player 2)

Figure 4: Driving Coordination Game (Normal Form)

Player 1 has a slight preference for driving on the left, player 2
for the right, but both care most about making the same decision.
(For that reason, this game is often labeled a *coordination game*.)
Neither player has a dominant strategy nor is any strategy a
dominated strategy. What then is the likely outcome? There is
another important approach to solving games, though it will be of
only some help here. Consider the following idea: If player 1 knew
that player 2 were to play "left," player 1 would play "left" also,
and the flipside of that is true as well. The same is true of the
combination (right, right): player 1 would play "right" in response
to player 2's "right" and player 2 would play "right" in response to
player 1's "right." (Left, right) and (right, left) lack this quality: if
player 1 chose to play "left" but before committing learned that
player 2 was going to play "right," player 1 would abandon "left"
and instead play "right." (Left, left) and (right, right) have a
stability that the other two outcomes lack. The game theory lingo
for this is that both (left, left) and (right, right) are Nash equilibria,
Nash coming from the great game theorist John Nash. This game
has two pure strategy Nash equilibria. (Pure strategy is more lingo
for saying that neither player is playing in a probabilistic fashion.)

In some settings, a game will have a unique Nash equilibrium
and it is perhaps understandable that such an equilibrium is
considered the most natural outcome to the game. Unfortunately,
as in figure 4, many games have multiple Nash equilibria and the
games themselves offer no good means for the players to coordinate
on those equilibria. As a consequence, if the game in figure 4 were
played in an experimental setting, I would expect to see a sizable
number of non-Nash (left, right) and (right, left) outcomes. The
players would not be happy about this, as this is the worst outcome
for them, but the problem with the game is that the players lack
any good means for coordinating their choices. Sometimes player 1
would hope that the (left, left) Nash outcome was going to be

played while player 2 would be hoping for the (right, right) Nash outcome and that puts the players squarely on (left, right).

Subject to the Churchill caveat, legal intervention might again be appropriate. To get at this and to introduce another form for representing games, suppose, for example, the government gave the first person the right to set the rules of the road. This game could be represented in the following way:

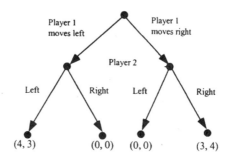

Payoffs: (Player 1, Player 2)

Figure 5: Driving Sequential Game (Extensive Form)

This game represents the players' choices through something akin to a decision tree. This representation is known as the *extensive form* of a game. Figure 5 differs from a decision tree in that it represents decisions by two players, but the basic idea is the same. Pursuant to governmental edict, player 1 chooses first, player 2 second, and each still chooses between "left" and "right." In this game, player 2 observes player 1's choice, which is the essential difference between this game and our prior game in figure 4.

This game can be solved using another solution technique, *backwards induction*. If player 1 moves "left," player 2 will choose between "left," with a payoff of 3, and "right" with a payoff of 0. Player 2 would clearly play "left." If player 1 moves "right," player 2 will choose between "left," with a payoff of 0, and "right" with a payoff of 4, and hence will choose "right." Player 1 thus faces moving "left," and receiving 4 and moving "right" and receiving 3, and hence would move "left." Legislation changing the sequence of moves turns a simultaneous decisionmaking game into a sequential game and establishes a clear outcome. The indeterminacy of the simultaneous game is eliminated. Note that the government allocation of the right to move first has distributional consequences. In this game, player 1 receives 4 and player 2 gets 3. If the right to move first were allocated to player 2, player 2 would get 4 and player 1 would receive 3.

Standard setting, such as establishing the rules of the road, is a conventional use of governmental power. The games in figures 4 and 5 should make clear the possible benefits associated with these activities.

4. Embedded Games: Caveat Legislator

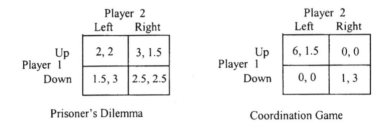

Payoffs: (Player 1, Player 2)

Figure 6: A Prisoner's Dilemma and a Coordination Game

I started the analysis with the Prisoner's Dilemma, as it is easily the best-known game and is most often invoked in defense of legal intervention. Such an analysis often does little more than to suggest that a particular situation has the form of the dilemma and then to claim that intervention would be appropriate. This may be a serious mistake. Whether a Prisoner's Dilemma creates problems depends on the larger structure in which the game exists. Put differently, a small game, such as the Prisoner's Dilemma, may arise in a much larger game. The very existence of the Prisoner's Dilemma in the large game may have beneficial, rather than negative, consequences. A simple example should make this clear. Consider the games set forth in figure 6 above.

Figure 6 illustrates a Prisoner's Dilemma and a coordination game. (I have changed the payoffs from the prior versions of these games, but that is irrelevant here.) In the first game in figure 6, player 1 will play "up," as that is his dominant strategy. (If player 2 were to play "left," player 1 gets a payoff of 2 from "up" and a payoff of 1.5 from "down;" if player 2 were to play "right," player 1 would get a payoff of 3 from "up" and of 2.5 from "down;" "up" is therefore a dominant strategy.) Players 1 and 2 are in symmetric positions in the first game, so player 2 has a dominant strategy of "left." Both players have dominant strategies, resulting in the payoff of (2, 2), which is worse than (2.5, 2.5) from (right, right).

Game 2 in figure 6 is a coordination game, meaning here, as before, that the game has two pure strategy Nash equilibria. The strategy combination (up, left) is one equilibrium: if player 1 were to play "up," player 2 would want to play "left," as that results in a payoff of 1.5 rather than the payoff of 0 obtained by playing "right." And if player 2 were to play "left," player 1 would prefer "up" and 6 to "down" and 0. Thus, (up, left) forms a Nash equilibrium. A similar analysis holds for (down, right). As before in figure 4, game theory offers us little basis for choosing between these two equilibria.

That's where the Prisoner's Dilemma comes in; it will take us two steps to get there. Start with the game set forth in figure 7:

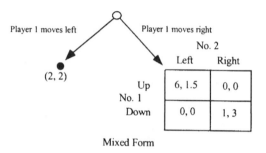

Payoffs: (Player 1, Player 2)

Figure 7: Embedded Coordination Game

I have embedded the coordination game from figure 6 into a larger game. In this game, player 1 makes an initial move in which player 1 has a chance to decide between taking a certain payoff of 2 or playing a coordination game. If the coordination game is played, player 2 knows that player 1 has elected to forego the certain payoff of 2 and has instead chosen to play the coordination game with player 2. This coordination game is identical to that in figure 6. In that game, players 1 and 2 move simultaneously, and, most importantly, neither can observe the choice of the other.

Now consider how players 1 and 2 should reason. Player 2 decides whether to play "left" or "right" only after observing that player 1 has moved "right." Player 2 does not know whether player 1 moved "up" or "down," but player 2 should not expect player 1 ever to move "down" after having moved "right." Moving "down" is dominated by any strategy in which player 1 moves "left." Player 1's maximum payoff of 1 in the game that follows after playing "right" followed by "down" is dominated by the payoff from playing "left." Hence, if player 1 moves "right," player 1 should follow that move by moving "up." Were player 1 to do otherwise, player 1 would have adopted a dominated strategy. Believing that others would not play dominated strategies, player 2 will play "left" in response to player 1's initial move of "right." Because player 2 believes player 1 will move "up" after moving "right," player 2 ensures a payoff of 1.5 rather than 0 by moving "up." Player 1, recognizing that player 2 will move "left," will play the strategy of moving "right" and "up" and enjoy a payoff of 6, rather than one in which player 1 moves "left" and enjoys a payoff of only 2. Even though this coordination game standing alone does not have a unique solution, it does have one when it is part of a larger game.[7]

Now take the next step. Replace the solitary payoff of (2, 2) with our Prisoner's Dilemma game from figure 6:

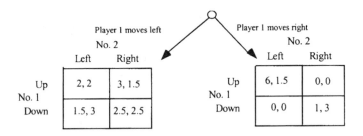

Payoffs: (Player 1, Player 2)

Figure 8: Embedded Prisoner's Dilemma and Coordination Games

In this game, player 1 moves "left" or "right" first, and this move is observed by player 2. If player 1 moves "left," the Prisoner's Dilemma game is played. If player 2 moves "right," the coordination game is played.

How should this game be solved? In the same way we solved the game in figure 7. In the Prisoner's Dilemma, each player has a dominant strategy and a payoff of (2,2) should result. If player 1 were to play "left," he would obtain 2. That payoff is better than any payoff that can result by playing "right" followed by "down." Hence, player 1 would follow "right" only with "up." Player 2 should understand this and play "left" following player 1's initial "right." This would result in a payoff of 6 to player 1. Player 1 should therefore play "right" followed by "up" and player 2 should play "left." This results in payoffs of 6 and 1.5, for a total of 7.5, the maximum available on these particular (and cooked) numbers.

7. This is an example of *forward induction*. For an introduction, see Drew Fudenberg and Jean Tirole, *Game Theory*, § 11.3 (MIT Press, 1991).

Step back and note what has happened. We started with two games in figure 6, the Prisoner's Dilemma and a coordination game. Taking either of these as freestanding games would suggest that legal intervention might be appropriate. The Prisoner's Dilemma plays out inefficiently, and the existence of multiple equilibria in the coordination game means we can have little confidence of an efficient outcome there. Yet bring these two games together in a single larger game, and private decisionmaking leads to an efficient outcome. The very existence of the Prisoner's Dilemma makes it possible to coordinate on a particular Nash equilibrium in the coordination game.

The punch line here is that game structure matters, and often matters a lot. Identification of the game itself is of great importance. Misidentification usually occurs when the small, freestanding game is viewed as *the* game. A modeler who focused on the interaction captured in the Prisoner's Dilemma in figure 8 rather than the entire game would be misled. It is a mistake to suggest that a Prisoner's Dilemma may arise in a particular context and to use that to justify legal intervention. The larger game structure must be understood, as these rather stylized games suggest. The counterintuitive (at least to me) suggestion of figure 8 is that the existence of a scenario in which a Prisoner's Dilemma game might arise actually *helps* the players to achieve the best outcome.

All of this should introduce a level of caution into willy-nilly invocations of the Prisoner's Dilemma as a basis for legislation. More generally, it is critical to understand the context in which a particular game occurs and the extent to which it is embedded in a larger game.[8] Understanding that may make it clear that the very form of the game is up for grabs. For example, the dominant theoretical justification for bankruptcy is that creditors of the failing firm face a collective action problem akin to that in the Prisoner's Dilemma.[9] (This is often called the common pool problem.) One solution is a government-created collective procedure, the modern bankruptcy proceeding. Nonetheless, to accept that the creditors of the firm must play the financial equivalent of the Prisoner's Dilemma is a mistake. Together with the debtor, the creditors have an interest in taking actions ahead of time to mitigate the possible harms of the dilemma. Security interests can be understood as one important way of completely avoiding the dilemma.[10] Again, the point here is that we must understand the

---

8. For a similar point in a political science context, see George Tsebelis, *Nested Games: Rational Choice in Comparative Politics* 7 (Univ. of California Press, 1990).

9. See Thomas H. Jackson, *The Logic and Limits of Bankruptcy Law* 10 (Harvard Univ. Press, 1986).

10. See Randal C. Picker, "*Security Interests, Misbehavior, and Common Pools,*" 59 U. Chi. L. Rev. 645 (1992).

context in which a game would otherwise take place. The game in figure 8 makes this point—I hope—in relatively stark fashion.

5. Conclusion

This talk sketches out some of the basic ideas of game theory. There is a standard language for representing situations, giving rise to the normal form and extensive form games, and ways to discuss solutions, such as dominant strategy solutions, Nash equilibria, backwards induction, and forward induction. I hope that I have suggested a number of ways in which these ideas help us generate counterintuitive insights about legal problems. The central lesson of the torts example is that a legal rule brings about changes through the consequences it attaches to behavior that never happens either when the legal rule is in place or when it is not. I found that surprising. I found even more surprising the notion that having a Prisoner's Dilemma handy might actually help solve collective action problems, rather than create them, and that this should make us cautious in relying on the Prisoner's Dilemma to justify legal intervention. I would have found it difficult to reach either of these points without using game theory, though there very well may be other routes.

I return to where I started. The bar stool test demands simplicity. The work of Ronald Coase, and a lecture worthy of his name, demands both simplicity and depth. I hope that the ideas set forth here at least come close on both scores. Nonetheless, if I have failed, I accept no blame and instead place it squarely on the shoulders of Dean Geoffrey Stone. Any failings must reflect the fact that I spent too little time in bars in preparing this talk and that in turn can be attributed to the measly research budget for it. Notwithstanding this, I am prepared to move forward and undertake more research and we can begin at the reception that immediately follows.

Study Questions:

1. It is often said that contract law is designed to solve a prisoner's dilemma. What is this prisoner's dilemma?

2. To what strategic problem might the commerce clause of the United States Constitution be a response?

3. International treaties establish technical standards for communication and transportation. What are the games that these treaties attempt to solve?

4. Analyze the common law from a game theoretic perspective. What about stare decisis?

5. Suppose that when parties have a dispute, they always have complete information about the interests of each other, and about how a court would apply the law to resolve their dispute. If this is the case, would there ever be a trial? A lawsuit?

*

3. The Law and Economics of Contract Damages

Douglas G. Baird[1]

Those of us who study contracts tend to forget that most people keep the promises they make. Contract law matters because of the way it affects the behavior of everyone who enters into a contract, not just those who end up in court. In this talk, I want to show that law and economics is useful for exactly this reason. It helps us to identify the effects that legal rules have on behavior.

I.

Let's start with a well-known case and a discrete problem of contract damages. The case is *Missouri Furnace Co. v. Cochran.*[2] The problem is measuring damages in the case of anticipatory breach.[3] The time is 1880. In early January, Cochrane promises to deliver 100 tons of coke to Missouri Furnace every working day of the year at a price of $1.20 a ton. There is a sudden rise in the price of coke in January and Cochrane breaches the contract in mid-February. Missouri Furnace immediately enters into a substantially similar contract with a different seller, but at the much higher price of $4 a ton.

This $4-per-ton price is less than the spot price for coke in February and it is the prevailing price for a forward contract in February. The spot price of coke, however, later falls far below $4. If Missouri Furnace had waited and purchased coke throughout the

---

1. Harry A. Bigelow Professor of Law and Dean. This lecture was delivered in February 1994.

This paper tries to distill the essence of the work of Richard Posner, William Landes, Steven Shavell, Ian Ayres, Robert Gertner, Thomas Jackson, and others. There are many important contributions that I do not cover explicitly. Given the state of the literature, this paper tries only to set out some basic landmarks.

One of the seminal treatments of contract damages remains Richard A. Posner, Economic Analysis of Law § 4.8, at 117–28 (4th ed. 1992). Other work has also made important contributions. See, e.g., Robert Cooter & Thomas Ulen, Law

and Economics (1988); Lewis A. Kornhauser, An Introduction to the Economic Analysis of Contract Remedies, 57 Univ. Colo. L. Rev. 683 (1986); A. Mitchell Polinsky, An Introduction to Law and Economics (2d ed. 1989).

2. 8 F. 463 (W.D. Pa. 1881).

3. The first comprehensive treatment of this question is Thomas H. Jackson, "Anticipatory Repudiation" and the Temporal Element in Contract Law: An Economic Inquiry into Contract Damages in Cases of Prospective Nonperformance, 31 Stan. L. Rev. 69 (1978). My discussion follows Jackson closely. For a critique, see Alan Schwartz & Robert Scott, Commercial Transactions: Principles and Policies 323–25 (1982).

year on the spot market it would have paid on average substantially less than $4 a ton for its coke.

Missouri Furnace argued that later changes in the price were irrelevant. It was entitled to the difference between the contract price of $1.20 and $4, the price of the forward contract at the time of the breach. Cochrane argued that Missouri Furnace was taking its chances when it entered into another forward contract. In its view, Missouri Furnace was entitled only to the difference between $1.20 and the spot price for the coke at the time it was to be delivered.

The court agreed with Cochrane and held that Missouri Furnace was not entitled to recover for the costs of entering into the forward contract that subsequently proved unfavorable:

> [Missouri Furnace was] not bound to enter into such a contract, which might be to [its] advantage or detriment, according as the market might fall or rise. If it fell, [Cochrane] might fairly say that [Missouri Furnace] had no right to enter into a speculative contract, and [Cochrane might fairly] insist that he was not called upon to pay a greater difference than would have existed had [Missouri Furnace] held its hand.... As [Missouri Furnace] was not bound to enter into the new forward contract, ... it did so at its own risk.

I want to use the tools of law and economics to examine whether the court's ruling in *Missouri Furnace* is consistent with its own first principles. The court in *Missouri Furnace*, like common law courts generally, accepts what is now called the expectation damages principle. The aggrieved party is entitled to those damages that put it in the same position that it would be in if the breach had not taken place. As the Uniform Commercial Code tells us in § 1–106, remedies for breach of contract are to be "liberally administered to the end that the aggrieved party may be put in as good a position as if the other party had fully performed." Is the decision in *Missouri Furnace* consistent with this idea?

Our intuition probably tells us that there is something suspect about what the court did. The day before Missouri Furnace breached, it had Cochrane's promise to take care of all its needs for coke for the whole year in exchange for its promise to pay $1.20 a ton. After Cochrane breached, Missouri Furnace had to promise to pay $4 a ton to get someone else to promise to do the same thing—to satisfy its need for coke for the entire year. To put Missouri Furnace in the same position it had been in before Cochrane broke its promise, it would seem Missouri Furnace needs damages based on the difference between $4 and $1.20.

Missouri Furnace entered into its contract with Cochrane in the first place because it had decided not to buy on the spot market.

Missouri Furnace bargained for the benefit of a forward contract. To make Missouri Furnace whole, the right question is how much more it would cost to enter into a forward contract with another seller.

The court in *Missouri Furnace* had it exactly backwards. Missouri Furnace did not want to speculate on the price of coke. It wanted to pay a fixed price for the coke. For that reason Missouri Furnace bargained for a forward contract with Cochrane and it is that benefit which it lost when Cochrane broke his contract.

We cannot stop our analysis here, however. In many cases, there won't be a forward market that the buyer can reenter. It may be much easier to figure out the spot price than the forward price. Even if the forward contract measure is conceptually correct, is there anything the matter with the spot price measure? The price could be higher or lower, but is there anything *systematically* wrong with it? After all, once this rule is in place, why should Missouri Furnace complain? It can just buy coke in the spot market and send Cochrane the bill. How is it any worse off?

Law and economics can answer this question for us. The spot price measure is systematically overcompensatory. In *Missouri Furnace*, the seller wanted the spot price after the fact, but, over the course of many cases and holding everything else constant, the seller more often favors the forward measure and the buyer the spot price.

The intuition is not that hard when one takes a step back. Assume we use the spot price measure. If the seller breaches and the price of coke continues to go up, the seller takes the entire loss. The seller pays the difference between the contract price and the market price. This amount just gets bigger as the spot price of coke rises.

But what if the price moves in the other direction? The seller gets the benefit of a fall in price only until the spot price falls to the original contract price. As soon as the spot price falls below the original contract price, the buyer gets all the benefit of further declines. (In the absence of the breach, in the face of this decline, the buyer would have to buy coke at the contract price, a price that was greater than the market price. The seller's breach frees the buyer from this obligation.) Under the spot price measure, the seller bears the entire risk if the price continues to rise, but does not capture the entire benefit when the price falls.

Let me make the point with a simple example. Before I do, however, I want to make an aside about methodology. My arithmetic example, consistent with the spirit of much of law and economics, simplifies things dramatically. We have to be careful that the assumptions we make do not eliminate the problem that we want to study. But simplifying assumptions have virtues that can offset this potential danger.

By stripping away the unnecessary, we can understand the basic forces at work much better than we could otherwise. I am going to use examples that make all sorts of unrealistic assumptions. I am not going to worry about litigation costs. I am also going to assume that people are risk neutral, even though I believe most people are risk averse. I do this not because economics isn't up to the task, but rather because it isn't necessary given the points I want to make.

The question you need to ask is not whether the model is too simple, but rather whether the basic force that is being identified in the example still remains in richer environments. Indeed, the single largest vice in modern law and economics is that we have become so compulsive about taking everything into account that we get caught up in the mathematics we need to do this. We then lose sight of the transactions we are trying to understand. As Ronald Coase put it:

> In my youth it was said that what was too silly to be said may be sung. In modern economics it may be put into mathematics.[4]

Let's look at a simple example. On January 1, you promise to sell me coke at $15 for delivery on July 1. It is now the end of February. You have decided to retire and you want to call off the contract. But there is now labor unrest in the coke industry. For this reason, I cannot find someone else who is willing to sell July 1 coke for $15.

Let me tell you exactly what the conditions are. If the labor disputes are resolved and the workers enter a new contract, the price of coke will be $10 on July 1. But if things do not settle down, mines will shut down and the price of coke will be $30 on July 1. Either event is equally likely. These possibilities are reflected in the forward price for coke of $20. ($20 is the average of $10 and $30.)

If you break your contract to sell me coke at $15, what damages should I recover? How much will it take to put me back into the same situation I was in before the breach? If others offer the same type of contract you offered me, I can simply enter into a forward contract. Because I have to promise this new seller $20 and I promised you only $15, I need $5 in damages to be made whole. ($5 is the difference between the $20 market price and the $15 contract price.)

But what is my recovery if contract law gives me the difference between the spot price and the contract price? There is a 50–50 chance that the spot price will be $30. In that case, I get the difference between $30 and the contract price of $15. This would

    4. R.H. Coase, The Firm, the Market, and the Law 185 (1988).

give me damages of $15. But let's consider the other possibility. If the spot price drops to $10, it is below the contract price. I have not been injured by your breach. Indeed, you turned out to do me a big favor by breaching. If I still want coke, I can go out and get it for less than I promised you. I don't need any damages to be made whole.

What are my expected damages then if we use the spot market measure? It is the average of $15 and $0 (or $7.50). An expected damage award of $7.50 is greater than the $5 I would get if we used the forward contract measure. The numbers are simple, but there is nothing cooked about them. The effect here is a quite general one. Over the course of many cases, the buyer is going to get more under a spot price measure than under the forward price measure. Because the forward price measure gives the buyer enough money to buy exactly that which the seller promised, the spot price measure gives the buyer more than is needed to make the buyer whole.

We should not rush to conclusions. A court might be justified in departing from the expectation damages principle in a case of anticipatory repudiation. The spot price may be readily ascertainable and the departure from the expectation damages principle may be negligible. The chance of the price falling below the original contract price may be small. Hence, the spot price may be a good approximation in cases in which the forward price is not available. Moreover, when the forward price is readily available, we do not need to be as worried about getting the damages remedy exactly right. In such cases, breach is less likely. A seller who wanted to retire could, instead of breaching, simply enter into the futures market and thereby find someone else to perform.

We should not, however, do what the court did in *Missouri Furnace*. That court did not recognize that it was departing from the expectation damages principle. If we want to depart from it, that may be fine, but we want to be aware of what we are doing. This naturally leads us to the question of whether the expectation damages rule itself is sensible.

II.

Let us imagine the prototypical contract. I agree to build a machine for you. I want the deal. I think I can make the machine for less than the contract price. You want the deal. You think that the machine will bring you more money over the long haul than the contract price. But none of this is certain. After we enter into the contract, but before performance, conditions can suddenly change. One of us may be tempted to breach. Legal rules can give each of us the right set of incentives. Or, to put it more cautiously, we want to be sure that we do not have legal rules in place that give us the wrong set of incentives. Let us see exactly how expectation damages changes the incentives of parties to a contract.

Let's use another example with stylized facts. We have a buyer who needs a new machine. Buyer could build the machine itself, but Seller has more expertise. It can build a better machine more cheaply. Buyer agrees to buy the machine for $125. Buyer is excited about getting the machine, because over the course of its life the machine will produce an extra $200 in income for Buyer. Buyer is going to be $75 richer with this machine than without it.

Seller is also happy with this deal. Seller believes it will cost about $100 to make the machine. It could cost more and it could cost less. Seller does not find out how much it will cost to make the machine until just before the time comes to build it, but on average Seller's profits on the deal will equal the difference between the $125 purchase price and the expected cost of $100. Seller's expected profit, in other words, is $25.

What is going to happen if the cost of building the machine suddenly rises? The machine turns out to cost $175. The contract is now a losing deal for Seller. If Seller performs, Seller will spend $175 building the machine and will get only $125 in return. But the machine is still worth building. The cost of the machine is still less than the $200 it is worth to Buyer.

We want Seller to take account of the loss Buyer will suffer when it is deciding whether to perform. How can we do this? How can we make Seller compare the cost of the machine to it against the benefits of the machine to Buyer? The answer is that we can use expectation damages.

Let's see how this works. Remember expectation damages. If Seller breaches, Seller has to make Buyer whole. Seller has to pay damages equal to the value of the machine to Buyer (or $200) less the contract price of $125. By contrast, if Seller performs, it incurs the costs of building the machine ($175), but Buyer pays it for the machine and Seller receives $125. When Seller thinks about breach, it will compare these two amounts: On the one hand, the value of the machine, less the contract price ($200 minus $125); on the other, Seller's cost, less the contract price ($175 minus $125).

The relationship between these two amounts does not change if we ignore the contract price, the $125, on both sides of the equation. Hence, under expectation damages, Seller is effectively comparing the $200 value of the machine to Buyer against its costs of $175. Seller won't breach because $200 is greater than $175. Under expectation damages, Seller is forced to internalize the benefit Buyer gets from the machine and to compare this benefit against its own costs.

Expectation damages forces someone who contemplates breaking a promise to take account of the harm others will suffer in the event of breach. One of the things legal rules can do is force people to internalize costs. We see legal rules with this feature everywhere from tort law to the law of agency.

Expectation damages also has the virtue of being informationally parsimonious. Expectation damages forces Seller to take account of the harm to Buyer when its own costs rise, but it does not require the court to measure Seller's costs. The court needs to know only the value of the machine to Buyer, not the costs to Seller of making it.

This rule, of course, doesn't overcome all our informational problems. The benefit Buyer enjoys from the machine may be hard to determine. Note, however, that it is exactly in those cases that determining Buyer's benefit is hard—when the goods are unique and have a great deal of subjective value—that we typically do not have a rule of expectation damages at common law, but rather the remedy of specific performance.

III.

The account I have given of contract damages so far, however, is incomplete. We must remember one of the central lessons of *The Problem of Social Cost*: It takes two to tango.[5] So far we have looked at how expectation damages affects the behavior of Seller. We must also ask how expectation damages affects the behavior of Buyer.[6]

Before we assumed that the new machine would be worth $200 regardless of what Buyer did. But this is too simple. After Buyer and Seller sign the contract, but before Seller builds the machine, Buyer may have the chance to spend money in anticipation of the delivery of the machine. For example, Buyer might begin training its workers to operate this particular machine so full advantage can be taken of the machine from the moment it arrives.

Let me offer a variation on our example to show how this complicates matters. Let's assume that the machine is worth $200 if Buyer makes no preparations. But the machine is worth $240 if Buyer spends $35 training workers to operate this particular model before the machine is delivered. These training costs are entirely wasted if Seller does not perform.

5. See R.H. Coase, The Problem of Social Cost, 3 J. Law & Econ. 1 (1960).

6. The pathbreaking work that analyzes the incentives of both parties to a contract is Steven Shavell, Damage Measures for Breach of Contract, 11 Bell J. Econ. 466 (1980). I follow Shavell's work closely in both this section and the next. Here, as elsewhere, there are complications that can be introduced into the analysis. See, e.g., David D. Friedman, An Economic Analysis of Alternative Damage Rules for Breach of Contract, 32 J. Law & Econ. 281 (1989).

Let us first ask what damages Seller must pay under an expectation damages regime. When Buyer spends $35 preparing for the performance, the value of the machine, under our assumptions, will be $240. Buyer gets a $240 benefit less the $125 contract price when Seller performs. Similarly, under a damage measure that puts Buyer in the same position as when Seller makes the machine, Seller must, when it breaches, pay the difference between $240 and the contract price of $125.

In all cases, the $35 investment in preparations increases what Buyer receives by $40. (Either the value of the performance increases by this amount or the damage recovery increases by this amount.) Hence, under expectation damages, Buyer will always train the workers before the machine arrives.

Do we want Buyer to do this, however? It is not obvious. If we are certain that building the machine makes sense and certain that Seller is going to perform, then we want Buyer to make this investment. The $35 in training costs brings a $40 benefit. There is a net gain of $5. But Seller is not always going to perform.

Let us assume that there is a 25% chance that it will cost so much to make the machine that it will not make sense to build it. Seller would rather pay expectation damages than perform. If the machine is going to be built only 75% of the time, Buyer should discount the $40 benefit accordingly. Preparations are worth $30 if the machine is built 75% of the time. Because training costs $35, it is not worth doing if it gives an expected benefit of only $30.

Expectation damages gives Buyer the incentive to invest too much in preparing for performance. Expectation damages induces Buyer to treat performance as a sure thing. This is wrong. If Buyer were making the machine itself, it would take into account the possibility that it might not acquire the machine and make the decision about training the workers accordingly.

Ideally, a damage measure should induce both Seller and Buyer to behave optimally, just as the ideal tort rule should induce the injurer and the victim to take due care. Can we modify expectation damages to take this into account? There is such a rule.[7] We could limit the amount of preparation costs that Buyer can recover. We could instruct a court to identify the optimal amount that Buyer should have spent preparing for the new machine. The court could then calculate the value of the machine to Buyer if it had invested this amount. It would then award Buyer the difference between this amount and the contract price.

7. K. Spier & M.D. Whinston, Legal Restrictions on Damages for Breach of Contract: Strategic Entry, Reliance, and Renegotiation (Harvard University manuscript 1993).

This rule, however, sacrifices a major benefit of expectation damages. A rule that requires a court to determine the optimal level of preparation is not informationally parsimonious. A damage measure that gives the correct incentives is not any good if a court has no way to calculate it.

IV.

So far we have seen that expectation damages does not give both Buyer and Seller the correct set of incentives, but is there any other rule that we can implement that is better? What about reliance damages? When we reward reliance damages, we award Buyer that amount of money necessary to put Buyer back in the position it would have been in if it had never entered into the contract. Reliance damages is the measure most commonly compared to expectation damages. Let's see how it affects the incentives of Seller and Buyer.

Let's first look at how reliance damages affects Seller's incentives. Under the reliance damage measure, Seller does not have to compensate Buyer for the value of the promise that has been broken. Buyer recovers only her out-of-pocket costs.

Let's see how reliance damages affects Seller's incentives in our example. When Seller breaches, it saves the $175 costs of building the machine. By contrast, when Seller performs, it enjoys the purchase price $125 and it avoids having to compensate Buyer for the $35 preparation costs. This is $160. Seller compares $175 to $160 and is therefore tempted to breach.

Note how this comparison under a reliance-based regime differs from the one Seller does under an expectation-based regime. The benchmark against which Seller compares its $175 costs in an expectation-damages regime is the value of the performance to Buyer ($240 in our example). The comparable benchmark in a reliance-based regime is the contract price and the amount spent in preparation ($160 in our example).

Note that the expectation benchmark is going to be consistently greater than the reliance benchmark. We are dealing with situations in which Buyer wants Seller to perform. This means that the machine brings Buyer a net benefit. For this reason, it must be that the value of the machine to Buyer is greater than what Buyer has to give up to get it. The value of the machine, the benchmark for expectation damages, is higher than contract price plus preparation costs, the benchmark for reliance damages.

As our example showed, costs of building the machine can be high enough to give Seller an incentive to breach under reliance damages, but not so high that Seller would breach in an expectations-based regime. Because Seller fully internalizes the costs of breach to Buyer under expectation damages, it follows that Seller is not fully internalizing them under reliance damages. Therefore, under reliance damages Seller does not take full account of the harm that Buyer will suffer in the event of breach.

But what is the effect of reliance damages on Buyer's incentives? Do reliance-based damages work better here than expectation damages?[8] Remember the problem with Buyer's incentives under expectation damages. Buyer prepares for performance as if performance were certain. Buyer spends $35 for something that has an expected benefit of only $30.

What does Buyer do under reliance damages? Buyer doesn't look at what happens when Seller breaches in calculating how much to invest in preparations. Buyer gets the $35 back in damages. Whenever Seller breaches, the money spent in preparation will be recovered.

Buyer therefore focuses on those cases in which Seller makes the machine and invests in preparations on the assumption that Seller will perform. Looked at from this point of view, Buyer will compare the $40 benefit with the $35 cost. But this is a bad idea. Because Buyer is fully compensated for preparation costs if Seller breaches, Buyer does not take the possibility that Seller will breach into account when deciding how much to invest in preparation.

We face exactly the same bad incentive as under expectation damages. Buyer makes investment in preparation as if performance were always going to happen even though it will not. Reliance damages are worse than expectation damages as far as the incentives it gives Seller and no better in the incentives it gives Buyer. Indeed, things are worse than this. There is another effect that we need to take into account.

In an expectation damages world, Buyer does not care whether Seller builds the machine. In theory, Buyer gets the same amount in all states of the world. But when Seller breaches in a reliance-based regime, Buyer loses out. Buyer loses a winning deal, a bargain in which it gets a machine that is worth more than the purchase price and preparation costs. Buyer would like to do something to encourage Seller to perform. Is there anything that Buyer can do?

There is. Remember that under a reliance damages regime Seller is going to breach when its cost of making the machine is greater than Buyer's preparation costs and the contract price. Buyer can influence Seller's decision about whether to make the

---

8. For the classic discussion of expectation and reliance damages, see Lon Fuller & William R. Perdue, The Reliance Interest in Contract Damages (Part I), 46 Yale L.J. 52 (1936).

machine (and increase the chance of getting a winning deal) by increasing the amount it invests in preparation.

As long as Buyer spends over $50 in preparation, Seller will perform when its costs are $175. Seller prefers to incur costs of $175 and get paid $125 (for a loss of $50) rather than repay Buyer's preparation costs of a greater amount. From Buyer's perspective, the additional preparation costs may be a good deal. It spends an extra $15 and ensures it gets a machine that it values a lot rather than a damage remedy that leaves it no better than when it started.

By increasing the investment in preparation, Buyer makes it less likely that Seller's manufacturing costs exceed the sum of the purchase price and Buyer's preparation costs. The more Buyer spends preparing for performance, the more likely that Seller will be better off making the machine rather than breaching.

Buyer does not make unlimited investments in preparation. After all, Seller will ordinarily make the machine and too much spent on preparing will cut down on Buyer's profits when Seller performs. But some additional expenditures on preparation, even though they don't bring a dollar for dollar increase in the value of the machine, are worth incurring from Buyer's perspective. Reliance damages gives Seller a bad incentive that was not there under expectation damages. Moreover, reliance damages gives Buyer an even worse set of incentives than expectation damages.

I have sketched all this out in very broad strokes. Steven Shavell, Kathy Spier, and others have explored this problem carefully. There are many complications, but the bottom line is pretty clear. Over two important dimensions—the incentives they give to Buyer and Seller respectively—reliance damages are unambiguously worse than expectation damages.

One cannot simply assume that expectation damages are therefore better than reliance damages. For example, reliance damages may be much easier to measure than expectation damages and in many instances reliance damages are an excellent proxy for expectation damages. But this way of looking at contract damages by looking at a model with very few elements tells us that using reliance damages comes at a cost.

V.

We should be careful about pursuing this mode of analysis too far, however. We have to remember another lesson of *The Problem of Social Cost*. We cannot make sense of legal rules without taking into account the frictions that exist in our world. We live in a world in which transaction costs are everywhere. Thus far, the account I have given of contract damages abstracts from transaction costs. We are bound to gain additional insights if we make an effort to take these into account. Let me spend a little time focusing on how we might do this by drawing on the work of Ian Ayres and Robert Gertner.[9]

Recall the facts of *Hadley v. Baxendale*.[10] In that case, a miller contracted with a carrier to transport a broken shaft from Glouces-ter to Greenwich. The shipment was delayed. The miller sued and the court had to decide whether the carrier should be liable for the profits lost for the increased time the mill was shut down. The court ruled that the miller could not recover the profits lost from the delay. The miller had not even told the carrier about its special needs. These damages from delay were not "reasonably foresee-able." Modern contract law continues to embrace this rule that a person is not entitled to its consequential damages when those damages are not reasonably foreseeable.

Let's see if we can identify the effects that this rule has. First, it is possible that there is relatively little that the carrier can do to prevent delays, but there is a lot that the miller can do to prevent the harm that can come from delay. A miller, for example, could have a back-up shaft. It is easier for a miller to have a back-up mill shaft than for a carrier to see that nothing gets delayed.

We want a legal rule to induce the person who can take steps to avoid the harm to have the incentive to do so. The rule in *Hadley v. Baxendale* may have this effect. I go to the Himalayas with one of those drug store cardboard cameras. The pictures of me on top of Mt. Everest do not come out. Can I get my money back plus the costs of a new trip? The rule of *Hadley v. Baxendale* tells me that I cannot. I am much better able to buy more suitable equipment that is less likely to fail than the drug store is able to ensure that the cardboard camera it sells me works. My damages—the cost of mounting an expedition to Mt. Everest—are not reasonably foresee-able.

But it is not clear this story does a good job of explaining *Hadley v. Baxendale*. It is worth remembering the source of delay in the actual case. The case arose in the 1850s. The economy was in transition between transport by canal and transport by rail. The carrier had a choice—to send the mill shaft by canal boat or train—and it made the wrong decision given the miller's need for speed. *Hadley* was a situation in which the carrier, unlike the drug store, could have prevented the harm if it had known about the miller's special needs.

9. Ian Ayres & Robert Gertner, Fill-ing Gaps in Incomplete Contracts: An Economic Theory of Default Rules, 99 Yale L.J. 87 (1989). For a critique of their work, see Jason Johnston, Strate-gic Bargaining and the Economic Theory of Contract Default Rules, 100 Yale L.J. 615 (1990).

10. 9 Ex. 341, 156 Eng. Rep. 145 (1854).

Second, the court suggests that it might have decided the case differently if the miller had told the carrier about the need for speed. For this reason, it may make sense to ask if we can understand the rule of *Hadley v. Baxendale* by looking explicitly at a transaction cost—the need for the miller to communicate information to the carrier.

Let's pursue the idea that contract law may provide default rules that induce the miller to disclose information. Once again, we can identify a force that might be at work by giving a simple example. There are two types of millers. One type of miller is low-damage. If Carrier fails to deliver the shaft on time, the low-damage miller will suffer damages of $100. The other type of miller is high-damage. These millers suffer $1000 in damages if Carrier fails to deliver the shaft on time. Carrier knows that 90% of the millers are low-damage and that 10% are high-damage, but has no way of telling one type from the other.

There are two ways to ship a shaft—by rail or by canal. Shipping by canal costs $10. Shipping by rail costs $15. When you ship by canal, there is a 1% chance of delay. When you ship by rail, there is no chance of delay. There is otherwise no difference between the two forms of transportation. It costs a miller $2 to contract around whatever legal rule we put in place.

What is going to happen if the *Hadley* legal rule is in effect? In the event of a delay, the carrier has to pay $100 in damages, regardless of the type of miller the carrier faces. In the absence of a special deal, Carrier ships by canal. It costs Carrier $10 to ship the mill shaft and Carrier expects to pay $100 in damages 1% of the time. Carrier therefore charges everyone $11.

The low-damage millers are fully compensated if there is a delay and they get their mill shafts shipped at Carrier's cost. It makes sense for Carrier to use the canal boat and pay $100 in damages one time in a hundred, rather than spend $5 extra for rail shipment each time to eliminate delay entirely.

What about the high-damage millers? If they say nothing and there is a delay, they will lose $1000 and recover only $100. This $900 loss happens 1% of the time, so they face expected damages of $9 in addition to the $11 they spend on shipping. Their total costs under this rule are $20 when their mill shafts are shipped by canal.

High-damage millers are better off identifying themselves as high-damage millers and having the shaft shipped by rail. High-damage millers would rather spend $2 negotiating a special deal and paying $15 for shipping by rail, than living with the status quo.

Under the *Hadley* rule, we have a good outcome. The appropriate mode of transportation is used for each type of miller. The $5 extra cost of shipping by rail is justified when there is a 1% risk of $1,000 loss, but not when there is a 1% chance of a $100 loss. In addition, we spend $2 opting out of the default rule only 10% of the time, so transaction costs are at a minimum.

Do we get the same result under a consequential damages rule? If Carrier shipped all mill shafts by canal, it would pay damages of $1000 in one time in a thousand and $100 in nine times in a thousand. Total damages would be $1900 over the course of 1,000 cases, so expected damages in a single case are therefore $1.90. Given that shipping by canal costs $10, total expected transportation costs for each miller are $11.90.

Under the consequential damages regime, Carrier is better off shipping by canal than by rail if no one opts out and bargains for a special deal. The $5 extra costs in shipping by rail is greater than the extra damages Carrier expects from shipping by canal boat. Carrier would prefer to face costs of $11.90, rather than costs of $15.

Does anyone opt out when we have the consequential damages rule in place? Let's see how each type of miller responds. The high-damage miller is happy to pay $11.90 and be treated the same as the low-damage millers. The high-damage miller is completely compensated in the event of delay. It is better off than it would be if it identified itself as a high-damage miller and had the mill shaft shipped by rail. If the high-damage miller did this, he would pay $15 rather than $11.90.

The low-damage millers would like to bargain for a different deal. They are paying $11.90 for a service that costs only $11 to provide. They are subsidizing the high-damage millers. They would be better off if they could agree ahead of time to limit their damages to $100. If they could do this, the carrier would provide them with the service for $11 rather than $11.90. But the low-damage millers can't do this, because it costs them $2 to negotiate a special deal. The $0.90 saved from the new deal does not offset the $2 transaction cost associated with opting out of the legal rule.

The *Hadley* foreseeable damages rule, unlike the consequential damages rule, allows the millers to sort themselves by type. In this example, it brings about a better outcome because Carrier uses the mode of shipping that is most appropriate for each type of miller. The rule of *Hadley v. Baxendale* forces one party to disclose information to another in way that the alternative rule would not.

The optimal contract default rule cannot focus merely on the bargain parties would strike in a world of no transaction costs. Our contract rules should bear in mind that parties may opt out of them and we need to pay attention to the transaction costs associated with opting out.

Once again, we have to be careful not to draw too many inferences from this example. This example identifies a force that we need to take into account in trying to understand how legal rules work. One cannot, however, use this highly stylized story to make a general point about the law that should govern carriers or anyone else. After all, someone who wants to ship a package quickly today goes to a carrier that specializes in overnight delivery. Millers with special needs sort themselves by going to a different type of carrier. There is no need for a legal rule to induce separation.

Once a market develops and specialized providers of services emerge, we can often see contract provisions that are tailored to the transaction. We should expect these provisions to depart from the default rules that contract law provides. (And, indeed, the contracts of carriers like Federal Express do not use either of the terms we have discussed. Instead, they provide that the carrier is not liable for *any* consequential damages in the event of a delay.)

Legal rules matter most, not in highly developed markets like the one that exists today for overnight shipping, but in places where commercial practices are still evolving. In this environment, information asymmetries and transaction costs may be quite high. It is here that the information-shifting properties of contract default rules should be studied.

VI.

The work that has been done on the law and economics of contracts is enormous and its achievement substantial. We now have a solid understanding of the way in which contract rules operate. They keep us from wandering astray. For example, they tell us that, given its own starting assumptions, the court in *Missouri Furnace* was wrong. They can identify a way in which reliance damages are unambiguously inferior to expectation damages. They can force us to recognize the different ways in which legal rules operate in a world in which transaction costs are high.

Nevertheless, there is still much work that remains to be done. Contract law operates in a world in which there are many other forces at work—such as custom and reputation. It is one thing to understand the effects that different rules of contract damages have. It is quite another to understand how these rules interact with other forces at work in a contractual relationship. Integrating the effects of law into the rest of the picture is the next challenge that we face and it is one that will surely begin, like all other quests in law and economics, with a focus on transaction costs.

Study Questions:

1. Restitution damages give the victim of breach the monetary value of the benefit that he or she confers on the promisor. How does this rule of damages compare to expectation and reliance damages?

2. Specific performance is an injunction requiring the promisor to perform his or her obligations. Is the rule of specific performance better or worse than expectation damages?

3. The mitigation rule holds that the victim of breach has an obligation not to run up damages after it is clear that the promisor has breached or will breach. Analyze the mitigation rule.

4. Some observers believe that the ordinary damages rules do not send the right signal. They believe that contract remedies should make it clear that the promisor has behaved immorally by breaching the promise. On this view, do punitive damages make sense? What would their effect be on people's behavior?

5. Parties sometimes set out the damages in the contract by including a liquidated damages clause. Courts do not enforce these clauses if they believe that they are "unreasonable." A reasonable doctrine?

4. Das Kapital: Solvency Regulation of the American Business Enterprise

Geoffrey P. Miller[1]

In this paper, I address the question of the legal regulation of corporate capital. This is a topic that cuts across a number of distinct areas of law, and that displays significant differences between the civil law used in Europe and elsewhere and the U.S. common law system. It is fundamental to the regulation of important economic institutions, notably banks, securities firms, and insurance companies. It is a question as well that lies at the core of the discipline of corporate finance. Surprisingly, however, scholars have not attempted to unify these disparate strands of theory and of legal regulation in a single analytical structure. In this paper I offer a preliminary attempt at such a unification.

I. Introduction

The attentive reader will not have missed the allusion to Karl Marx in the title. Capital is not only a basic organizing principle for law and theory in developed economic systems. It is also a subject that formed the central focus of Karl Marx's later work.[2] And, although Marx's predictions that capital would be increasingly concentrated in fewer and fewer hands turns out to have been erroneous, at least for modern industrialized nations, his insight that capital is fundamental was not. That the concentration of capital predicted by Marx did not happen is largely due to the fact that capital ended up being dispersed in the population: a rising middle class came to own much of the means of production, and social wealth began to be distributed to the needy through an increasingly active welfare state.

This triumph of capitalism may be something to celebrate, but it would be a mistake to view the dispersion of the means of production as costless in itself. On the contrary, as the means of production became dispersed in the large industrial enterprise, a whole new set of problems arose which had their origin exactly in the fact that capital *was* dispersed. It turned out that as the number of owners of the business enterprise increased, and as their respective share in the total ownership decreased, it became more and more difficult for those who provided capital to the enterprise

---

1. Professor of Law, New York University. This lecture was delivered in April 1994.

2. Karl Marx, Capital: Volume I (1976).

to control its behavior. Free-rider and collective action problems entered the picture with a vengeance.

The result was that effective control of the large-scale business enterprise became lodged in a managerial class who were not themselves the major owners of the firm. Adolph Berle and Gardiner Means recognized this fact in their classic 1932 book, *The Modern Corporation and Private Property*,[3] which identified the separation of ownership and control as the leading problem of the modern business enterprise. Berle and Means viewed the gap between ownership and control as a danger because corporate managers could abuse their trust and run the corporation to serve their own interests rather than the interests of those who provided capital to the firm.

The law and economics analysis of the corporate form, pioneered by Frank Easterbrook, Dan Fischel, Henry Manne, Ralph Winter, and others, in many respects adopts a stance antithetical to the pro-regulatory views of Berle and Means. Nevertheless, law and economics draws its central inspiration from the Berle and Means insight that ownership and control are separated in the large business enterprise. Law and economics has a different terminology from Berle and Means, of course: instead of managerial "abuse," law and economics prefers the ostensibly less value-laden term "agency costs." But, moral connotations aside, the fundamental insight is the same: the agents—that is, the managers of the large corporation—have interests which differ from those of the principals—that is, the providers of capital to the firm; and because effective control over the firm's actions lies in the agents, there is the danger that the agents will act in a self-serving fashion to the detriment of the owners. Many rules of corporate law, as well as many privately-negotiated contractual arrangements, are then analyzed as means for limiting, although not eliminating these agency costs of management.[4]

At the same time, law and economics recognized, as the Berle–Means tradition did not, that the conflict of interest was not limited to discontinuities between capital providers and managers. There were also important conflicts between different classes of capital providers. Those who own corporate debt have a prior claim on the firm's assets and income stream, but only for the amount of principal and interest specified in the debt contract. This makes debt holders risk averse, to the point where debt holders would prefer that the firm not engage in risky ventures even when the profits expected from the venture if it succeeds are very high.

3. Adolph A. Berle and Gardiner C. Means, The Modern Corporation and Private Property (1932).

4. The most comprehensive analysis by two of the pioneers is Frank Easterbrook and Daniel Fischel, The Economic Structure of Corporate Law (1991).

Those who hold the firm's equity—the legal owners—have a residual claim on the firm's assets and income stream, in an amount restricted, on the down side, only by the protection of limited liability. This makes equity holders risk-preferrers, in the sense that if the firm engages in a risky venture, the profits from the venture if it is successful, after debt service, are appropriated by the equity holders, while the losses if the venture is unsuccessful are shared by the debt holders if the firm becomes insolvent as a result.

These are significant differences between the law and economics and Berle–Means traditions. But each is based on the fundamental problem of conflicts of interest that result from the dispersal of the firm's capital among different investors. Notice further that both the Berle and Means and the law and economics traditions really grow out of this basic failure of Marx's theory, namely, that capital did not in the end become concentrated in a few hands, but rather became so widely dispersed that the owners of the means of production lost control over the ways in which the productive capacities of society were utilized.

II.   The (Uneasy) Case for Capital Regulation

With this background, let us consider the possible reasons why a legal system might elect to regulate capital structure. By capital structure regulation, I mean regulation that controls in some fashion the amount of *equity* capital in a firm. This is different from the economist's definition of capital, which includes all claims on the firm's assets and income stream, debt as well as equity. To avoid confusion in terminology, the term "capital" in American regulation refers, roughly, to equity capital only, not to equity and debt together.

The basic puzzle of capital regulation can be understood in light of the Modigliani–Miller (M–M) irrelevance hypothesis.[5] Modigliani and Miller demonstrated that under certain assumptions— such as ignoring tax consequences and assuming frictionless capital markets and perfect information—a corporation's capital structure is irrelevant to its value. In the world posited by M–M, a firm has precisely the same value whether it is financed 100% by debt, 100% by equity, or with any combination of debt and equity you choose.

In the M–M world, the question naturally arises: Why should we have any type of capital regulation? If capital structure is irrelevant to firm value, there would seem to be no reason at all to regulate the amount of equity capital in a firm.

5. Franco Modigliani and Merton Miller, The Cost of Capital, Corporation Finance, and the Theory of Investment, 48 American Economic Review 261 (1958).

Add to this another puzzle we can draw from basic economic theory. Ordinarily, in a capitalist economy, we think it is appropriate and necessary, even if unfortunate for the owners, that some firms should fail. Failure of some firms is the inevitable consequence of competition among many; and if we tried to prevent firms from failing by insisting that they remain solvent at all times, the fundamental economic benefits of competition might be jeopardized.

So is there any possible justification for capital regulation? To see the reasons for capital regulation, we must leave the perfect world of M–M and enter the world of taxes and transactions costs in which we live our imperfect lives. In the real world, we can posit at least four principal reasons for requiring corporations to establish or maintain certain levels of capital. These reasons may not be completely persuasive; indeed, the case for capital regulation is quite problematic. But the justifications for capital regulation are sufficiently plausible to be worth serious consideration.

The first, most obvious reason for capital regulation is that it protects a firm against insolvency and all the attendant costs of bankruptcy. If a firm's capital is effectively regulated, it will never become insolvent. Either the firm will earn a profit from its operations, which will be applied, in part at least, to increase its capital, or the firm will lose money and run up against its required capital ratios. When a firm has reached the point of legally inadequate capital, its managers face a choice of actions: they can seek to recapitalize the firm, say with a subscription offering to existing equity holders or by inviting a new investor to stake a claim; they can seek a merger partner with adequate capital; they can sell assets if doing so will enhance the firm's capital position; or they can arrange for the voluntary dissolution of the firm's affairs before the capital becomes impaired. Note that none of these actions necessarily represents a social cost aside from the transactions costs of organizing the transaction. Capital regulation does not require that inefficient firms remain in business; it is not the same, for example, as the conduct of business through a government-owned enterprise that can never become insolvent. Capital regulation simply shifts the point at which reorganization of a firm's capital structure is likely to occur, and this in itself has no obvious efficiency implications. Since under capital regulation reorganization occurs prior to bankruptcy, this administrative technique offers the potential to significantly reduce bankruptcy costs.

A second possible rationale for capital regulation is that it can protect investors, particularly debt holders, who are not well situated to protect themselves. In a world of high transactions costs, debt holders may not be able to safeguard their interests adequately against the threat that equity holders will take undue risks with the firm's assets and drive it into insolvency. Capital regulation might provide debt holders with some assurance that the firm is solvent, at least in its early days, and thus reduce the need for costly contracting and monitoring of management to guard against excessively risky ventures.

A third reason for capital regulation is that it can protect society against inefficient activities by corporations which reduce social wealth. We have noted that equity holders tend to be risk preferrers. And, while some risk is desirable, there comes a point as the firm's equity capital becomes thin—that is, as a firm approaches insolvency—when the equity holder would prefer almost any level of risk, even if the project in question is a loser for the firm on a present value basis. To take an extreme example, assume that the firm has already lost so much money that there is only one dollar left in net worth. At this point the equity holders have an incentive to take wild risks—even causing the firm to invest in lottery tickets—because they stand to lose, at most, only one dollar if the risks don't pan out, while if the unexpected happens and the firm wins the lottery, the equity holders get all the benefit of the payoff. Capital regulation tends to mitigate this problem of inefficient investment.

A final possible argument in favor of capital regulation is that, despite its shortcomings, it is arguably the best available strategy for accomplishing the social objectives of reducing bankruptcy costs, protecting debt holders, and policing against socially inefficient corporate behavior. We could, for example, imagine a system of command-and-control regulation under which the state scrutinizes the actions of corporate managers in order to ensure that they are not excessively risky. But command-and-control regulation arguably would be undesirable, since it would effectively substitute the state as corporate manager, and states have not shown themselves as particularly effective in managing business corporations. Capital regulation is a potentially better alternative to command-and-control regulation because it leaves the fundamental business decisions up to the professional managers of firms, subject only to the constraint that they must meet the applicable minimum capital rules.

Note that the case for capital regulation appears to be strongest in two situations: where dispersed debt holders lack the means or the incentive to protect their interests effectively; and where as a result of thin capital equity holders develop an extreme taste for risk. It turns out that these are indeed situations where we observe capital regulations having bite in the real world.

As will be seen, there are quite a variety of different sorts of capital regulation, but to simplify the analysis we can sort them into two general categories: ex ante regulations and ex post regulations. The distinction turns on how capital requirements are enforced. Imagine that the government wants a firm to maintain a specified level of capital. To enforce this requirement, the government has basically two choices. It can monitor the firm's capital on an ongoing basis and can regulate the firm's behavior that poses a potential threat to the maintenance of adequate capital levels. This is ex ante regulation: the government monitors and regulates ex ante to ensure that capital does not become depleted.

Alternatively, the government can adopt a hands-off strategy, allowing the firm to make its own choices but imposing sanctions in the event that the firm's capital does fall below the specified levels. This is the ex post approach. Obviously, the ex ante and ex post approaches are not mutually exclusive: a state could impose a combination of both strategies if it so chose.

Both the ex ante and the ex post approaches have encountered serious obstacles in the American regulatory environment. Because it entails pervasive and continuous monitoring of a firm's affairs, the ex ante approach requires a well-funded, active, and powerful administrative agency to enforce it. The American system of corporate federalism, in which states compete to provide corporate charters and regulatory regimes for business enterprises, deters the creation of any such agency. There are no administrative agencies at the state level capable of undertaking the task of regulating firm capital, especially in a world in which business is increasingly conducted on an interstate and even global scale. The federal government would be equipped to handle the task; and it is no coincidence that most instances of ex ante regulation that are observed in the United States are administered by the federal government. But the American system has elected to retain substantive corporate law regulation at the state level, with only minimal federal involvement. Ex ante capital regulation, accordingly, is simply not feasible for the average American corporation.

The ex post approach generally requires that providers of equity capital to the firm stand ready to make good some or all of the shortfall, and thus it runs squarely into the basic rule of limited liability for corporate shareholders. If shareholder liability is to be limited, then holders of the firm's equity capital cannot be required to pay into the firm treasury additional amounts beyond their initial investments.

Both the ex post and the ex ante approaches, in short, face severe difficulties, and it is these difficulties that have prevented capital regulation from assuming a central a place in the American system.

III. Types of Capital Regulation in the United States

It turns out that capital regulation in this sense was an important form of social control of the business enterprise in the nineteenth century. During most of the twentieth century, however, capital regulation ebbed in importance and became nearly vestigial, although it has never disappeared entirely. More recently, capital regulation has experienced a resurgence of importance in financial services industries such as banking, insurance, and securities; and it has suddenly become an important topic of scholarly debate in the general corporate context as well. I will start with general corporate regulation and then turn to capital adequacy regulation in the financial services sector.

A. General Corporate Regulation

We do, in fact, have rules in corporate law regulating firm capital in the United States.[6] Examine a corporate law statute today and you will find provisions referring to the par value of stock—stating, however, that a stock can have a par value or no par as the organizers choose. Some states require that corporations start business with a minimum capitalization that must be paid in before the firm can commence business. And in disclosure statements under the securities law we routinely find the mysterious intonation that the shares being sold are "fully paid and nonassessable." These are vestiges of what in the nineteenth century was a leading, if not the dominant form of corporate law regulation in the United States: the par value system.

The par value system required that a corporation start business with an initial capitalization. There was a minimum, but the organizers of a corporation could establish any initial capitalization they chose above the minimum. The capitalization had to be embodied in par value stock, so if initial capital was set at $50,000, a firm would have to distribute stock with a total par value of $50,000—for example, 5,000 shares of $10 par value each.

The catch was that the initial capitalization had to be actually paid in. If stock was distributed without payment of the par value, the holder of the stock was liable for assessment in the event of subsequent insolvency. A receiver in bankruptcy would sue the holder of the stock for the difference between the par value and what was actually paid in to the corporation for the stock. These par value rules were very important at the time—if you examine nineteenth-century reporters, you will discover literally thousands of assessment lawsuits based on the par value system.

---

6. See, e.g., Bayless Manning, A Concise Textbook on Legal Capital 13–15 (2d ed. 1982); William A. Klein & John C. Coffee, Jr., Business Organization and Finance 210–15 (5th ed. 1992).

It is easy to see that the par value system was a form of capital regulation. It required that firms have an initial capitalization and provided a system of penalties if the capitalization was not paid in. The purpose of the system was to protect creditors, who could look to the par value for some indication of the value of the firm. The system was also designed to protect members of the public who bought equity in firms by assuring them that their stock was not "watered"—that is, that the insiders who received the initial distribution had paid full price.

The par value system had many problems and ultimately failed. Its defects included the following:

—Par value rules never coped adequately with the problem of insiders purchasing stock in exchange for services or property as opposed to cash. The danger of insider manipulation in this setting is obvious, but the difficulty in valuing services or property made fraud difficult to establish. While the system could have simply prohibited the issuance of stock to insiders in exchange for property or services, this was not a realistic option because in practice it is necessary for corporate promoters to be compensated for their noncash contributions.

—The par value system provided very little information about the valuation of a firm after its initial capitalization, since profits or losses from operation were not reflected in the par value account. Thus the informational content of the system degraded quickly over time.

—The par value system impaired the marketability of stock since liability followed the holder; purchasers of stock faced the possibility of being assessed if the initial purchaser had failed to pay in the par value. Par value stock could even obtain a negative value when the value of the claim on the corporation's assets and income stream fell short of the assessment exposure. In such a setting, holders would try to foist stock off on impecunious persons in order to avoid their assessment obligations.

—Assessment litigation was time consuming and expensive, since holders had to be tracked down and assessed. Moreover, in many cases the holders of the par value stock were also officers or directors of the failed firms; these people were likely to be in personal financial distress when their firms failed, and therefore were often unable to pay out on assessments even if they were ordered.

Ultimately, business lawyers vitiated the par value system by developing low par and no par stock. The market price of such stock was far above the par value, so there was little or no danger that the holder of low par or no par stock would be assessed. Moreover, with no par or low par stock there was no real prospect that the insiders would be held liable for fraud in the public securities flotation, since the value of the shares being distributed was sure to be higher than the stated par value. These advantages came at the cost of eliminating any residual utility the par value system might have held as a mechanism for regulating corporate capital structure. With low par and no par stock, corporations operated free of any realistic requirements that they start with, or maintain, any particular level of capital. In place of par value, the legal system developed a philosophy of disclosure, both at the federal level and at the state level with the enactment of "blue sky" securities laws.

One important reason for the failure of the American par value system of capital regulation is the fact that there was no administrative agency in place capable of enforcing the system effectively. The secretary of state who issued the corporate charter did not monitor the corporate capital structure. The states had little incentive to take on the burden of regulating corporate capital structure. In the case of large corporations where the par value system was important, any attempt by the secretary of state to exercise a significant supervisory power would be met with a likely decision by the corporation to move to another, less restrictive jurisdiction. The result would merely be the loss of corporate franchise taxes for the state. It was simply not in a state's interest to administer an effective system of capital regulation.

We can usefully contrast the American experience with that of many European countries, where capital regulation of corporations is much more important. Because most European countries operate under unitary systems of corporate law where the competition for charters is not a factor, administrative agencies can police the capital rules effectively. In Belgium, for example, a relatively stringent system of ex ante monitoring and enforcement ensures that minimum capital regulations remain effective throughout a corporation's existence. Formal appraisals are required for all insider transfers to ensure that capital is fully subscribed. If a corporation's equity becomes less than half the issued capital, the board of directors has the obligation to organize a shareholders meeting to discuss dissolution of the company or restoration of capital. The system is backed up by a system of supervision by powerful administrative officials.

In Switzerland, the law requires that corporations maintain capital stock and statutory reserves. If the annual balance sheet shows that half of the capital stock and reserves is no longer covered, the board of directors is obligated to call a meeting of shareholders and to propose measures for restructuring. Failure to comply with this law subjects the board members to personal liability. Moreover, it is a crime in Switzerland to go bankrupt either through fraud or carelessness, or to fail to keep accurate records.

Similar provisions for minimum capital exist in most European countries, as well as in countries elsewhere in the world. But a system such as that which exists in these countries could not exist in the United States under our current system of corporate law. The United States is actually an anomalous jurisdiction in this respect: the considerable majority of countries around the world maintain a level of capital regulation for their corporations that far exceeds that obtaining in the United States under the vestigial par value system.

However, par value is not the only form of capital regulation for corporations in the United States. We also have a number of explicit ex post remedies for capital shortfall. The most prominent of these remedies is piercing the corporate veil, a doctrine which allows creditors of a corporation to proceed against the shareholders notwithstanding the "veil" of limited liability. Veil-piercing is a form of ex post capital regulation, since it imposes liability after insolvency on the shareholders of a firm that has been operated with inadequate capital. Although the stated requirements for piercing the veil are complex and indeterminate, the central issue is capital adequacy. If a corporation is being run on inadequate capital, the likelihood that a court will hold its shareholders liable for the corporation's debts and torts is much higher than if capital is considered to be adequate. Note that while par value is a mixture of ex ante and ex post regulation, albeit an unsuccessful one, veil piercing is purely ex post: there is no official monitor of a firm's capital and the sanction is administered only after insolvency.

The problem with veil piercing, of course, is that of determining how much capital is enough. Any firm that fails has by definition been run on inadequate capital at some point; but if this were enough to pierce the veil, we would not have a doctrine of limited liability at all. The legal decisions often refer to the fact that a corporation has been operated on insufficient capital, but never do the courts come up with any workable definition of how much capital is enough. Largely for this reason, the corporate veil is pierced only very rarely and in extreme circumstances in the United States. Veil piercing is not a particularly effective form of capital regulation.

In addition to veil piercing, capital adequacy is policed, to an extent, by bankruptcy rules that allow the trustee in bankruptcy to recapture certain transfers made to corporate shareholders in contemplation of or within a specific time before the insolvency. Other rules of equitable subordination in bankruptcy allow the bankruptcy judge to subordinate debt claims of shareholders to the claims of others in cases where the shareholder has used his or her insider status to obtain an inequitable position vis-à-vis other creditors. These bankruptcy rules are also a form of capital regulation, but, as in the case of veil piercing, they are limited in their application, largely because they are in tension with the general rule of limited liability for corporate shareholders.

Recently, corporate law scholarship has begun to revisit the basic question of limited liability. Professors Hansmann and Kraakman have written a controversial article in which they claim that the benefits of limited liability are overstated and recommend exploration of unlimited liability for corporate shareholders, at least for tort liability.[7] Note that, from the perspective of this lecture, Hansmann and Kraakman have recommended a form of capital regulation. For, to the extent that a firm's shareholders have unlimited liability, the firm's effective capital is greatly increased— to the point where the capital of a widely held firm, if such could exist under a regime of unlimited liability, would be virtually infinite.

Hansmann and Kraakman's argument for unlimited liability has not persuaded many in the academic community—and certainly very few outside the ivory tower—because of the perception that unlimited liability would be extremely disruptive to capital formation and quite expensive to administer.[8] Imagine a capital market where there is unlimited liability. Stock would be worth more in some hands than others. The rich might not want to buy stock at all. People would make efforts to disguise their ownership by vesting legal title in impecunious individuals while keeping some form of beneficial title for themselves. At some point, when a firm approached insolvency, its stock would actually take on a negative value—much as in the case of the old system of par value stock. People who held unlimited liability stock would be willing to pay others to take it off their hands. Those who were willing to hold the stock would not have the assets to pay on the assessments. The system appears so fraught with problems as to be nearly unworkable.

But, while unlimited, joint and several liability may not make sense, there are other ways to structure a liability regime to give shareholders some responsibility for a corporation's debts or torts. The most viable system is a form of multiple liability, where shareholders take on a liability for assessment when they purchase stock, but only up to a specific and defined amount. Such a system actually existed in the American banking industry for more than 75

---

7. Henry Hansmann and Reinier Kraakman, Toward Unlimited Shareholder Liability for Corporate Torts, 100 Yale Law Journal 1879 (1991).

8. For a justification of limited liability from the law-and-economics perspective, see Easterbrook and Fischel, supra note 4, at 40–62.

years, prior to the Great Depression; similar rules obtained in England, Scotland, Australia, Canada, and New Zealand. This was a system of double liability, under which a bank shareholder would be liable for assessment for the benefit of creditors in the event the bank failed, but only up to the par value of the shareholder's stock.

Professor Macey and I have studied the operation of this system and found that, in general, it was a success.[9] About half the amounts assessed were actually collected, a good recovery figure given the fact that many bank shareholders became personally insolvent when their banks failed. Beyond this, the assessment remedy tended to discourage risk taking by bank managers at the point where the bank's capital became impaired: instead of becoming risk preferrers at this point, the shareholders became risk avoiders, because they knew that if the bank were to become insolvent, they would be personally liable for its debts. Thousands of banks voluntarily liquidated during this period, evidently because the owners recognized that the institution was in danger of failing and chose to wind up or sell its operations while it was still solvent rather than risk personal assessment liability. Some of the perverse effects of unlimited liability were observed: for example, when a bank was close to failure, people became extremely generous with their stock, foisting it off on their children or any impecunious person they could find; but the courts were very effective at tracking down these transfers and fixing the assessment liability on the prior holder. The system of double liability was vigorously enforced during this period. There are over 100 decisions by the United States Supreme Court on this topic, and thousands of cases in the lower courts. Ironically, Congress and the states repealed the double liability regime during the 1930s because of the belief that federal deposit insurance was a cheaper and preferable method for protecting bank creditors.

Although multiple liability would appear to be a potentially viable ex post system of capital regulation, one with good monitoring effects and a workable, if somewhat cumbersome, legal structure, the U.S. legal system has not opted for such a regime outside the financial services area. The general rule has been one of limited liability.

B.   Regulation of Financial Firms

In general, therefore, the regulatory system in the United States has elected not to regulate firm capital, beyond the vestigial par value system, the specialized bankruptcy rules, and the doctrine of corporate veil piercing. There is one area, however, where far from being moribund, capital regulation is alive and growing: the financial services industry. Banks, savings and loans, broker-deal-

---

9. Jonathan R. Macey and Geoffrey P. Miller, Double Liability of Bank   Shareholders: History and Implications, 27 Wake Forest Law Review 31 (1992).

ers, commodities brokers, and insurance firms are all required to meet minimum capital standards. These standards have not been losing force over time; on the contrary, capital regulation is increasingly viewed as an essential part of the regulatory landscape for these firms. Why is it that capital regulation has been so important in these industries, whereas it has been much less important elsewhere?

The significance of capital adequacy regulations in the financial services sector is largely due to the presence for each industry of regulatory bodies with sufficient powers and jurisdiction to impose a form of ex ante capital regulation—the federal and state banking regulators, the SEC, the CFTC, the state insurance commissioners. The American system of regulatory federalism which prevents effective capital regulation for corporations generally does not affect these financial service industries in the same way. Thus, these industries are regulated much more like the European system than the American one so far as capital adequacy is concerned.

Beyond this, financial services is a field where the justifications for capital regulation appear particularly strong. Creditors in such industries—bank depositors, private customers of securities firms, holders of insurance policies—are often dispersed and unsophisticated. They may lack effective means for protecting their own interests against expropriation by the equity holders. Further, creditors often lack the financial incentive to monitor against risk taking by corporate managers. Depositors in banks and savings and loans are protected by federal deposit insurance and accordingly have no incentive whatever to monitor their institutions (unless they are foolish enough to have more than the insurance ceiling on deposit at a bank). Insurance policy holders are protected by insurance guarantee systems, and securities customers are insured by the SIPC. These protections for creditors take them out of danger, but place the insurance funds at even more severe risk, because the insurance removes the marketplace discipline against excessive risk taking by corporate managers that would otherwise exist.

Moreover, some of these industries—banking and insurance are examples—operate at high leverage ratios relative to industrial firms. That is, a bank's equity capital is typically only a small percentage of its total capitalization. This means that there is a relatively thin margin against insolvency, so that if a bank suffers unanticipated losses, there is a serious risk that it will become insolvent. And, once a bank is insolvent, the risk taking incentives of its owners go wild; the owners will be willing to take on nearly any sort of risk in order to gamble on a possible return to solvency, knowing that if the risks do not pay off, others will pick up the tab.

This combination of factors—powerful regulators, unsophisticated and dispersed creditors, moral hazard created by insurance,

and highly leveraged capital structures—makes the financial services industry particularly suitable for capital regulation. In the
banking area, capital regulation is now viewed in some quarters as
nearly a panacea to all the problems which have afflicted that
industry over the past ten years.

Although there is good reason to suppose that capital regulation may be beneficial in the financial services sector, those who
view such a regulatory system as any sort of panacea are excessively optimistic. It is certainly true that capital regulation is preferable
to command-and-control regulation because it leaves much greater
room for entrepreneurship and private decision making. But capital
regulation has in no way displaced command-and-control regulation
for financial services firms; on the contrary, the enhanced capital
rules have merely supplemented the existing regulatory framework.
This is perhaps not so much a conceptual as a political point:
Congress in its wisdom does not want to be criticized for failing to
regulate the financial services industry in light of the catastrophe
that happened in the banking and savings and loan industries.
State regulators of insurance firms are equally averse to criticism
for alleged shortfalls on their watch. Enhanced capital standards
have not, in practice, led to any form of deregulation in the
command-and-control system.

More fundamentally, the justifications for capital adequacy
regulation mentioned at the outset of this paper may not be
entirely persuasive. A fundamental problem with capital regulation
is simply that we have no idea how much capital is enough. The
rules we have in place for the banking industry now are not based
on any kind of systematic analysis; they were adopted by bureau-
crats in Basle, Switzerland, based on no discernible theory other
than expediency. The rules largely reflect political tradeoffs among
the signatories of the Basle accord rather than any sort of objective
analysis.

Even if we assume that the rules now in place are roughly
appropriate, there are serious questions as to the efficacy of capital
regulation as a means of measuring insolvency risk. Capital tends
to be a lagging indicator of insolvency: many banks and savings and
loans that failed drastically had perfectly adequate capital ratios
only a few months before the disaster. Capital regulation is inevitably built on accounting conventions that may be only a very
imperfect indicator of true market values or business prospects.

Further, capital regulation is inevitably imperfect in its application and encourages all sorts of regulatory avoidance measures.
For example, the rule used to be that banks had to hold a certain
amount of equity capital as a percentage of their assets. This was a
very ineffective way to deter risk taking, because any bank that
wanted to achieve a given level of risk could simply step up the
riskiness of its assets—a three percent capital ratio may be perfect-

ly fine when held against a portfolio of treasury bonds, but not when offset against speculative derivative instruments. The new rules attempt to correct for this problem by weighting the assets according to risk, but to be administrable, the risk weightings have to be exceedingly gross. For example, nearly all unsecured private debt has a hundred percent risk weighting—so that an unsecured loan to a local dry cleaner has the same risk weighting as a loan to General Motors. A bank can easily arbitrage within asset categories in order to increase its level of risk.

Finally, there are real problems about what to do when there is a capital shortfall. The old rules gave the agencies a great deal of discretion about whether to shut down a capital-impaired bank or not. This resulted in fiascos in which important politicians did political favors for friends by intervening with the regulators in order to keep insolvent institutions open. Congress reacted by adopting a regime of nondiscretionary administrative sanctions under which the agencies are required to take increasingly stringent steps to rectify capital impairment as an institution slides toward insolvency.

Although this system of prompt corrective action is nearly universally admired, there are obvious problems with it. How soon should an institution be closed? If you close it while it is still solvent, you are going to prevent losses to creditors, but there will be significant social costs because a potentially viable institution is being closed. If we look at private contracts, we do not see creditors automatically closing down debtors even on default. The creditor will renegotiate the debt if, in its judgment, the insolvency costs exceed the losses from renegotiation. But under our system of prompt correction action, the agencies have no power to act as private creditors would in a similar situation; they have to close the institution under penalty of law.

My own mind is still unsettled with respect to the value of solvency regulation. It is true that capital regulation can offer potential efficiencies to solve free-rider and collective action problems for creditors and can mitigate problems associated with inefficiently risky investments and insolvency costs. On the other hand, capital regulation has significant problems and costs of its own. For the foreseeable future, we are unlikely to observe effective capital regulation much beyond the financial services area in the United States, although, as we have seen, capital requirements are a much more significant part of the regulatory landscape in Europe. But within the U.S. financial services sector, capital has become an important regulatory strategy. It is therefore appropriate that business lawyers and business law scholars begin to grapple intensively with the complex issues posed by this interesting and potentially far-reaching approach to the legal control of the American corporation.

Study Questions:

1. During the Great Depression the New Deal government enacted laws that prohibited a single firm from offering insurance, deposit accounts, and investment services. These functions had to be divided among different firms. Why might these laws have seemed to make sense?

2. In recent years, regulatory and legislative reform has largely eliminated the old walls between insurance, banking, and investment services. Why might attitudes be changing?

3. The corporation has famously been described as a "nexus of contracts." What does this phrase mean?

4. The last several decades have seen the rise of enormous pension funds. Their managers aggressively monitor the firms in which they invest. What are the regulatory implications of this trend?

5. There has also been a very rapid increase in the percentage of ordinary people who invest a substantial amount of their assets in stocks and bonds. Many ordinary people seem to monitor their investments quite attentively, but there are also concerns that they are vulnerable to faddish investment advice. What are the regulatory implications of this trend?

5. Freedom of Contract

Richard Craswell[1]

Talking about freedom of contract is tricky, because the topic carries a heavy ideological charge. Depending on one's point of view, freedom of contract can be seen as a choice between individual liberty and heavy-handed government control, or between communitarian consensus and the worst excesses of laissez-faire capitalism. In other words, freedom of contract is a sort of lightning rod, which always attracts strongly-held political beliefs.

In fact, freedom of contract is such a charged topic that I have to start with a disclaimer, and point out that most of what we know as contract law has very little to do with freedom of contract as such. Most of contract law consists of default rules, or rules that apply when parties fail to address a topic one way or the other in their contracts. For example, most of the rules governing offer and acceptance, or implied warranties, or implied excuses such as impracticability or mistake, apply only if the parties have not agreed otherwise. And as long as the parties are free to agree otherwise, it is hard to see how freedom of contract is at all affected by these default rules. There are lots of other arguments that might bear on the desirability of any particular default rule, but arguments about "freedom of contract" are largely irrelevant.[2]

There are some parts of contract law, though, that do raise freedom of contract issues. The rules against excessive liquidated damage clauses, for example, or the rules blocking enforcement of promises unsupported by consideration, both limit the freedom of contracting parties to some extent. The same is true, in at least some cases, when enforcement of harsh contract terms is deemed unconscionable by courts. And outside of contract law itself, limits on freedom of contract can also be found in insurance law, labor law, landlord-tenant law, products liability law, and in many other doctrinal fields.

1. Professor of Law, University of Chicago. I am grateful for financial support from the Harry and Lynde Bradley Foundation, the John M. Olin Foundation, and the Sarah Scaife Foundation. This lecture was delivered in December 1994.

2. For discussions of possible bases for choosing default rules, see Ian Ayres & Robert Gertner, Filling Gaps in Incomplete Contracts: An Economic Theory of Default Rules, 99 Yale L.J. 87 (1989); Richard Craswell, Contract Law, Default Rules, and the Philosophy of Promising, 88 Mich. L. Rev. 489 (1989); Symposium on Default Rules and Contractual Consent, 3 S. Cal. Interdisc. L.J. 1 (1993).

Since this is supposed to be a *short* lecture, I'm going to set aside some of the relatively uncontroversial doctrines like fraud and duress. It's not that these doctrines are uninteresting, from either an economic or a philosophic point of view. Indeed, as many writers have discovered, it's not at all easy to explain just why a contract induced by fraud or duress should not be enforced.[3] Still, most people would agree that no one should be held to a contract that was signed at the point of a gun, or a contract signed as a result of fraud. Most people would also agree that there may be a case for limiting contract terms that create externalities, or effects on people who aren't parties to the contract.[4] Since I don't want to talk about things that everybody agrees on, I'm going to focus instead on some of the more controversial limits on the enforceability of contract terms.

To give us some examples, think about a clause that gives a creditor the right to repossess all of the debtor's furniture if the debtor misses a payment,[5] or a clause that releases a manufacturer from all liability—including liability for physical injury—if its product turns out to be defective.[6] These are the kind of clauses that are often challenged under the contract-law doctrine of unconscionability. My topic is, what can economics tell us about when clauses like these ought to be restricted?

At this point, though, I have to make another disclaimer. The question that economics tries to answer is whether clauses like these are efficient or not. In other words, economics has nothing directly to say about whether these clauses are fair, or just, or whether a buyer's freedoms have been infringed. There are of course political and moral theories which speak to those questions, and I think economics does have something to contribute to these theories. In this lecture, though, I'm going to be speaking primarily about questions of efficiency. In other words, we can rephrase the question I'm addressing here as, "When can legal restrictions on contract clauses be efficient?"

I.   An Example of a Perfect Market

To answer this question, let me start with a story in which restrictions on contract clauses would never be efficient. (If this were a technical economic paper, what I'm about to say would be

---

3. For a survey of some possible arguments, see Anthony T. Kronman, Paternalism and the Law of Contracts, 92 Yale L.J. 763 (1983); Michael J. Trebilcock, The Limits of Freedom of Contract chs. 4–5 (Cambridge: Harvard University Press, 1993).

4. For discussions of this issue see, e.g., Richard A. Epstein, Why Restrain Alienation? 85 Colum. L. Rev. 970 (1985); Susan Rose–Ackerman, Inalienability and the Theory of Property Rights, 85 Colum. L. Rev. 931 (1985).

5. E.g., Williams v. Walker–Thomas Furniture Co., 350 F.2d 445 (D.C. Cir. 1965).

6. E.g., Henningsen v. Bloomfield Motors, Inc., 32 N.J. 359, 161 A.2d 69 (1960).

called a *model*—but since this is a nonmathematical lecture, you can think of it as a story.) The moral of this story is that if the market is working perfectly, there should never be any inefficient contract terms, so efficiency can never be improved by forbidding certain terms. I'm not going to end my analysis with this story— but it does make for a convenient starting point, if only by way of illustration.

Suppose, then that we have a market that's highly competitive, in the sense that there are lots of sellers competing for buyers' business. Even more important, suppose buyers in this market are perfectly informed about what they are buying. By this, I mean not only that buyers know what kind of product they're buying, but also that they know everything there is to know about the risks they have to bear, given the contracts that sellers use. For example, if one seller's contract limits the seller's liability for damages caused by a defective product, buyers not only know that they have to bear that risk, they also know just how likely a defective product is, and just how much damage a defective product is likely to do. This is an extreme assumption, in some ways—but, as I said, it's useful to start with an extreme case to use as a benchmark.

A. The Efficiency of Perfect Markets

In this market, economists would claim, any contract clause which survives very long must be an efficient one. Efficiency, in this context, is defined in cost-benefit terms: A clause is inefficient if the harms it inflicts on buyers are greater than the savings it creates for sellers. There are of course difficulties in how we measure these harms, and how we compare the harm to buyers against the benefits to sellers—but it will be easier to talk about these difficulties later, after I've finished this story. Let me focus first on the claim this story attempts to illustrate: the claim that, in a market such as this, the only clauses that survive will be the ones whose net benefits are positive. If this claim is right, it follows that prohibiting those clauses could only reduce efficiency, by getting rid of clauses whose net benefits were positive.

Why would only efficient clauses survive in this market? If buyers in this market know exactly what risks a clause imposes on them, any seller can make her product more attractive by getting rid of terms that impose risks on buyers.[7] Of course, the seller will lose something by getting rid of those terms: she'll lose whatever benefits the terms gave her. If a seller gets rid of the limitations on her warranty, for example, her product will then be more attractive to buyers, but the seller's own costs will go up because she'll have

---

7. For convenience in the use of pro-   sellers and male buyers.
nouns, all of my examples involve female

to pay more warranty claims. Still, the seller can make up for her own higher costs by raising the product's price to cover her costs. And here's the key: if buyers know exactly what risks the seller's contract does or does not impose, the higher price won't necessarily scare buyers away. Instead, buyers will be more attracted to the product (on balance) whenever the higher price is outweighed by the better contract terms they're now getting. Conversely, buyers will be less attracted to the product whenever the better contract terms are not enough to outweigh the higher price. And that's exactly what we want to happen, from an efficiency point of view.[8]

Another way to put this point is to think of the risks that a product imposes as just one more element of the product's total price. By "total price," I mean not just the monetary price the buyer has to pay, but also the expected costs of all the risks the buyer has to assume. If getting rid of a particular clause will make the total price go down, from the buyer's point of view, that will make the product more attractive to the buyer, and sellers in a competitive market will have an incentive to get rid of that clause in order to make their products more attractive. But if getting rid of that clause will make the total price go down, this means that the benefits to the buyer must exceed the costs to the seller (i.e., the costs reflected in the higher monetary price), so getting rid of that clause must also be efficient. This is why, in markets where buyers are perfectly informed, the only clauses which survive should be those that are efficient.

II.   Market failures

In a perfect market like this, then, there would never be an efficiency case for any restrictions on freedom of contract. Indeed, if all markets were this perfect, economists would have very little to say about freedom of contract: I could end the lecture right now, and we could all go home. However, much of economics consists of studying markets that are not this perfect, and then trying to figure out which institutions could arise to deal with the imperfections. Let me talk now about this branch of economics: the branch that analyzes what are sometimes called *market failures*. As I'll use the term here, a "market failure" is simply anything that prevents a market from operating as perfectly as it did in the scenario I just described.

A.   Monopoly

I'm going to spend most of my time talking about market failures that result from imperfect information. First, though, I

---

8.   The fact that the sellers' costs can be passed on to buyers in the form of a higher price also eliminates some of the difficulties involved in comparing gains to buyers and costs to sellers. For a more complete discussion of this point, see Richard Craswell, Passing On the Costs of Legal Rules: Efficiency and Distribution in Buyer–Seller Relationships, 43 Stan. L. Rev. 361 (1991).

should say something about markets where the problem is a monopoly. Economists have known for a long time that monopolized markets may not behave as well as markets where there's lots of competition. As a result, monopoly is the kind of market failure that's become most familiar to laypeople. Indeed, for a long time many courts and legal scholars assumed that, if inefficient contract terms seemed to be persisting in certain markets, it must be due to monopoly power.[9]

Today, though, most economists would not list monopoly power as a likely source of inefficient contract terms. Moreover, even in those cases where a monopolist did have an incentive to choose inefficient contract terms, most economists would not say that prohibiting the inefficient terms would necessarily improve things for consumers. While I don't want to spend too much time talking about monopolized markets, let me give you a brief sketch of the economic argument.

First, monopolists usually will not have an incentive to choose inefficient contract terms. The monopolist may have an incentive to charge a high price, of course, but this does not mean that she'll also have an incentive to distort any of the other contract clauses. If consumers know what the monopolist is doing—an important qualification that I'll come back to in a minute—then any attempt by the monopolist to insert an inefficient term will be seen by consumers as an increase in the "total price" of the product. In other words, the effect will be much the same as if the monopolist had not introduced the inefficient clause, but had simply raised the monetary price of the product by an equivalent amount. But if the monopolist wants to exploit buyers, she can usually do better by raising the monetary price of the product, rather than by raising the "total price" by using an inefficient contract term. The problem with raising the total price indirectly, by using an inefficient contract term, is that—by definition—an inefficient contract term hurts buyers by more than it benefits the monopolist. By contrast, a higher monetary price helps the monopolist by exactly the same amount that it hurts buyers: the amount of the higher price. This is why the monopolist will usually be better off exploiting buyers by charging a higher monetary price, rather than by inserting an inefficient contract term.[10]

9. For example, the link between unfair contract terms and market power was asserted in an influential article by Friedrich Kessler, Contracts of Adhesion—Some Thoughts About Freedom of Contract, 43 Colum. L. Rev. 629 (1943). In Henningsen, supra note 6, the market power of automobile manufacturers was put forward as one explanation for the persistence of the (allegedly) inefficient limitations on the manufacturers' warranties.

10. This issue is analogous to the question, often addressed in the economic literature, of whether a monopolist will have an incentive to produce a level of product quality or durability that differs from that produced by a competitive

Now, I have to add that there are some situations where a monopolist might indeed profit by using certain kinds of inefficient contract terms. Monopolists can sometimes increase their profits by dividing their customers into different groups, so that they can charge each group a different price, and sometimes the introduction of an inefficient contract term can help sort out the buyers who would be willing to pay the highest price. Even in these situations, though, it does not follow that buyers would necessarily be made better off if the law were to prohibit the inefficient term *without doing anything about the monopoly power*. If the law prohibits the monopolist from using the inefficient term, the monopolist can simply go back to charging all consumers the same price, and it is very difficult to define the circumstances under which buyers will be benefited rather than being hurt by this response.[11] Indeed, in some cases the only way to benefit buyers as a class would be to make the monopolist adopt a term that was *less* favorable to buyers than the term the monopolist would prefer—which might suggest that the legal system should try to strike down terms that were unduly *generous* to buyers.[12] Fortunately, these cases are very difficult to identify in practice, so no court that I know of has ever felt compelled to try to carry out this theory.

To be sure, there are other arguments that might be made about a monopolist's incentives to choose efficient nonprice terms. If the monopolist is securely protected from competition, she might not face as much pressure to maximize her own profits, and thus might not take as much trouble to use efficient terms, even if using efficient terms would be more profitable. On the other hand, a monopolist is not subject to some of the free-rider problems that

firm. For a survey of the economic literature on this point, see Richard Schmalansee, Market Structure, Durability, and Quality: A Selective Survey, 17 Econ. Inquiry 177 (1979); see also the articles cited infra in note 11. Discussions in the legal literature include M.J. Trebilcock, The Doctrine of Inequality of Bargaining Power: Post–Benthamite Economics in the House of Lords, 26 U. Tor. L.J. 359 (1976); Alan Schwartz, A Re-examination of Nonsubstantive Unconscionability, 63 Va. L. Rev. 1053, 1071–76 (1977); Duncan Kennedy, Distributive and Paternalistic Motives in Contract and Tort Law, With Special Reference to Compulsory Terms and Unequal Bargaining Power, 41 Md. L. Rev. 563, 617–18 (1982).

11. For formal economic models of this problem, see A. Michael Spence, Monopoly, Quality, and Regulation, 6 Bell J. Econ. 417 (1975); David Besanko, Shabtai Donnenfeld & Lawrence J. White, Monopoly and Quality Distortion: Effects and Remedies, 102 Q.J. Econ. 743 (1987); Avery Katz, Your Terms or Mine? The Duty to Read the Fine Print in Contracts, 21 Rand J. Econ. 518, 531–33 (1990).

12. For example, if a liquidated damage clause exposing the monopolist to large damage payments would assist the monopolist in sorting its customers, overall consumer welfare could conceivably be improved if the law required the monopolist to set a lower limit on her potential damage liability. For formal models with this characteristic, see Jason Scott Johnston, Strategic Bargaining and the Economic Theory of Contract Default Rules, 100 Yale L.J. 615, 661–64 (1990); Ian Ayres & Robert Gertner, Strategic Contractual Inefficiency and the Optimal Choice of Legal Rules, 101 Yale L.J. 729, 744 (1992).

affect competitive firms, and this might make it easier for the monopolist to offer more efficient terms. In short, the theoretical case for being particularly suspicious of contract terms in monopolized markets is, at best, weak. Significantly, an empirical study of warranties in monopolized and non-monopolized markets found no appreciable difference between the two.[13] This is not to say that the monopolists' terms were always efficient, of course—just that they were no more and no less likely to be inefficient than the terms used in competitive markets.

For now let me return to something I mentioned earlier. I said that if the monopolist tried to introduce an inefficient contract term, consumers would perceive that as an increase in the "total price" of the product, *if* consumers were aware of the inefficient term. If consumers didn't realize the monopolist had inserted an inefficient term—for example, if the inefficient term were hidden in thirty pages of fine print—then the monopolist might well be able to exploit consumers by using an inefficient contract term. In other words, it might seem that, when we have a combination of a monopoly seller and uninformed buyers, we would then have reason to worry about inefficient contract terms.

Once we introduce imperfect information into the story, however, the presence of a monopoly becomes largely irrelevant. As I'll explain in a minute, if buyers don't realize what clauses are hidden away in the fine print, then even markets with lots of competitors may still generate inefficient contract terms. This is what I'm going to talk about for most of the rest of the lecture: the market failures that can arise from imperfect information, regardless of whether the market is monopolized or has many competing sellers.

In short, I think the focus on monopoly power is really a red herring where contract terms are concerned. If courts and laypeople tend to associate inefficient terms with monopolies, it's probably because monopoly is the only form of market failure that courts and laypeople are familiar with. The economic analysis of imperfect information came along much more recently in economic history— most of it in the last twenty years or so—so information economics hasn't yet had time to sink into the collective legal consciousness. But this is where these Coase Lectures come in: One of the goals here is to introduce lawyers and law students to more recent developments in economic analysis. With that in mind, let me now turn to some of the market failures that might arise from imperfect information. I'll then talk about the implications that these market failures might have for the regulation of contract terms.

13. George L. Priest, A Theory of   Yale L.J. 1297 (1981).
the Consumer Product Warranty, 90

B.   Imperfect Information

In particular, I want to talk about three distinct kinds of information problems, so I'll be introducing three more models (or stories). The first two both have to do with imperfect information on the part of buyers. The third story is more paradoxical: it shows how terms that are unduly harsh to buyers might also arise if *sellers* are the ones who are not perfectly informed.

1.   Buyer misperception of risks

Let me start, though, with the simplest of these stories. This is the story that I've already alluded to: Suppose buyers simply don't know all the risks associated with the products and contracts they buy. For example, suppose they don't know that the seller's contract makes buyers bear all the losses if the product turns out to be defective—or suppose that they know they'll bear all the losses, but they don't know how likely it is that any losses will occur (i.e., they don't know the defect rate). In other words, in this story buyers are aware of the *monetary* price the seller is charging, but they do not correctly estimate the *total* price of the product (the monetary price plus the expected cost of the risks they have to assume).

Obviously, in markets like this there is no guarantee that sellers' contract terms will be efficient ones. If buyers don't know enough to evaluate the total price they're paying, an inefficient term could survive simply because buyers didn't realize how costly the term was likely to be. In fact, in addition to inefficient contract terms being provided, buyers might also end up purchasing too much of the product in question, if they didn't fully appreciate the risks associated with the product. To be sure, this problem doesn't mean that laws attempting to prohibit inefficient terms will necessarily improve matters: I'll return to that issue a little later. Still, in the market I've just described, there's at least a *potential* for improvements in efficiency from legal rules banning certain contract terms.

Indeed, this market problem could be analogized to a kind of fraud, or (at least) to a kind of misrepresentation. That is, the effect on buyers is the same as if they had been defrauded: buyers end up with inaccurate beliefs about the purchases they make. To be sure, common-law fraud required that the seller play an active and knowing role in creating the buyer's inaccurate beliefs, and that may not be the case with the problem I have just described.[14]

---

14. Of course, the line between affirmatively creating a false belief, on the one hand, and merely failing to correct an existing false belief, on the other, is not easy to define. For a discussion of this issue, see Howard Beales, Richard Craswell & Steven Salop, The Efficient Regulation of Consumer Information, 24 J. Law & Econ. 491, 499–501 (1981). Indeed, many states now treat the mere failure to disclose information as actionable (in certain cases), while others

The problem described here could arise simply because buyers are inattentive, or because the cost of reading detailed contracts makes such close attention inefficient for buyers. Nonetheless, the economic *effect* of this problem is very similar to the economic effect of fraud—and since I said I wasn't going to say very much about fraud, I won't say very much about this problem, either.

2. Buyer misperception of changes in risks

My second story involves a more complicated sort of market failure. In this story, buyers can be perfectly informed about all the risks associated with the products they actually buy, but they might not be perfectly informed if any seller were to change the risks associated with her product. In technical terms, buyers might not be perfectly informed about possible actions off the equilibrium path. If buyers would not accurately evaluate any change in the level of risks, sellers might then have no incentive to change their products, and the market could get stuck in an inefficient equilibrium. Even though buyers would be accurately informed about all the risks actually created in that equilibrium, no seller will have an incentive to offer a more favorable level of risks, because buyers would not accurately perceive the significance of the seller's change.[15]

Let me make this more concrete. Suppose that buyers are accurately informed about the scope of the average warranty in some market. Suppose, though, that buyers get this information not from reading each warranty carefully before they buy, but from their own personal experiences (or from the experiences of friends) in cases where they were or were not allowed to collect on the warranty. Suppose, finally, that this general perception about the scope of the average warranty is perfectly accurate. That is, suppose that all sellers do limit their warranties to exactly the extent that buyers expect them to, meaning that no buyer is misinformed about the extent of any existing warranty.

Now consider a seller who is thinking of improving her warranty, to make it a little more generous to buyers. If buyers only have

reach similar results by being quite willing to treat silence as an *implied* representation. Compare, e.g. Swinton v. Whitinsville Savings Bank, 311 Mass. 677, 42 N.E. 2d 808 (1942) (mere failure to disclose that house was infested by termites held not actionable), with Kannavos v. Annino, 356 Mass. 42, 247 N.E. 708 (1969) (failure to disclose that apartment building was in violation of local codes was held actionable, because the appearance of the building implicitly represented that it was suitable for use as an apartment house). See generally W. Page Keeton, Dan B. Dobbs, Robert E. Keeton & David G. Owen, Prosser and Keeton on the Law of Torts § 106 (5th ed. 1984).

15. For a formal economic model, see Michael Spence, Consumer Misperceptions, Product Failure and Producer Liability, 44 Rev. Econ. Stud. 561 (1977). Nontechnical discussions in the legal literature include Victor P. Goldberg, Institutional Change and the Quasi-Invisible Hand, 17 J. Law & Econ. 461 (1974); Kennedy, supra note 10, 41 Md. L. Rev. at 597–603.

a general idea about the average warranty offered by all sellers, buyers might fail to notice if this particular seller improved her warranty. Moreover, if this seller improves her warranty, her costs will probably also go up, so she'll have to raise the price of her product to compensate. And if buyers don't realize that her warranty is now more generous, they'll only see the higher price, and will shy away from buying her product. In such a market, the seller will have no incentive to make this improvement in her warranty. Instead, she'll continue to offer the less generous warranty that buyers already expect—thus turning buyers' beliefs about the average warranty into a self-fulfilling prophecy.

Indeed, we could get even worse results than this. Some other seller might decide to offer a slightly *less* generous warranty—and if consumers know only the average level of warranty in the industry, they might not realize that this particular seller's warranty has gotten worse. Moreover, since this seller will be able to reduce her costs by offering a stingier warranty, she'll now be able to reduce her price. If buyers see only the lower price, and do not see the less generous warranty, this seller's sales should increase. In the extreme case, other sellers will be forced by competition to follow her example and we'll have a "race to the bottom," at the end of which all sellers will be offering stingy warranties. This is what George Akerlof has called the "market for lemons": in the end, only lemons are left on the market.[16] Once again, consumers' information may be perfectly accurate after this end-state is reached—that is, consumers may soon become perfectly aware that every seller offers a stingy warranty, so they may continue to have accurate beliefs about all existing warranties. The problem is that, under these assumptions, consumers would *not* be perfectly aware if any seller were to change her warranty, so the market will never get out of this equilibrium.

Now, having sketched out the theory behind this story I should mention that there are several factors which in practice may prevent the result from being so bad. For one thing, consumers don't always buy from whichever seller charges the lowest price. In some markets a low price may be a signal that the seller is probably cutting corners somewhere, maybe by offering a stingy warranty. Another check comes from the fact that a seller who offers a better warranty may be able to advertise that fact, thus bringing the better warranty to buyers' attention.[17] (The occasional outbreaks of warranty advertising in the automobile industry show that this is not impossible.) A third possible check comes from the fact that a

---

16. George A. Akerlof, The Market for "Lemons": Quality Uncertainty and the Market Mechanism, 84 Q.J. Econ. 488 (1970).

17. See Ronald H. Coase, The Choice of the Institutional Framework: A Comment, 17 J. Law & Econ. 493 (1974).

seller who offers less generous terms will have more disappointed customers than a seller who offers more generous terms. If these disappointed customers repeat their stories often enough to other potential buyers—and if enough buyers remember the particular seller associated with this story—sellers who reduce their warranty coverage may suffer the reputational loss they deserve.

Still, I also have to mention that these countervailing factors may not work perfectly in every market. Sellers' advertising claims may not always be believed by buyers, or it may simply be too expensive for sellers to convey the level of detail needed to inform buyers correctly. Reputations may not work perfectly, either: in some industries, the repeat business of buyers may not be important, or it may be too hard for buyers to remember which sellers were associated with good experiences and which were associated with bad ones. In short, the possibility that inefficient terms might persist because of imperfections in buyers' information cannot be ruled out purely as a matter of theory. And if this last theory I've been discussing is sound, imperfections in buyers' information can't be ruled out even if, in equilibrium, buyers are perfectly informed about all the warranties actually offered by sellers.

3. Imperfect seller information

Finally, let me also mention that it's possible to get inefficient contract terms if *buyers* are perfectly informed and *sellers* are the ones who lack information. This is most likely to be a problem when different buyers bring different degrees of risk to the transaction, and sellers don't know how risky any particular buyer is. In technical terms, buyers may have an incentive to agree to certain contract clauses to *signal* their level of risk, even if the clause is inefficient in the sense that its total benefits are less than its total costs.[18]

For example, suppose that some credit buyers (the good credit risks) have a very low probability of defaulting on their loans, while other buyers (the bad risks) are six times as likely to default. Suppose, though, that sellers can't tell which buyers are good risks and which ones are bad risks. Sellers can, of course, get a lot of information by looking at buyers' credit records and employment histories. However, within any group of buyers with similar credit records and employment histories, there will always be some unob-

---

18. For technical economic models, see Janusz Ordover & Andrew Weiss, Information and the Law: Evaluating Legal Restrictions on Competitive Contracts, 71 Am. Econ. Rev. Papers & Proceedings 399, 403–04 (1981); Samuel A. Rea, Jr., Arm–Breaking, Consumer Credit, and Personal Bankruptcy, 22 Econ. Inquiry 188 (1984); Philippe Aghion & Benjamin Hermalin, Legal Restrictions on Private Contracts Can Enhance Efficiency, 6 J. Law, Econ., & Org. 381 (1990). A more accessible explanation can be found in Douglas G. Baird, Robert H. Gertner & Randal C. Picker, Game Theory and the Law 142–47 (1994).

servable factors that make some of these buyers relatively good risks and others relatively bad risks. These differences in risk that remain, after sellers have done whatever screening they can, are the differences I want to focus on here.

To make the example more concrete, suppose that if sellers could find out who the good-risk buyers are, they would be willing to loan to those buyers at a 10% interest rate, while they would only be willing to loan to the bad-risk buyers at an interest rate of 20%. That is, a 10% interest rate would cover the sellers' expected losses to the good-risk group of buyers, but a 20% interest rate would be necessary to cover the higher expected losses to the bad-risk buyers. But if sellers don't know which buyers are which, they won't be able to charge one group of buyers 10% and the other group 20%. Instead, they'll have to charge a rate that's somewhere in between, to cover their expected losses from both groups of buyers. For example, if there are an equal number of good-risk and bad-risk buyers, sellers might have to charge an interest rate of 15% to cover their expected losses from both groups.

Now let's introduce a potentially inefficient contract term. Specifically, consider a clause in which buyers agree to let the seller repossess all their furniture if they default on their loan. Since I want to set the example up so that the clause *is* inefficient, let's assume that the threat of losing their furniture has no effect on the likelihood that buyers of either type will repay their loan. (Maybe the probability of being able to repay depends on events that are entirely beyond the buyer's control.) In fact, let's assume that the threat of repossession has no effect on anyone's behavior: all it does is transfer assets from the buyers to the seller. Finally, let's assume that this transfer creates a net loss, thus making the repossession clause inefficient overall. (The net loss might be because the used furniture is worth more to the buyers that it is to the seller, or it might just be because of the transaction costs associated with repossession.) These assumptions may be unrealistic—but I already told you that I was cooking the example to make sure repossession is inefficient.

I now have to make the example both more concrete and also a little more complicated. Let's quantify the inefficiencies associated with repossession by saying that the right to repossess reduces the interest rate sellers can charge by one percentage point, because it reduces the seller's losses if the buyer doesn't repay. That is, if sellers have a repossession clause in their contracts, they can afford to loan to all buyers at an interest rate of 14%, rather than the 15% rate they'd have to charge without the repossession clause. (If sellers could tell the two groups of buyers apart, they could loan at rates of 9% and 19%, rather than the 10% and 20% they have to charge without the right to repossess.[19])

Suppose, though, that a repossession clause inflicts expected costs on the buyers which are equivalent to *more* than one percentage point in the interest rate. (This is what makes the repossession clause inefficient.) Specifically, suppose that the expected cost of the repossession clause to low-risk buyers is equivalent to two percentage points of interest, while the expected cost of the repossession clause to high-risk buyers is the equivalent of twelve percentage points of interest. The expected cost is greater to high-risk buyers because they're the ones that are most likely to default, and thus most likely to have their furniture repossessed. But as I've set up the numbers, the repossession clause is actually inefficient for both groups of buyers. In each case, the expected cost to the buyers exceeds the expected savings the clause yields for sellers.

Now we come to the potential for market failure. Even if the repossession clause is inefficient for both groups of buyers, the low-risk buyers may nonetheless find that it pays to agree to this clause, in spite of the clause's inefficiency. Here's why. No high-risk buyer would ever agree to this clause, because the expected cost to a high-risk buyer (the equivalent of twelve percentage points of interest) is far too high. But this means that any buyer who does agree to the repossession clause must be a low-risk buyer. If sellers are smart enough to figure this out, that means they can lend to anybody who's willing to agree to a repossession clause at the low-risk buyer rate (9%). And if low-risk buyers can get credit at 9% by agreeing to a repossession clause, that's a better deal than refusing to agree to the repossession clause and having to pay 15%. (If the low-risk buyers don't agree to the repossession clause, the seller won't have any way of telling them from the high-risk buyers, and she'll have to charge them all 15%).

Meanwhile, once the low-risk buyers all agree to the repossession clause, sellers will then be able to figure out that anybody who refuses to agree to that clause is a high-risk borrower. Consequently, sellers will charge anybody who doesn't agree to the repossession clause the interest rate appropriate to high-risk buyers: 20%. High-risk buyers cannot do better by agreeing to the repossession clause and paying a nominal rate of 9%, since (as noted above) the clause inflicts expected costs on high-risk buyers equal to an

19. In a more realistic example, the repossession clause might reduce the interest rate sellers charged the high-risk buyers by more than it would reduce the interest rate they could charge the low-risk buyers, as the repossession clause would be more likely to come into play against the high-risk buyers (who, by definition, are more likely to default). Introducing this refinement, though, would merely make the example more complex without changing the basic point.

additional twelve percentage points, which more than wipes out the reduction in the nominal interest rate. In the end, therefore, all high-risk buyers will pay a 20% rate and will not be subject to a repossession clause; while all low-risk buyers will pay a 9% nominal rate but will agree to a repossession clause, thus paying an effective rate equal to 11%. (The two contracts offered and accepted in equilibrium are shown in bold in Table I.)

Table 1: Effective Interest Rates to Buyers

	Low-risk Buyers	**High-risk Buyers**	**All Buyers (pooled)**
Without repossession clause	10%	**20%**	15%
With repossession clause	**11%** (9% + 2%	31% (19% + 12%)	—

Note: The repossession clause yields a 1% benefit to sellers, but has an expected cost equal to 2% for low-risk buyers and 12% for high-risk buyers.

In this example, then, the low-risk buyers agree to the repossession clause as a way of distinguishing themselves from the high-risk buyers. By distinguishing themselves from the high-risk buyers, the low-risk buyers get an interest rate six points lower than the 15% rate they would have to pay if all buyers refused to agree to the clause. This six-point savings is more than enough to offset the expected costs these low-risk buyers suffer as a result of the clause. But this savings to the low-risk buyers is mostly a transfer from the high-risk buyers, who are now going to have to pay an interest rate of 20% (rather than the 15% rate that they, too, would pay if all buyers refused to agree to the clause). The "market failure" involved here is thus a form of externality, in which low-risk buyers are able to shift some costs to the high-risk buyers by agreeing to a clause which signals their low level of risk. The overall effect, though, is a loss in efficiency. The gains to the low-risk buyers and the losses to the high-risk buyers cancel out, and the only thing left is the cost imposed by the repossession clause itself.[20]

20. In mathematical terms, the equilibrium involves the high-risk buyers paying an interest rate of 20% (with no repossession clause) and the low-risk buyers paying an effective rate of 11% (with a repossession clause). The average rate paid by all buyers is thus (11% + 20%) ÷ 2, or 15.5%. This is 0.5% higher than the 15% rate that all buyers would pay (with a repossession clause) if the repossession clause were banned, and sellers could no longer distinguish between high-risk and low-risk buyers. The 0.5% average loss comes from the

At this point, let me repeat that I've cooked the numbers to make the example come out this way. It's just as easy to come up with variations on these numbers in which a repossession clause would be efficient. For example, in some cases it might not be efficient for sellers to loan to high-risk buyers, and a repossession clause might then be an effective way of preventing this inefficient result. In other cases, low-risk buyers might not be willing to borrow if they have to pay a 15% interest rate, in which case the only way those loans would ever take place is if low-risk buyers can distinguish themselves by agreeing to a repossession clause. In still other cases, the repossession clause might be efficient for all buyers—for example, if the threat of repossession creates more efficient incentives for buyers to take precautions against accidents that might leave them unable to repay.

In short, all I've shown so far is that it's *possible* for imperfect information to cause inefficient contract terms to persist in competitive markets. For this to justify the legal regulations of contract terms, we have to look at how effective the regulation will be at preventing these inefficiencies without creating new ones. In other words—and I promise this will be the last topic—we now have to turn to the question of legal remedies.

III. Remedies

One remedy that I'm not going to address attempts to solve the information problem directly, by mandating the disclosure of information. This kind of remedy will not always be workable, for disclosure itself has costs, and sometimes there may be no information that could usefully (or practicably) be disclosed. In the high-risk/low-risk buyer example, for instance, it is hard to think of any specific piece of information that buyers could possibly disclose. Still, in any case in which disclosure *can* be used to restore the market to something close to the perfect information that I described earlier, a disclosure remedy is certainly worth considering. If disclosure rules could recreate the perfect market described earlier, it would then be unnecessary for courts to try to decide which contract terms were inefficient.[21]

My focus here, though, is on direct restrictions on freedom of contract, in the form of bans on the enforcement of certain contractual terms. I showed earlier that there could be cases where the

---

fact that the clause inflicts a 1% dead-weight loss on all loans to low-risk buyers, who make up exactly half of the population in this example. (The 1% deadweight loss on loans to low-risk buyers is because the repossession clause inflicts costs on those buyers equal to 2%, but benefits sellers by only 1%.)

21. For more extended discussions of the costs and benefits of information disclosure, see Beales, Craswell & Salop, supra note 14; Alan Schwartz & Louis L. Wilde, Intervening in Markets on the Basis of Imperfect Information: A Legal and Economic Analysis, 127 U. Pa. L. Rev. 630 (1979).

market could generate inefficient terms. The problem I want to point to now is that, even if we're certain that the market is working inefficiently, we still may not know which terms we ought to ban.

This is easiest to see in the high-risk/low-risk example I just described. In my example, the repossession clause was in fact inefficient—but I also pointed out that, if the example were changed slightly, the repossession clause might well be efficient. The problem that a court or legislature is going to face is that it won't know for sure which theoretical model best describes any particular real-world contract. This problem introduces another risk: the risk that the legal system, in attempting to increase the efficiency of markets, may make a mistake and end up reducing efficiency.

The same problem comes up in my first two examples, stories, where buyers were the ones who were imperfectly informed about sellers' contract terms. Even when buyers know nothing at all about the contracts they sign, it hardly follows that *every* term ought to be prohibited, for if every term were prohibited then no enforceable contract could ever be signed. Instead, even in such an extreme case of imperfect information, courts still have to be able to tell whether any given clause produces net efficiency benefits or net efficiency losses. You can think of this as the economic analog of the legal distinction between procedural unconscionability and substantive unconscionability.[22] Even if we're sure there's something wrong with the market processes that generated the contract terms—the economic equivalent of procedural unconscionability—we also have to be sure the clause is substantively undesirable before it makes sense to ban the clause.[23]

In other words, even when we are quite sure that the market is not working perfectly, the market can be improved upon only if a court or legislature can ban the inefficient terms without also banning the efficient ones. This requires the court to be able to determine whether any given clause is inefficient or not. But a direct analysis of the efficiency of any given clause will often be

22. The legal distinction is due to Arthur Alan Leff, Unconscionability and the Code—The Emperor's New Clause, 115 U. Pa. L. Rev. 485, 487 (1967). For more on an economic interpretation of this distinction, see Richard Craswell, Property Rules and Liability Rules in Unconscionability and Related Doctrines, 60 U. Chi. L. Rev. 1, 17–20 (1993).

23. A ban on the enforcement of even efficient terms could be justified as a kind of penalty against sellers who fail to comply with a mandatory disclosure program of the sort described at the beginning of this section (see text supra at note 21). However, this makes sense only when disclosure is both feasible and desirable. For a further discussion of this possibility, see Craswell, supra note 22, at 7–12.

very difficult, and courts (or other legal institutions) may not be very good at this task.

Think about it this way: most challenged contract terms produce both good and bad effects. For example, a term limiting a manufacturer's liability under a product warranty might, on the one hand, reduce the manufacturer's incentive to produce a reliable product. This effect, taken by itself, would probably be a bad one (in efficiency terms), since it could lead to an inefficiently low level of product reliability. On the other hand, the same term might increase the customer's incentive to use the product more carefully. This effect, taken by itself, would probably be a good one in efficiency terms. On the third hand—for those of you who have three hands—the same term would also reduce the extent of customers' insurance, by limiting the compensation they would receive if the product was defective. This effect could be either good or bad, depending on the degree of consumers' risk-aversion.[24]

Now, there's a lot more that could be said about each of these three effects, as well as other effects that I haven't even mentioned. However, this is enough to give you a general idea of the kind of things that a court would have to consider in any direct evaluation of the efficiency or inefficiency of a challenged term. Moreover, the court would also need some way to estimate the approximate size of the good and bad effects, to figure out whether the net effect was good or bad. But measuring the actual size of any of these effects will usually be extremely difficult, at least at the present state of our knowledge. While there's been a great deal of theoretical work identifying the effects that *might* be present in any given case, there's been much less empirical work aimed at measuring the exact size of those effects. Moreover, the size of the effects will probably vary from market to market or from industry to industry, so empirical studies of the size of the effects in one kind of contract may not tell us much about the size of the effects in other contracts. This could make it difficult for even a trained analyst to decide whether any particular contract term is inefficient or not. And if we're imagining a legal test in which courts (and not trained analysts) would have to figure out whether a contract term is inefficient, the problems become even greater.

In short, the appropriate comparison here (as in so many other areas) is not between an imperfect market and a perfectly functioning legal system. Instead, the relevant comparison is between an admittedly imperfect market, on the one hand; and an admittedly imperfect legal system, on the other. Moreover, the imperfections of

---

24. Risk-aversion, in this context, is just economic jargon for, "depending on whether consumers want insurance strongly enough to be willing to pay for it."

each institution are likely to vary significantly from case to case, or from industry to industry. In some industries, buyers may be quite well-informed and the market may work very well; in other industries, market imperfections may be much more serious. Presumably, the same is true of the imperfections of the legal system—though these imperfections are, at present, much less understood.

What this means is that we have a good deal more to learn about the potential inefficiencies of markets, on the one hand, and the potential inefficiencies of governmental efforts to improve those markets, on the other. I realize that it may be a bit self-serving for an academic professor to conclude "further research is needed," but I think that's the only conclusion possible here. We've certainly come a long way in our understanding of the economic effects of limits on contract terms—but we've also got a long way to go.

IV. Conclusion

To some of you, it might seem odd that I've devoted most of a Coase Lecture to talking about market failures. There's a popular impression that economists in general, and maybe University of Chicago economists in particular, spend most of their time proving that markets do *not* fail. I want to close, though, by suggesting that the comparative analysis I've just highlighted is actually in the best Chicago tradition, if that tradition is properly understood. Indeed, this sort of comparative analysis is similar in many ways to the comparison called for in Ronald Coase's pathbreaking 1937 article, "The Nature of the Firm."[25]

Coase's article did not begin by assuming that prices and markets always worked perfectly. Instead, he pointed out that many economic activities—specifically, the production and allocation decisions that take place within a firm—have deliberately been removed from the workings of ordinary markets and subjected instead to a sort of hierarchical or command-control ordering system. For example, factory managers don't normally put each day's jobs out to bid to the different members of the factory's work force, or require their workers to buy each day's supplies from the inventory room at a market-clearing price. Instead, the question of how many workers to hire and how many supplies to stock is generally decided centrally by the factory's management. The allocation of those workers and supplies on a day-to-day basis also is usually left to centralized planning within the factory.

For Coase, the question was what explained the existence of these "islands" of centralized planning within an otherwise market economy. His insight was to realize that this question could not be answered from a theoretical framework which assumed that mar-

25. Ronald H. Coase, The Nature of
the Firm, 4 Economica 386 (1937).

kets always worked perfectly. Instead, the way to answer a question like this was (a) to recognize that markets generally entail frictions or costs; (b) to recognize that the alternatives to markets (in this case, hierarchical allocation systems) also have costs; and (c) to begin the inquiry into the exact nature and extent of those costs, in order to figure out where and when each regime would minimize the total costs. (Of course, Coase's insistence on the importance of transaction costs was also to lead to his "Coase Theorem" article,[26] and eventually to a Nobel prize in economics.)

Coase's insights into the nature of the firm have since become the basis for an entire branch of industrial organization economics. For citations to this literature see, e.g., Oliver Hart, An Economist's Perspective on the Theory of the Firm, 90 Colum. L. Rev. 1757 (1989); Conference Issue, Contracts and the Activities of Firms, 34 J. Law & Econ. 451 (1991); Oliver E. Williamson, Markets and Hierarchies: Analysis and Antitrust Implications (1975).

In short, one of Coase's insights was that both markets and their alternatives have imperfections, and that the most interesting questions concern the nature and degree of the imperfections of each. I believe that this same insight must drive any inquiries into the efficiency of restrictions on freedom of contract. If one starts with the premise that markets are always efficient, the inquiry will be over as soon as it is begun, and any analysis of the comparative efficiency or inefficiency of judicial and regulatory regimes will never get off the ground. If we instead recognize that markets may not always work perfectly, and we also recognize that this conclusion is not itself sufficient to justify the legal regulation of contract terms, we can then proceed to the questions that are really worth studying.

---

26. Ronald H. Coase, "The Problem of Social Cost," 3 J. Law & Econ. 1 (1960). (The phrase, "Coase Theorem"—never mentioned in the article itself—was coined by later scholars.)

Study Questions:

1. Usury laws restrict the amount of interest that a creditor may charge a debtor. Are they consistent with freedom of contract? What market failures might they be a response to?

2. Minimum wage laws forbid employers from paying employees below a certain wage. Evaluate them.

3. Rent control restricts the rents that can be charged by landlords. What market failures are they a response to?

4. List doctrines of contract law that appear to violate the principle of freedom of contract.

5. Are the capital regulations described by Geoffrey Miller (Chapter 4) consistent with the principle of freedom of contract?

6. Public Choice

J. Mark Ramseyer[1]

As everyone here probably knows, the point of this lecture series is to explore the many ways that economics has reshaped the fields in which we work. Within the series, my assigned topic is "public choice." If you think of this as the political science analogue to law and economics, you won't be that far off. Just as some scholars have been using economic models to understand legal phenomena for over three decades, others have been applying them relentlessly to political phenomena.

Thinking of the subject as the economic analysis of politics should also clarify just how intractable a topic this is. Essentially, it's as large as law and economics itself—and my job is to explain it all to you in 40 minutes. That being silly, I won't pretend to do the topic justice. Instead, I'll simply outline a few of its more important implications for legal work. If an issue doesn't relate fairly directly to the law, I'll ignore it. And if I ignore points fundamental to political science—well if political scientists don't like it they can fund their own lecture series.

Let me make three basic points, and a series of digressions. First—and most basically—in modern democracies, politicians must work to compete in electoral markets or they do not stay politicians. As a result, there's a market constraint to politics. Second, because of this constraint, when constituents don't much care about an issue, rational politicians will likely trade their vote on it for a vote on something their constituents do care about. There's simply no such thing as a free vote. Last (a subtheme throughout this lecture), institutions decisively shape the way voter preferences get mapped onto legislation. Often, the institutional structure of the electoral market itself determines what becomes law.

Thesis I: There is a market constraint to politics.

The central observation of public choice is simple: politicians in modern democracies operate within the constraints of a competitive electoral market. Many of you will protest that you knew this. And as a profession we have indeed collectively known it, and known it

1. Mitsubishi Professor of Japanese Legal Studies, Harvard Law School, formerly Professor of Law, University of Chicago Law School. This paper was prepared for the Coase Lecture at the University of Chicago Law School on February 21, 1995. I received helpful suggestions on this draft from Eric Rasmusen and the many participants of the Coase lecture series.

for decades. But we've known it in the same way that before law and economics we claimed to know that firms competed in economic markets. We knew it. And we blew it. We blithely proceeded to theorize in ways that ignored the point entirely.

More than anything else, politicians need to win elections. Granted, if we surveyed them most probably would not volunteer that they consciously try to maximize their chance of reelection. But what they tell us they do is beside the point. For whatever they say they do, those that don't work to maximize their odds of reelection will less likely stay in office. As two scholars recently put it, "legislators who indulge their preferences at the expense of their constituents' preferences put themselves at a competitive electoral disadvantage."[2] According to an enormous array of empirical studies, legislators who change the way they vote and ignore their constituents' preferences regularly lose their jobs.

To illustrate some of the consequences of this for legal scholarship, let me give an example. Lest anyone take it personally, let me pick on someone who teaches somewhere else. Recently, a visiting scholar argued here that legislators should deliberate more about constitutional matters. When they want to decide whether to pass a bill, said he, they should talk about whether it's constitutional. Courts should not be the only voice on whether something is constitutional. Instead, our legislators should discuss the constitutionality of what they do, and only do things they think constitutional.

Is this a good idea? Sure. And so is Santa Claus. The world might indeed be a better place if legislators honestly debated the constitutionality of statutes, but the question is whether we have any reason to think that real-world legislators would hold those debates. Restated, the question is whether we have any reason to think that legislators who conscientiously debate the constitutionality of statutes increase their odds of reelection. Because unless we do, this entire proposal is yet another professorial mind game of no real-world significance.

Digression 1: What do voters really want?

All this raises the first digression: what, as Freud would have put it had he studied public choice, do voters really want? If voters in fact valued constitutional deliberation, then our visitor's proposal might indeed have some significance. And at the level of unhelpful abstraction, the answer is relatively clear: voters want a mix of private and public goods. On the one hand, they want some private goods. They want assets and services (like wealth and pork) that they can enjoy to the exclusion of others. Routinely, they reward

2. Bruce Bender & John R. Lott, Jr., Legislator Voting and Shirking: A Criti- cal Review of the Literature, 87 Public Choice 67 (1996).

legislators who redistribute wealth to their districts. On the other hand, any model that relies exclusively on pork-maximizing politicians will miss much of real-world politics. Voters don't just want pork. They also want a broad portfolio of public goods—policies (like low taxes and a stable currency) whose benefits extend beyond them and their own districts.

The question here is whether voters also care about constitutional deliberation. To my knowledge, no one has directly studied the issue. But there is a fairly direct market test. To be sure (as noted later), because institutions mediate voter preferences we have no reason to think political outcomes necessarily track voter preferences. Yet if voters highly valued constitutional deliberation, one would think at least some legislators would find such deliberation advantageous. Notwithstanding, few do. In turn, that fact itself suggests that constitutional deliberation would not help them in the ballot box.

Digression 2: Pork is endogenous.

As a second digression, note that the amount of pork one observes is endogenous to the system: the equilibrium ratio of public to private goods dispensed in any political environment will depend on the institutional structure of the electoral market. More simply, how one structures electoral incentives will determine the amount of pork (or anything else) that politicians provide. Take a polar example from Japan.[3]

Under the post-war Japanese electoral system for the national Lower House, voters cast ballots (a single non-transferable vote, SNTV) for individual candidates (not for parties), but elected several representatives from each district (multi-member districts, MMD). Consider the problem that this posed for a party that hoped to amass a legislative majority. Because it needed to elect several candidates from most districts, it didn't just need to maximize the votes it obtained. It also needed to divide those votes evenly among several candidates in most districts. Ironically, if instead it ran a fabulously popular candidate, that candidate could take votes away from other candidates in the party and thereby reduce the total number of party candidates elected.

An ideal system for dividing such votes would have been cheap and predictable. Suppose party leaders thought they had enough support in a district to elect two representatives. Ideally, they might have told their supporters to vote for candidate A if their telephone number ended in an even digit, and for B if it ended in an odd. Unfortunately, such mechanical schemes work only if voters are willing to follow instructions from party headquarters.

---

3. Drawn from J. Mark Ramseyer & Frances McCall Rosenbluth, Japan's Political Marketplace ch. 2 (Cambridge: Harvard University Press, 1993).

During the post-war decades, voters of the long-ruling Liberal Democratic Party (LDP) were seldom that loyal.

Under a more intuitively obvious system, party candidates would have competed against each other on ideological grounds. If party leaders thought they could field two representatives in a district, they would have fielded both a relatively left-ish candidate and a relatively right-ish one. Relatively left-ish supporters would have voted for the first. The more right-ish would have voted for the second. Unfortunately again, the scheme raised basic problems. First, it was inherently unpredictable. As lines go, the one between "left-ish" and "right-ish" is hardly the cleanest. Second, when they compete on ideological lines, candidates depreciate the value of the party label itself (as American parties routinely find during presidential primaries). One of the more valuable things a political party can provide is a standard portfolio of public goods for which its candidates stand. By disputing the contents of that portfolio, candidates reduce the value of the ideological label that the party would otherwise provide them.

Instead, the LDP divided its supporters through candidate-specific support groups. To build those groups, its candidates dispensed an elaborate array of private goods. To their supporters, they gave pork galore: from sewers and train stations to vacation packages and cash. Through their money machines, they amassed voters who were loyal to them personally. And through that personalized loyalty, party leaders divided the vote.

Two points: First, the amount of pork the LDP dispensed was neither a historical accident nor a cultural artifact. Instead, it was a predictable and rational response to the institutional structure of the electoral market. Indeed, scholars have told much the same story of 19th Century Britain. During the course of the century, Britain gradually eliminated multi-member districts. And as district magnitudes fell, so too did the relative electoral importance of pork. Second—and more basically—legislative outcomes don't just track voter preferences. Instead, they reflect the institutional design of the market through which those preferences get transformed into policies.

Digression 3: Interest groups are endogenous.

Much the same logic applies to the influence interest groups wield. One of the earliest accomplishments of public choice was to show how interest groups often had an influence all out of proportion to the number of their members.[4] The reason was simple: smaller groups (i) generally could organize more cheaply than larger ones, and (ii) often cared more deeply about certain issues

---

4. See Mancur Olson, The Logic of Collective Action: Public Goods and the Theory of Groups (Cambridge: Harvard University Press, 1965).

than the larger groups did. Milk producers had a larger impact on dairy policy than milk consumers, for example, even though more voters drank milk than produced it and even though cows didn't vote. Producers had a larger impact because they could organize more cheaply and because they cared more deeply about milk prices than did consumers.

The interesting point is that the influence that interest groups wield depends—again—on the institutional structure of the electoral market. In effect, early public choice scholars modeled the demand for statutes. Institutional analysis helps us understand the supply.[5] The basic logic is simple: Interest groups will provide legislators with money, and legislators will then use that money to buy (usually figuratively) votes. Because the ability of a legislator to use money to buy votes depends on the institutional structure of the electoral market, the influence of the groups which provide that money will depend on that structure as well.

Again, Japan provides a polar case. Because LDP politicians needed to cultivate large personal support groups to compete under the SNTV–MMD electoral system, they needed huge amounts of money. Because interest groups could provide that money, they had a relatively greater impact in Japan than they have had in most other functioning democracies.

In effect, politicians face a trade-off: They can (a) give policies to their constituents for votes, or (b) give policies to interest groups for money, and use that money to obtain votes. Rational politicians will sell policies for money to interest groups, up to the point at which the votes they lose from catering to such interest groups equal the votes they can acquire with the money the interest groups pay them. In turn, the amount of legislation they sell to interest groups will depend on (i) how much (stated in terms of legislative favors) an interest group charges for its support, (ii) how much (stated in terms of private goods) voters demand for their votes, and (iii) how much an interest-group-biased statute outrages voters. The answers to those questions, however, depend crucially on the institutional structure of the electoral market.

Thesis II: The electoral market constraint leads to vote trading.

Consider now a basic consequence of competition in the electoral market: vote trading. When a legislator's constituents don't care intensely about issue *A*, a vote-maximizing legislator won't vote his principles on *A*. Instead, he'll find an issue *B* that his constituents do care about, and trade his vote on *A* for another legislator's vote on *B*.

5. See Kenneth Shepsle, Congress Is a "They," Not an "It": Legislative Intent as an Oxymoron, 12 International Review of Law and Economics 239 (1992).

Again, take the proposal that legislators deliberate about the constitutionality of bills. When asked whether electoral market constraints would allow legislators to indulge in such principled exercises, our visitor said something like this: "Well, sure. Sometimes legislators won't have the leeway to do it. But there's a lot of room for principles, because most of the stuff legislators vote on are issues that their constituents don't care about." The point is true. And horribly misleading.

To explore the impact of constituent apathy more fully, take an issue of *real* national importance—whether *Casablanca* should be declared a National Historical Treasure on the order of Robie House, such that colorizing it would be a felony. I'd think the interest in this issue would be regional. Somewhere in southern California, somewhere in Burbank, there's probably an army of people with green eyeshades and tiny brushes, painting Ilsa's dress blue, frame after frame. "Sure, the Burbank legislator will have to vote the self-interest of his voters," our visitor might have argued. "But most other legislators can be principled. They ought to be able to debate the constitutionality of declaring *Casablanca* a National Treasure."

Suppose, though, that you're a legislator from a district where voters don't much care about the color of Ilsa's dress, but do care about school prayer. Will you vote your principles on *Casablanca*? Maybe, but the market constraints are that if you do you throw away a chance to raise your reelection odds. If you do care about your reelection, you'll instead go to your Burbank friend and cut a deal. "I'll vote your way on colorization," you'll say, "if you vote my way on school prayer." In doing so you increase the welfare of your constituents. In the process, you also increase your odds of winning the next election. The key here is that voters in different districts often care intensely about different issues. Burbank voters care intensely about colorization; voters elsewhere care intensely about other things. Given this disparity, a trade necessarily can make voters in both places better off; a politician who negotiates such a trade necessarily endears himself to them.

Digression 1: So what did legislators really want?

The possibility of these trades takes us to a discussion of "legislative intent." Although a few sophisticated commentators use the phrase to refer to the vote trades that the legislators thought they had negotiated,[6] most scholars and judges use the phrase to mean something very different: What policies did the legislators think would be best? What programs did they want to

---

6. E.g., Richard A. Posner, The Problems of Jurisprudence ch. 9 (Cam-   bridge: Harvard University Press, 1990).

see implemented? Consider the implications of vote trading for such questions.

Suppose there are four legislators in a legislature (if you want to be more realistic, suppose there are four roughly equal coalitions of legislators). Legislator *A* is from Burbank. He wants a statute declaring movie studios free to paint all movies any way they wish. He calls it the Colorization Liberty Act (CLA).

Legislator *B* opposes colorization. He thinks Casablanca should be a National Treasure, and should forever remain black and white. Did Ilsa really wear blue the day the Germans marched into Paris? He thinks the visual text ambiguous, and would leave that ambiguity ambiguous. *C* and *D* agree with *B*.

What can *A* do? Can he get the CLA passed, when *B*, *C*, and *D* think it a travesty? The answer is "maybe." Maybe, because he may be able to cut a deal with *B* and *C*, and leave *D* rotting with Ugarte in a north African jail. Suppose *B* comes from a district with fertile but dry land. *A* will promise him support for an expensive hydroelectric dam. Suppose *C* comes from a retirement community. *A* will promise her a vote for higher Medicare payments.

If *A* can put together the package, the legislature will then pass three statutes: the CLA, a dam in *B*'s district, and enhanced Medicare. The incomes of voters in *A*, *B*, and *C*'s districts will rise. Faced with funding dams and Medicare programs that disproportionately benefit voters elsewhere, the incomes of voters in *D*'s district will fall. Faced with badly painted movies, even their utility from cinematic leisure will decline.

Now suppose that the new CLA is ambiguous. In interpreting its terms, what should a court do? Traditionally, commentators and judges urged courts to explore the "legislative intent" behind the statute. If by that intent, they mean the deal that *A*, *B*, and *C* thought they were cutting, fine (although even that will often be ambiguous). Yet most commentators and judges use "legislative intent" to ask what legislators thought would be good policy. In our example, though, a majority of the legislators thought the statute terrible policy. *A* thought it was a good idea, but *B*, *C*, and *D* detested it. *B* and *C* voted for it anyway because they were bought. In exchange for statutes that redistributed wealth to their districts, they voted for what they thought was a bad bill.

Note two points about such exchanges. First, sometimes you won't have a clue that they occur. Legislators don't register their deals in the *Congressional Record*. Second, they're perfectly legal. You may think they stink, and courts may too. Tough cookies. Courts don't have the option of striking down a statute on the grounds that most of the legislators thought it outrageous but voted for it because some of them got money routed to their district. At root, vote trades are not a subversion of democracy. They follow directly from competitive elections.

Digression 2: Political parties facilitate vote trades.

This discussion suggests a new perspective on political parties. For one of the major functions that parties perform is to provide a forum where legislators can arrange these trades.[7] Parties can facilitate vote trades for two reasons. First, transactions costs are generally lower for intra-party trades. Because of the repeated nature to intra-party negotiations, legislators will generally find it cheaper to cut deals within the party than without.

Second, the default risk is lower for intra-party trades than for others. In part, this results (again) from the repeated nature of intra-party transactions. As scholars in law and economics have shown time and again, most people more readily honor trades with people with whom they regularly cut deals than with those whom they do not know. In part too, it results from the resources that party leaders control. In most modern democracies, those leaders control access to a wide variety of resources (like wealth) that the rank and file need. By using their control strategically, they can help ensure that the rank and file honor the promises they make.

All this has implications for how we understand party-line votes. Typically, we argue that such votes show that the party holds the issue dear. In fact, they show no such thing. Instead, they may simply show that the party has organized a log-roll, and convinced party members to keep their bargains. Even where a majority party has organized a straight party-line vote, in other words, it's possible that only a small minority within the party supports the bill.

Digression 3: Preferences can cycle.

This analysis of vote trading suggests that congressional votes need not reflect congressional preferences about the policy at issue. Instead, the votes may reflect the trades the legislators organized to pass a larger package of statutes—and a majority of legislators may have opposed every component statute within that package. Yet the opacity of legislative votes is more basic: even absent trades, legislative votes may not represent legislative preference. Instead, under plausible conditions, there may be no proposal that a legislative majority prefers to all other proposals. Legislative preferences may "cycle," such that for every proposal there is another proposal that a majority prefers to it.[8]

7. Keith T. Poole & Howard Rosenthal, Congress and Railroad Regulation: 1874 to 1877, in Claudia Goldin & Gary D. Libecap, eds., The Regulated Economy: A Historical Approach to Political Economy (Chicago: University of Chicago Press, 1994).

8. Kenneth J. Arrow, Social Choice and Individual Values (New Haven: Yale University Press, 1951).

This is tough to see in the abstract, so let's take another North African example. It is a dark and stormy night. The pilot of the Lisbon-bound plane has started the engines, but our three lonely people are still on the runway trying to decide who will get on. As it actually happened, of course, Richard acted as autocrat. He recited that marvelous speech that Real Men everywhere dream of giving, and ordered Victor and Ilsa on. Suppose, though, that the three-some decided instead to vote (after all, they were doing this To Defend Democracy). Suppose that they had three options: Richard and Ilsa board the plane, Victor and Ilsa board it, and Ilsa boards it alone. Suppose that they will vote the first two options against each other, and then the winner against the third. And suppose, finally, that they hold the preferences that appear on Table 1.

Table 1
Preference Rankings

	First Choice	Second Choice	Third Choice
Richard	Victor & Ilsa	Richard & Ilsa	Ilsa alone
Ilsa	Ilsa alone	Victor and Ilsa	Richard and Ilsa
Victor	Richard & Ilsa	Ilsa alone	Victor and Ilsa

We know Richard's first choice: being noble and courageous, he wants Ilsa on that plane with Victor. As a second choice, if Victor does not take her home he will. Even he isn't totally selfless. Under his last choice, Victor will stay and fight the Nazis, he will run off with Captain Renault, and she will fly home alone.

Quixotic as you may consider this, I think Ilsa wanted to ditch both men and head to Lisbon alone. Think about it. She's had these wimps whining over her all week. "Enough already," she says to herself. "I'm high-tailing it out of here alone. You clowns can deal with Major Strasser on your own." Her second choice is to return with Victor, and her last is to return with Richard. At least once she misses her first choice, virtue will triumph over love.

And Victor? Well, we can guess his preferences from his earlier conversation with Richard at the Cafe: he wants Richard to use the letters of transit and take Ilsa with him—"because I love her that much," he explains. His second choice is for Ilsa to return alone, and his last is to take her home himself.

Now as a matter of cinematic hermeneutics, you can plausibly question whether I properly understand the movie. But save those questions for my panel at the next MLA.[9] Assume, for our limited

---

9. "Ilsa's Choice: Gendered Rationality and the Cultural Construction of Mating Patterns in North African Cinematic Texts."

purposes, that these are indeed their real preferences. The interesting point is that Richard, Ilsa, and Victor cannot solve their problem by the vote we proposed. If they vote "Richard and Ilsa" against "Victor and Ilsa," Richard and Ilsa will both vote for the latter. If they then vote "Victor and Ilsa" against "Ilsa alone," Ilsa and Victor will vote for the latter. So "Ilsa alone" would seem to represent their preferred choice—except that if they vote "Ilsa alone" against "Richard and Ilsa," both Richard and Victor will vote for the latter. Effectively, they will cycle over and over—and stand there voting on the runway until Major Strasser arrives and carts them all off to jail. For every outcome, it seems, there will be another that a majority prefers.

In turn, this point raises a basic puzzle: why do we seldom observe such cycling in actual legislatures? The question puzzled public choice scholars for much of the 1970s, but the answer seems to lie in institutions. Through what scholars call "gate-keeping rules," legislatures can prevent the chaotic cycling that might otherwise ensue. In the case of Richard, Victor, and Ilsa, a simple rule giving one of them the power to set the agenda (the number and order of votes to take) would resolve the issue. In American legislatures, the committee system performs much the same function.[10]

As a result, when votes would otherwise cycle, relatively mechanical gate-keeping rules will effectively determine legislative outcomes. If so, however, then even without vote trading we have no assurance that legislative votes reflect any legislative preference. Instead, legislative votes may simply reflect the institutional rules that resolve voting cycles. In this regard, remember that those rules (the institutions that make the crucial difference) are often utterly arbitrary rules (like seniority) that bear no resemblance to majority preferences on any given issue. Yet those rules—not preferences—determine what becomes law.

Conclusions

Where does this leave us? It suggests, I think, three basic points. First, in modern democracies legislators face highly competitive electoral markets. Unless they maximize their reelection probabilities, they will not likely stay legislators. In politics as in economics, people face a fundamental market constraint.

Second, because of this market constraint legislators will often trade their votes. When a rational legislator faces a vote on an issue that his constituents don't much care about, he'll trade it for a vote

10. Kenneth A. Shepsle & Barry R. Weingast, Structure Induced Equilibrium and Legislative Change, 37 Public Choice 503 (1981).

on something about which they do intensely care. Consequently, the votes one sees on a bill do not necessarily reflect legislative preferences about that bill. They may just reflect legislative trades.

Last, institutions matter. In many ways, legislative outcomes are artifacts—even arbitrary ones—of the institutional rules that structure electoral market competition. Even in a world without trades, the votes one sees on a bill may not reflect legislative preferences. They may just reflect the institutional rules by which legislators structure their votes.

Study Questions:

1. So what *is* legislative intent?

2. Public choice analysis is well-known for showing that many statutes that appear to be in the public interest may actually be designed to transfer income to powerful interest groups. Safety regulation, for example, might raise barriers to entry to an industry, thus benefiting incumbents, while not providing much in the way of safety. Can you name some statutes for which this might be true?

3. What might be the role of bicameralism in legislatures?

4. What is the purpose of judicial review when statutes are deals struck by interest groups?

5. Discuss campaign finance reform from a public choice perspective. Which politicians benefit from reform? Which interest groups?

6. Craswell (Chapter 5) discusses "market failure." What's the public choice analogy ("political failure")?

7. Intellectual Property in an Age of Software and Biotechnology

Kenneth W. Dam[1]

The basic economic foundations of intellectual property are straightforward and increasingly recognized by the courts. The problems lie in applying those principles in particular situations. That theme can be highlighted by considering how intellectual property deals with new technologies. This essay will emphasize the two latest technologies to create major intellectual property problems for courts and legislatures—namely, software and biotechnology.

New technologies drive courts and legislatures back to basic principles. For example, new technologies frequently raise the question whether intellectual property rights should be accorded.

The way in which this question arises has traditionally been somewhat different in copyright from patent, largely for historical rather than analytical reasons. In the case of copyright the issue has usually been decided by the Congress, technology by technology. But even after Congress decides for copyright protection, the scope of that protection can be enlarged or cut back sharply by the way the courts apply traditional copyright doctrines. By finding, for example, that the "writing" in question is an idea[2] or a method of operation[3] or that copying constitutes fair use,[4] courts have it within their power to restrict drastically the scope of the property right.

In the case of patents in contrast, the Congress has played little role in the decision whether or not to protect the new technology. Courts have normally made that determination. But here too the courts have the power to narrow patent protection by applying technical patent doctrines so as to leave the property right for a new technology more theoretical than real.[5]

1. Max Pam Professor of American and Foreign Law, University of Chicago Law School. This article is based on a Coase Lecture delivered at the University of Chicago Law School on May 16, 1995, and does not reflect subsequent case law. The author would like to thank Douglas Baird, Jack Brown, Mark Ramseyer, and Sandra Panem for their helpful comments.

2. Computer Associates Int'l v. Altai, Inc., 982 F.2d 693 (2d Cir.1992).

3. Lotus Development Corp. v. Borland Int'l, Inc., 49 F.3d 807 (1st Cir. 1995).

4. Sega Enterprises, Ltd. v. Accolade, Inc., 977 F.2d 1510 (9th Cir.1992).

5. The Congress has, of course, the power to legislate to change any judicial decision narrowing, or for that matter broadening, the scope of protection. For

Even where the societal consensus is that a new technology should be accorded legal protection, the question often arises whether protection should take the form not of traditional intellectual property—say copyright or patent—but rather some new sui generis form.

Sometimes, even after the decision has been reached to use a traditional form of protection, strong and persistent voices will be heard arguing for sui generis protection. For example, a recent massive "Manifesto" in the Columbia Law Review argued for abandoning both software and patent protection of computer software in favor of a new, specially tailored statutory scheme.[6]

This essay discusses the economic principles of intellectual property not just in the abstract but especially as they apply to the decision framework for new technologies. It is limited to patents and copyrights, leaving out of account trademarks, trade secrets and other forms of protection (where other considerations come into play).

I.   The Economic Foundations of Intellectual Property

What are the basic economic principles underlying intellectual property protection?

The first derives from the simple observation that innovation takes the form of information. To be sure, for innovators to profit from innovation and for consumers to benefit, it is often necessary for the innovation to be found in some physical form, if only as the medium in which the innovation is transmitted. Still, the need for protection arises from the simple fact that the innovation itself is information and therefore creates a condition often called the public goods problem. Information is costly to produce, yet cheap to copy. Indeed, it is often said that my use of information does not exclude or place any costs on your use of the same information: hence, the notion of public goods.

Looked at from the standpoint of the innovator, we often describe the same phenomenon as the appropriability problem. If the information can be copied at little or no cost, then the price for using the innovation is likely to be driven down through competition to the costs of copying. As a result, the innovator will not be able to appropriate the benefits of the innovation and recoup his

example, a 1988 amendment to the Patent Code cut back substantially on prior judicial decisions rendering patents unenforceable for patent misuse. See 102 Stat. 4674, incorporated in 35 U.S.C. § 271(d)(4) and (5). This kind of Congressional response is relatively rare in intellectual property scope-of-protection decisions.

6. Pamela Samuelson, Randall Davis, Mitchell D. Kapor and J.H. Richman, A Manifesto Concerning the Legal Protection of Computer Programs, 94 Colum. L. Rev. 2308 (1994).

costs of generating the information in the first place.[7] And if this condition were generalized to innovation as an economy-wide process, then there would be a less than optimal economic incentive to innovate. We can, of course, imagine other motives than direct profit—prestige, other nonmonetary returns, monetary returns from being first to market, and the like—but still the need to protect innovators through according intellectual property rights is generally accepted and widely understood.

This incentive-to-innovate principle is quite general. It applies not only to inventions in the patent sense but also to a wide range of human activities including the writing and publishing of books, the traditional realm of copyright. Moreover, even businessmen and judges who have never heard of public goods or of the appropriation problem recognize the need to accord intellectual property protection to support research and development and to support investments necessary to commercialization of new technology.

So too, everyone—economist, lawyer, businessman—understands that intellectual property rights can be on balance harmful if they are too broad in scope or too rigidly applied. Here we come to a second well-recognized economic principle underlying intellectual property. Even conceding the need to accord intellectual property protection in order to give an incentive, innovation is not a once-for-all matter. We are interested in innovation over time.[8]

If giving too broad protection today arrests future innovation, then we will not have an optimum rate of innovation over time, and the economy will suffer. This is particularly the case because in the overwhelming majority of instances each innovation builds on past innovations. Each innovator stands on the shoulders of the innovators of the past, even where those past innovators were not giants but just a wee bit taller than the crowd. Hence, to obtain an appropriate balance between innovation today and innovation tomorrow, it is essential to allow access.

How much access, under what conditions, and when are major topics in the law of patents and copyrights, whatever the legal rubric used—whether it be, in the case of patents, disclosure, length of term, or the reverse doctrine of equivalents, or, in the case of copyrights, such doctrines as fair use.[9] Sometimes this

7. William M. Landes & Richard A. Posner, An Economic Analysis of Copyright Law, 18 J. Legal Stud. 325, 328 (1989).

8. See Douglas G. Baird, Changing Technology and Unchanging Doctrine: Sony Corporation v. Universal Studios, Inc., 1984 Sup. Ct. Rev. 237, 239 (1985).

9. See Kenneth W. Dam, The Economic Underpinnings of Patent Law, 23 J. Legal Stud. 247, 266–267 (1994). A third economic principle of intellectual property not specially relevant to new technologies is the need to reduce the incidence of rent seeking. Patent law, for example, needs to be constructed in such a way that it does not lead to

access principle is so strongly valued by a society, especially in the case of new technologies, that it is allowed to overwhelm completely the incentive-to-innovate principle and no intellectual property right is accorded. In the case of patents, this judgment favoring access over incentives is expressed in the legal conclusion that the invention is nonpatentable subject matter.

II.   Protecting New Technologies

In considering the new technologies of software and biotechnology, it is useful to keep in mind that there are in principle three options for each new technology. First, do not protect at all. Second, protect in principle while applying the rules in such a way as to balance incentive and access. A variant of this second option is to protect in principle but, because of some societal judgment, to decide—often case by case—to emphasize access over incentive in particular situations.[10] Third, protect not through patent or copyright but through a tailored, sui generis system.

A related preliminary point is that new technology protection has evolved in somewhat different ways in the copyright and patent regimes. For the first century of the Republic, and even to some extent today, Congress has made a separate decision as to whether each new technology should be protected and, if so, how. This pattern was set in the very first copyright statute. In 1790 Congress accorded copyright protection to any "map, chart, book or books"[11] and to no other category of writings. In 1802 it added prints, clearly extending copyright into the realm of technology, albeit not a new technology.[12] In 1831 Congress added musical compositions[13] and in 1856 dramatic compositions.[14] In 1865 it added a new technology—photographs.[15]

Congress did not get around to covering paintings, drawings, sculpture and fine arts models and designs until 1870.[16] When one considers that Congress covered maps and charts in 1790 and added photography as soon as the Civil War revealed the power of that technology, while not even dealing with the fine arts until 1870, we

undue investment in innovation in the race to obtain the governmentally-accorded privilege of excluding competitors. Id. at 251–153, 261–266.

10.   A variant of this second option is to emphasize incentive over access. Although in the application of the second option, the balancing of incentive and access may have been done by some courts in such a way as to unduly emphasize incentive, no system appears to have explicitly downgraded the access principle.

11.   1 Stat. 124 (1790).

12.   2 Stat. 171 (1802). It is significant that in referring to prints, section 2 of the 1802 Act speaks of persons "who shall *invent* and design, engrave, etch or work" prints. (Emphasis supplied) See William F. Patry, Copyright Law and Practice, Vol. I, p. 36 n. 108 (1994) (hereafter "Patry").

13.   4 Stat. 436 (1831).

14.   11 Stat. 138 (1856).

15.   13 Stat. 540 (1865).

16.   Section 86, 16 Stat. 198, 312 (1870).

can deduce that Congress had technology very much in mind in the first century of American copyright.[17]

In the twentieth century Congress began to legislate more generically, presumably leaving to the courts a greater role in deciding to what extent new technologies were to be protected by copyright. For example, the 1976 comprehensive revision uses the format of protecting "works of authorship" (in the 1909 copyright revision called "writings of an author"[18]) which "include" certain stated categories. Examples are literary works and musical works.[19] Some of these categories are defined, other not. Thus, in principle a new technology could come into existence and be covered under one of the already listed categories.

But old habits die hard and when it came time to protect some new technologies, they were legislatively added to the list. Motion pictures were included in 1912.[20] Sound recordings, as opposed to long-protected musical compositions,[21] did not receive explicit protection until 1971.[22] When computer software came on the scene, Congress established a commission to study the problem, but even before the commission reported, Congress confirmed through legislative history that software would be covered under the existing category of "literary works," thereby resolving an already long-standing controversy on the protection issue.[23] Later legislation nailed down copyright protection for software.[24] Indeed, the copyright tradition required special legislation in 1990 simply to include "architectural works," even though such works have been around much longer than any U.S. copyright statute.[25]

17. See the correlative point that Congress in the first century of American copyright was at least as concerned with protection of labor-intensive informational writings as with creative writings. Jane C. Ginsburg, Creation and Commercial Value: Copyright Protection of Works of Information, 90 Colum. L. Rev. 1865, 1873–1881 (1990).

18. Section 4, 35 Stat. 1075, 1077 (1909).

19. 17 U.S.C. § 102.

20. 37 Stat. 488 (1912).

21. Patry, Vol. I, 234–235.

22. 85 Stat. 391. Sound recordings received state law protection earlier, and there was controversy and ambiguity about pre–1971 federal protection for sound recordings. Donald S. Chisum and Michael A. Jacobs, Understanding Intellectual Property Law § 4C[1][c]. See Goldstein v. California, 412 U.S. 546 (1973). See Patry, Vol. I, 73–74, 294–297 and Vol. II, 830–831 (1994), concerning the history of protection of sound recordings as well as their indirect protection as derivative works.

23. See discussion in Kenneth W. Dam, Some Economic Considerations in the Intellectual Property Protection of Software, 24 J. Legal Stud. 321, 322 n. 5 (1995) (hereafter Dam, Protection of Software); and Arthur R. Miller, Copyright Protection for Computer Programs, Databases, and Computer–Generated Works: Is Anything New since CONTU?, 106 Harv. L. Rev. 977, 978–80 (1993).

24. 94 Stat. 3015 (1980).

25. 104 Stat. 5089, 5133 (1991), now 17 U.S.C. § 102(a)(8). For the background of this enactment, see Patry, Vol. I, 302–304.

Since the 1976 Act the copyright statute has grown increasingly complex. Congress has attempted to deal with competitive fights between industries based on different technologies by adjusting rights and obligations. The names of some of the statutes tell the story: the Satellite Home Viewer Act,[26] the Audio Home Recording Act,[27] and the Cable Television Consumer Protection and Competition Act.[28] Without too much exaggeration, one could summarize the copyright approach as a separate statutory scheme for each new technology.

Congress has played other roles in deciding on protection. For example, when the question of protection for semiconductor mask works arose, Congress decided that, rather than establishing a new copyright category, a brand new property rights scheme—a sui generis scheme—should be used. We find it in the Semiconductor Chip Protection Act of 1984.[29]

The pattern in patent law was completely different. The first patent statute set out to give protection to inventions of every kind. The original 1790 statute broadly authorized patents on "any useful art, manufacture, engine, machine, or device."[30] Thanks to the draftsman Thomas Jefferson, something of an inventor himself, a 1793 amendment broadened the categories to "art, machine, manufacturer or composition of matter."[31] Today, the list of categories remains the same, substituting only "process" for "art" to reflect contemporary usage.[32]

To be sure, the form of the patent code is somewhat analogous to that of the copyright act in the sense that both list categories that are to be covered. In principle, an invention has to fall within one of the four patent categories or no patent will issue. However, the four patent categories are broader and more general than the eight copyright categories. For example, "machine" in the patent statute is an altogether broader concept than "sound recording" or "architectural works" in the copyright act. Hence, though the four patent categories could be thought to fail to exhaust the universe of things that ought to be patented, that view does not reflect the history of patent law. Under the patent law in action, new technolo-

---

26. 102 Stat. 3949 (1988).

27. 106 Stat. 4237 (1992).

28. 106 Stat. 1460 (1992). New technologies have led to a large volume of statutory enactments to define narrow technology-specific rules with regard, for example, to limitations on rights. See examples in Patry, Vol. 1, pp. 89–115. For an extensive explanation of this copyright phenomenon, see Jessica Litman, Copyright Legislation and Techno-

logical Change, 68 Oregon L. Rev. 275 (1989).

29. 98 Stat. 3347, now 17 U.S.C. §§ 901–914.

30. 1 Stat. 109, 110 (1790).

31. 1 Stat. 318, 319 (1793). See Diamond v. Chakrabarty, 447 U.S. 303, 308–309 (1980); Graham v. John Deere Co., 383 U.S. 1, 7–10 (1966).

32. 35 U.S.C. § 101.

gies were automatically covered as they came along. There was no need for Congressional action.[33]

Perhaps the different pattern in patent from copyright is not a question so much of statutory drafting or of inherent differences in the two types of protection but rather of the very idea of invention, which presupposes technological change.[34] In any event, the patent law approach focuses attention not on the kind of technology, but rather on whether the particular invention is new, useful and, to use the neologism of the current statute, "non-obvious."[35]

For example, when the question of patent protection for computer software arose, the Congress felt no need to confront the issue. Nor did the courts decide in principle whether patents could provide protection. It was assumed that in some cases software patents were possible, and the struggle was over the circumstances. Specifically, the courts, especially the Supreme Court, invoked a judge-made mathematical algorithm exception to patentable subject matter, thereby making it hard to sustain software-related patents.[36] But as discussed below, this objection has been largely overcome,[37] and, in any event, the courts have never ruled out software-related patents in principle but have considered only the particular circumstances of each software innovation so long as it fell within the statutory categories of "process, machine, manufacture, or composition of matter."[38]

A caveat is, however, in order. Despite this rather clear positive direction on coverage, the courts took it upon themselves to declare that certain kinds of inventions were not patentable subject matter. Although some courts had declared that a "product of nature" could not be patented because it was not in one of the patentable categories,[39] the courts later took to declaring certain things not patentable without too much attention to the categories.[40]

---

33. A fuller discussion of the four patent categories would consider the definition of "process" in 35 U.S.C. § 100(b), which includes in that term "a new use of a known process, machine, manufacture, composition of matter, or material."

34. Diamond v. Chakrabarty, 447 U.S. 303, 316 (1980); and see U.S. Patent and Trademark Office, Revolutionary Ideas, Patents and Progress in America (1976).

35. The statutory term "non-obvious" appears in the Patent Code in the title to Section 103. The section itself refers to whether the subject matter sought to be patented "would have been obvious at the time the invention was made to a person having ordinary skill in the art to which said subject matter pertains." 35 U.S.C. § 103. This essay will use, in following the tradition of patent law commentary, the terms "obviousness" and "nonobviousness."

36. See Gottschalk v. Benson, 409 U.S. 63 (1972); Parker v. Flook, 437 U.S. 584 (1978). But see Diamond v. Diehr, 450 U.S. 175 (1981).

37. See discussion infra at notes 53–58 and accompanying text.

38. 35 U.S.C. § 101. See Diamond v. Diehr, 450 U.S. 175 (1981).

39. Merck & Co. v. Olin Mathieson Chemical Corp., 253 F.2d 156, 162 (4th Cir.1958); Parke–Davis & Co. v. H. K. Mulford Co., 189 Fed. 95, 103 (S.D.N.Y. 1911).

To summarize, patent protection for computer software and biotechnology did not require a go/no go decision by either legislature or courts. The only question was under what circumstances software and biotech patents met the standards of novelty, usefulness and nonobviousness. However, as we shall see, the courts did have to wrestle with some judicially created exceptions to patentable subject matter. In contrast, returning to copyright, we have seen that a legislative decision was necessary to ensure protection for software.

This difference between the copyright and patent traditions is illustrated by biotechnology. Since Congress did not undertake to protect biotechnology by copyright, protection has been sought and accorded only by patent despite the fact that Congress also took no action under the patent code. This differential result of Congressional non-action in both fields is significant not just because there is a secondary literature suggesting copyright protection for biotechnology[41] but because at least some of the field would lend itself to copyright protection insofar as it has the equivalent of letters, words and sentences. The genetic code in DNA has only four letters, one for each of the building blocks (nucleotides) that comprised DNA. This is a remarkably efficient alphabet, indeed one in which all substantive "words" are only three letters long with each different three-letter "word" coding for an amino acid. With this language cells are able to express thousands, probably hundreds of thousands of proteins, and—equally remarkably—to do so with only twenty naturally occurring amino acids. These amino acids are, if you like, the "letters" of protein words and sentences. Be that as it may, patents, not copyrights, are the weapons of choice for biotechnology.

III. Software and Copyright

Copyright protection for software, though widely considered necessary for the incentive effect, clearly risks denying a desirable and even a necessary degree of access to follow-on innovators. And this is true even though independent creation is a complete defense to a charge of copyright infringement. In part this fear of denying access is based on the quite legitimate need of computer programs to attach to other programs and to computer hardware. But in part this fear has also been fed by economists and economics-oriented

---

40. See discussion of the mathematical algorithm exception infra at notes 53–58 and accompanying text.

41. For suggestions in the secondary literature that copyright be used for biotechnology, see, e.g., Dan L. Burk, Copyrightability of Recombinant DNA Sequences, 29 Jurimetrics J. 469, 492–512 (1989); Irving Kayton, Copyright in Living Genetically Engineered Works, 50 George Washington L. Rev. 191, 216–218 (1982).

lawyers who, with a raft of arguments concerning compatibility, de facto standards, network externalities, switching costs and lock-in, have sought to argue that at least some outright copying, not just of software and hardware interfaces but of baseline programming itself, should be permitted.[42]

I have argued elsewhere that despite the extraordinary versatility of these economic constructs, which incidentally boil down to essentially the same argument, the basic case for copyright protection of software is quite strong, with only two possible exceptions: first, where attachment interfaces are involved and second, where the follow-on innovator substantially improves and adds value to the software.[43] Both of these two possible exceptions involve a special need for access and the latter is simply a copyright law analogue, via the "fair use" principle, for what in patent law is called an "improvement patent."

The courts have tended in recent years to concentrate on developing theories by which to deny copyright protection to certain features of particular software programs despite the presence, often conceded by infringement defendants, of outright wholesale copying. In arriving at these results, the courts in those software cases have sometimes downplayed the need to balance incentive and access, settling instead on two quite simple legal theories—one, that the copied programming involved ideas rather than expression[44] and two, that it involved a system or method of operation.[45] In short, those courts have simply applied the statute which denies copyright protection "to any idea, procedure, process, system, method of operation, concept, principle, or discovery,"[46] a litany that is hardly self-defining.

Most of those software cases fall in the first category, denying protection to an idea, which necessarily involves a continuum between unprotected "ideas" and protected "expression." As Judge Easterbrook said in *Nash v. CBS*, a case outside the software field, the courts must find where on that continuum to draw the line, yet "[n]either Congress nor the courts has the information" necessary to draw the line in particular cases.[47] What we do know, he said, is that "it is a mistake to hitch up at either pole of the continuum."[48] So the courts have been drawing the line using a variety of techniques and labels. Perhaps some courts have drawn the line too

42. See the analysis of these economic arguments in Dam, Protection of Software, supra.

43. See discussion in Protection of Software, supra.

44. See, e.g., Computer Associates Int'l v. Altai, Inc., 982 F.2d 693 (2d Cir.1992).

45. See, e.g., Lotus Development Corp. v. Borland International, Inc., 49 F.3d 807 (1st Cir.1995).

46. 17 U.S.C. § 102(b).

47. Nash v. CBS, Inc., 899 F.2d 1537, 1541 (7th Cir.1990).

48. 899 F.2d at 1543.

far in one direction, undercutting the incentive function of copyright protection. Perhaps some have undervalued the importance of access. On the whole the courts have done a reasonable job in approaching the balancing task, even though they have not usually recognized the two economic principles of incentive and access. Indeed, looking beyond the software cases to the general issue of incentive and access, the courts have long been aware, at least intuitively, of the need to balance these two principles.[49]

Some commentators argue that software so poorly fits the copyright paradigm that it would have been better to choose a sui generis approach more conducive to the technical nature of software.[50] When one looks at the results of the 1974 Semiconductor Chip Protection Act, one is left with doubts about a sui generis approach. There Congress set forth detailed rules but, by failing to consider amendments over time, Congress has failed to keep progress with rapidly changing technology and thereby has left the statute essentially irrelevant to present-day semiconductor technology. As the 1992 Patent Advisory Commission found, "[S]ome of the basic definitions [of the Act] are already obsolete, leaving important parts of mask work technology outside the protection of that legislation."[51] One can conclude that the general intellectual property law has a flexibility that sui generis statutes are unlikely to have where fast-moving technology is involved. This conclusion may be somewhat counter-intuitive, for one might suppose that a specialized statute should usually be better at dealing with a specialized field of endeavor, but that conclusion about the superiority of Congress over the courts is not obvious where rapidly advancing technology is concerned.[52]

IV. Software and Patents

As we have seen, software has also benefited from patent protection. But there too the courts have, on a case by case basis, tried to balance the incentive and access principles. They have done so, however, with less clarity of view than in the software copyright

---

49. See Gerald Gunther, Learned Hand: The Man and the Judge 316 (1994); Paul Goldstein, The Competitive Mandate: From Sears to Lear, 59 Calif. L. Rev. 873 (1971). And see Benjamin Kaplan, An Unhurried View of Copyright 89–92 (1967).

50. See the Columbia Manifesto, cited supra, and citations to earlier articles along the same line therein.

51. Advisory Commission on Patent Law Reform, A Report to the Secretary of Commerce 151 (August 1992). Moreover, according to Rauch, the rapid change in process technologies creates opportunity for piratical exploitation of the reverse engineering exception to the relatively narrow protection accorded by the statute. John G. Rauch, The Realities of Our Times: The Semiconductor Chip Protection Act of 1984 and the Evolution of the Semiconductor Industry, 75 J. Pat. & Trademark Office Soc'y 93 (1993).

52. See Protection of Software, supra at 371–376. Several minor amendments have been made to the Chip Protection Act concerning procedural, rather than substantive, matters.

cases. In software patent cases the main field of battle has been a legal principle not to be found in the statute, namely the principle that mathematical algorithms are not patentable subject matter.

Several decades of time and vats of judicial ink have been spilled in deciding whether particular software-related inventions constitute patentable subject matter. The Supreme Court and the Federal Circuit have wrestled with the issue without bringing much clarity.[53] The issues have been how much physical interaction between software and hardware must be present and whether the software produces a physical change. To be sure, part of the problem has been that the Patent and Trademark Office until recently has fought a rearguard action against enlarging the sphere of software patent protection, leading to repeated appeals by patent applicants—frequently successful but not always with well-reasoned resulting opinions.[54] The practical effect of these decisions has been to cause many patent lawyers to draft software claims as so-called apparatus or machine claims. The applications say, in effect, that the invention is a machine, not software and certainly not a mathematical algorithm, and the software is simply a means by which the machine does its work.

In a recent case, *In re Allapat*,[55] the Federal Circuit—which has become de facto the Supreme Court of patent law—took a long step toward drastically restricting the mathematical algorithm exception by allowing, in an *en banc* decision, a patent on a software program whose instructions were executed by well-known computer components. Indeed, the *Allapat* court emphasized that when a general purpose computer is programmed, it becomes a special purpose computer and hence, if the claimed invention is new, useful and nonobvious, a patent is appropriate even if a mathematical algorithm is central to the software itself.[56]

Suggestive of what is actually at stake is Judge Newman's concurring opinion in which she argues that "mathematics is not a monster to be struck down or out of the patent system, but simply

---

53. See generally Robert Patrick Merges, Patent Law and Policy 45–100 (1992)

54. See, however, the PTO's proposed guidelines for reviewing "computer-implemented inventions." 60 Fed. Reg. 28778 (1995), reprinted in 50 BNA Patent, Trademark & Copyright J. 164 (1995), and the supporting legal analysis, reprinted id. at 659. The proposed guidelines, while directed to patent examiners, not only promise a more receptive attitude toward software patents but also provide a blueprint for patent claim drafting.

55. 33 F.3d 1526 (Fed.Cir.1994).

56. See also In re Lowry, 32 F.3d (1994), applying analogous reasoning in reversing a "printed matter" rejection concerning data structures in computer memory. On the issue of the relevance of a programmed computer as a statutory "machine" in software cases, see also In re Warmerdam, 33 F.3d 1354 (Fed.Cir. 1994), and the Federal Circuit's vacation and remand (July 25, 1995) of In re Trovato, 42 F.3d 1376 (Fed.Cir.1994).

another resource whereby technological advance is achieved."[57] She went on to observe that modern technology such as software and electronics inevitably relies heavily on mathematics, that mathematics is "simply another resource whereby technological advance is achieved," that there has been "no major technological advance, no new industry or evolving technology, that has not participated in the patent system" and therefore the fact that a new technology relies heavily on mathematics should no more disqualify an innovation than if it relied on the principles of chemistry.[58]

The Federal Circuit rarely articulates what is really at stake in its decisions, but it seems apparent that the mathematical algorithm principle is an attempt to prevent a patent applicant from preempting an abstract principle of human knowledge. To allow such an abstract principle to be preempted would completely imbalance the trade-off between incentive and access and would gravely impede future innovation.

Under this analysis software-related patents can be seen to raise few access problems with regard to abstract mathematical principles because a patent on the application of particular software to a computer or to some specialized machine in no ways precludes others from applying the same mathematical principles to achieve some other result in a computer or specialized machine. It is the application of the mathematics for a narrow practical use, not the mathematics itself, from which the patentee can exclude the competitor.

Obviously the application of this concept of a balance between the two economic principles of incentive and access is not self-executing. All of the tools of legal process, including fact-finding and reasoning, are still required. But explicit attention to this balance would make patent law decisions more understandable and predictable.

V.   Biotechnology and Patents

Biotechnology is another new technology that has faced problems in achieving equal protection in the patent system. Nearly every principle of patent law has to be rethought and interpreted anew in biotechnology, which is a reason why so many leading patent law decisions of the last decade have been biotech cases.[59] For this reason and in order to explore more deeply the application of the incentive and access principles to contemporary patent law, it is worth reviewing not merely patentable subject matter but also

---

57.   33 F.3d at 1568, 1570.

58.   33 F.3d at 1568, 1570–1571.

59.   See Diamond v. Chakrabarty, 447 U.S. 303 (1980) (patentable subject matter); In re Bell, 991 F.2d 781 (Fed. Cir.1993) (obviousness); In re Vaeck, 947 F.2d 488 (Fed.Cir.1991) (enablement); Fiers v. Revel, 984 F.2d 1164 (Fed.Cir.1993) (conception).

how the courts have handled other core patent issues, such as novelty, nonobviousness and utility in the biotechnology field.

With respect to the threshold issue of patentable subject matter, the underlying question is, as in the case of software, one of balancing the two grand economic principles of intellectual property—incentive and access. Under this economic approach, we should take care to ensure that principles of the biological sciences not be preempted through patents but rather only specific technological applications, so that the basic scientific principles remain open to future innovators. Still the question whether biotech innovations are patentable subject matter has had to be fought out in the courts.

What has particularly bedeviled the courts and many opponents of biotechnological research has been the frightening notion that life itself might be patented. As usually argued, this is predominantly a religious or ethical concern, but it obviously relates to the question of what is being preempted if patents are granted.

In the United States the threshold issue was left to the courts and, as in the case of software, the issue was phrased as whether patentable subject matter was presented by the patent application. The breakthrough in the United States was the Supreme Court decision in the 1980 *Chakrabarty* case involving a patent on a living bacterium that could break crude oil down into its chemical components, a highly useful property in fighting crude oil spills.[60] The Court simply concluded that the bacterium was "not nature's handiwork," but the inventor's, and that Congress had got it right in the 1952 patent codification when it said in a committee report that patentable subject matter "include[d] everything under the sun that is made by man."[61]

Converting this approach to my language, one can summarize by saying that since neither naturally occurring bacteria nor the principles of life but rather just a newly created bacterium was the subject matter from which the patentee could exclude others, the incentive principle clearly dominated any concerns about the access principle. It is thanks to this decision that we now have patents on such things as the famous Harvard mouse, an *onco*mouse that rather perversely had the highly useful property that it was particularly susceptible to carcinogens and therefore lent itself to cancer research.[62]

The problem in that patent has nothing to do with mice for one can invent any other kind of non-oncomouse one pleases and so

---

60. Diamond v. Chakrabarty, 447 U.S. 303 (1980). See also In re Allen, 2 USPQ2d 1425 (Bd. Pat. App. & Int. 1987), aff'd, 846 F.2d 77 (Fed. Cir. 1988).

61. 447 U.S. at 309–310.

62. P. Leder and T. Stewart, Transgenic Non–Human Mammals, U.S. Pat. 4,736,866 (1988).

access is not compromised. Rather an access problem lurks in its broadest claims, including the claim to all transgenic non-human mammals with increased susceptibilities to cancer. Not just mice but elephants and whales are excluded too, so long as they show the same susceptibility to carcinogens.[63] Of course, one can still invent a new elephant if it is made especially susceptible to say malaria rather than cancer.

More important than transgenic creatures has been the fact that biotechnology inventions now enjoy patent protection without unnecessary squabbles about threshold life-related subject matter issues. The situation has been fundamentally different in some foreign countries that impose major restrictions on biotechnology patents, just as indeed some still do on pharmaceuticals,[64] though the TRIPS agreement in the Uruguay Round should help because it is a violation of that agreement to exclude any "field of technology" from patent protection.[65]

One general point is that although Congress had previously enacted two sui generis plant patent statutes to protect innovations in plants,[66] in part to avoid lurking doubts about the "product of nature" exception to conventional patent coverage,[67] the courts have wisely found a sui generis approach unnecessary for biotechnology. Indeed, new man-made plants, whether or not created by biotech methods, have been held eligible for conventional patents—that is, eligible for what are called utility patents in order to distinguish them from plant and design patents.[68]

VI.   Biotech Patent Doctrine

In addition to the patentable subject matter issue, biotech product patent applications must face the three hurdles faced by all

---

63. The European Patent Office rejected the broader claims. See Robert P. Merges and Richard R. Nelson, On the Complex Economics of Patent Scope, 90 Colum. L. Rev. 839, 847 (1990).

64. Harold C. Wegener, Patent Harmonization §§ 2311–2312 (1993); Gerald J. Mossinghoff, Research–Based Pharmaceutical Companies: The Need for Improved Patent Protection Worldwide, 2 J. of Law & Tech. 307 (1987); Michael L. Doane, TRIPS and Int'l Intellectual Property Protection in an Age of Advancing Technology, 9 Am. U. J. Int'l Law and Policy 465, 479 (1994).

65. Agreement on Trade–Related Aspects of Intellectual Property Rights, Including Trade in Counterfeit Goods, Art. 27(1). However, Article 27(3) has certain exceptions with regard to biotechnology.

See also the transitional provisions of Article 65. See J.H. Reichman, Universal Minimum Standards of Intellectual Property Protection under the TRIPS Component of the WTO Agreement, 29 Int'l Lawyer 345, 352–353, 358–360 (1995).

66. The two statutes are the Plant Patent Act of 1930, 35 U.S.C. § 161, and the Plant Variety Protection Act of 1970, 7 U.S.C. § 2402.

67. This was a major motivation of the 1930 Act. Diamond v. Chakrabarty, 447 U.S. 303, 311–313 (1980). The 1970 Act extended coverage to sexually reproduced plants. 447 U.S. at 313–314.

68. Ex parte Hibberd, 227 USPQ 443 (Bd. of Pat. App. 1985). See Animal Legal Defense Fund v. Quigg, 932 F.2d 920, 923 (Fed.Cir.1991).

patents; the product must be novel, nonobvious and useful.[69] For commercial efforts in biotechnology, which at least initially were mostly concerned with using biotech methods to make what already existed in nature (say a human protein), one can readily see that these hurdles are not automatically cleared. The key in that context to meeting these three requirements lies in the fact that biotech provides the product in a form that is purer and easier to administer in the treatment of disease, while at the same time being cheaper to produce than through conventional pharmaceutical processes. As Sandra Panem has concisely summarized the early promise of biotechnology, "The power of this new technology lies in the ability to produce rare biological products in large quantity, with high purity, and at low cost."[70]

1. *Novelty.* The courts, particularly the Federal Circuit, have approached the biotech cases in the traditional patent law manner, which is to treat patent law as unitary and then to apply that law to the facts as if there were nothing extraordinary about the new technology. The novelty question, which is simply whether the naturally occurring product is new, had already been answered in the pharmaceutical cases. Those cases held that if a protein is isolated and purified, then it is new for the purpose of the novelty test.[71] This result not only solves a riddle inherent in the nature of biotechnology but does so in a way that promotes the incentive principle.[72]

2. *Nonobviousness.* The novelty cases do not answer the obviousness question, the second hurdle to patentability. How, one might ask, can the isolated, purified form of a protein fail to be obvious if it is otherwise identical to a naturally occurring protein, which we already know about? This is a complicated question that the courts have struggled with.[73] But the courts have not tried to

---

69. A further hurdle is the enablement requirement. 15 U.S.C. § 112. See Amgen, Inc. v. Chugai Pharmaceutical Co., 13 USPQ2d 1737 (D.Mass.1989), 927 F.2d 1200 (Fed.Cir.1991). This requirement has the effect of narrowing the scope of biotech patents by limiting the ability of the applicant to make generic product claims covering more than the applicant has actually made, In re Vaeck, 947 F.2d 488 (Fed.Cir.1991), and thereby balances the incentive and access principle by granting the first innovator a narrow patent while leaving room for follow-on innovators to make claims for other species within the genus, assuming that the obviousness hurdle can be overcome. For a discussion of the significance of the enablement requirement to the biotech industry, see

Kenneth J. Burchfield, Biotechnology and the Federal Circuit 208–210 (1995).

70. Sandra Panem, The Interferon Crusade, back cover (1984).

71. Merck v. Olin Mathieson Chemical, 253 F.2d 156 (4th Cir.1958); In re Bergstrom, 427 F.2d 1394 (CCPA 1970).

72. To the extent that biotech innovation has expanded to include substances not found in nature, the novelty requirement no longer presents a special barrier to patentability. See Burchfield, supra, at 66.

73. The pharmaceutical cases used a variant of the purification rationale to deal with the obviousness doctrine as well. See Merck v. Olin Mathieson Chemical, 253 F.2d 156, 164 (4th Cir.

construct a separate biotechnology patent doctrine. Rather they have used the traditional approach of comparing what is claimed with the prior art. The crucial point is that the prior art is not what is known to nature but what is known to man. For example, if what is known to man is a protein and what is claimed is a gene and the gene has been isolated and purified so that it clears the novelty hurdle, then the obviousness question is not whether it is obvious that a particular gene having a particular nucleotide sequence exists in principle, but whether it would be obvious to one skilled in the art how to identify and isolate it.

The leading case of *In re Bell* held that while "[i]t may be true that knowing the structure of the protein, one can use the genetic code to hypothesize possible structures for the corresponding gene and that one thus has the potential for obtaining that gene," nevertheless the degeneracy of the genetic code is such that there are more than 1036 different possible nucleotide sequences in a gene that might code for that protein.[74] This recognition of the special nature of the genetic code does not involve, however, any separate doctrine favoring biotechnology patents but rather constitutes an application of the long-established principle applied across a wide range of technologies that simply because a new research approach is "obvious to try" does not mean that a resulting product would be obvious. Thus, unless there is something in the prior art that would suggest to a researcher a particular gene in question, as opposed to the thousands or millions of other possible nucleotide sequences that might possibly encode the particular protein, the resulting isolated and purified DNA molecules are not obvious and may be patented. While the processes for looking for the right nucleotide sequence might be known, it is not obvious how to pick the right one out of this human haystack.

This approach seems eminently good common sense in the protein-to-gene case, but it does not provide a rule for the protein-to-protein situation where biotech methods are used to produce a protein identical to a protein found in nature. Yes, the patent application may meet the novelty test if the protein is isolated and purified, but does it meet the obviousness test? One possible, but inadequate answer is that if the biotech *process* used to obtain the biotech form of the protein is new and nonobvious, then of course the patentability standard is met.[75] But the problem is that the

1958) ("It did not exist in nature in *the form* in which the patentees produced it and it was produced by them only after lengthy experiments. Nothing in the prior art ... suggested it." (emphasis supplied)).

74. 991 F.2d 781, 784 (Fed.Cir.1993). See also In re Deuel, 51 F.3d 1552 (1995).

75. Process (or "method") patents are of course also subject to the nonobviousness requirement. See In re O'Farrell, 853 F.2d 894 (Fed.Cir.1988).

inventor can obtain a process patent, not a product patent,[76] and as the courts have recognized in the pharmaceutical cases, process patents may be so hard to enforce that they do not provide a sufficient property rights basis to finance the risky development and clinical trials necessary to bring a new drug to market.[77]

The effort to emphasize the incentive function through the isolation-and-purification rationale has created a problem of deterring future innovation. In the *Scripps* case a patent involving a blood growth factor produced by a chemical purification process was held potentially infringed by the biotech version of the same product.[78] The full impact of that decision on innovation over time becomes clearer when one considers that its doctrine could presumably preclude a subsequent biotech firm from producing the same growth factor through still newer and even more superior biotech processes.[79]

As biotechnology has progressed, the obviousness question tends not to arise in the simplistic way just discussed in which the

76. The 1988 process patent amendments provide product protection in the sense that 35 U.S.C. § 154 makes "sale or use" in the United States of a product made by a patent process an independent act of infringement. However, the use of the patent process must still be established. Although the amendment was aimed at imported goods, it was not so limited. See the legislative history cited in Burchfield, supra, at 313 n. 10.

77. See statement of Judge Rich, dissenting in Atlantic Thermoplastics Co. v. Faytex Corp., 974 F.2d 1279, 1280–1281 (1992), that the cost in 1990 of moving a new chemical entity from laboratory to market was over $230 million and that only one of 5,000 to 10,000 compounds discovered ever make it to market. Some attempts to find a solution to this problem have involved so-called product-by-process claims. Such claims have sometimes sought to give product protection where the essence of the invention is in truth a nonobvious process. However, the justification for such claims, which are not mentioned in the patent code, is to permit a patent on "an otherwise patentable product that resists definition by other than the process by which it is made." In re Thorpe, 777 F.2d 695, 697 (Fed.Cir.1985). Compare Atlantic Thermoplastics Co. v. Faytex Corp., 970 F.2d 834 (Fed.Cir.1992), holding that the process is a limitation on a product-by-process claim so that making the

product by a different process would not constitute infringement with Scripps Clinic & Research Foundation v. Genentech, Inc., 927 F.2d 1565 (Fed.Cir.1991), and the dissents of Judges Rich and Newman in the Atlantic Thermoplastics case, supra.

78. Scripps Clinic & Research Foundation v. Genentech, Inc., 666 F. Supp. 1379 (N.D.Cal.1987), but see a later decision in same case holding many claims invalid, 707 F. Supp. 1547 (N.D.Cal. 1989), aff'd in part, rev'd in part, 927 F.2d 1565 (Fed.Cir.1991). See discussion in Robert Patrick Merges, Patent Law and Policy 488–489 (1992), and Robert P. Merges and Richard R. Nelson, On the Complex Economics of Patent Scope, 90 Colum. L. Rev. 839, 914–915 (1990). The Federal Circuit pointed a way out of the dilemma thus created by the Scripps lower court holding by remanding the case to the trial court to determine whether the reverse doctrine of equivalents, a seldom applied doctrine, avoided the dilemma by absolving the biotech firm from infringement liability. 927 F.2d 1565 (Fed.Cir.1991).

79. See, however, Genentech, Inc. v. Wellcome Foundation, 29 F.3d 1555 (Fed.Cir.1994), a doctrine of equivalents case, implicitly distinguishing the situation where an allegedly infringing protein was superior in therapeutic application to the patented protein.

applicant claims the biotech equivalent of the naturally occurring substance—for example, a protein or a gene—but rather claims some new biotechnological half-way house. To the extent that biotechnology today creates substances that do not exist in nature, the obviousness issue rather becomes the generic issue of what would have been obvious to one skilled in the art.[80]

3. *Utility.* The third hurdle to patentability, namely the utility doctrine, has become in some ways the front line in the biotech patent wars. The Constitution's reference to the "useful Arts" has led to the statutory requirement of utility. Put abstractly, the threshold utility issue is whether any utility has been shown if a substance simply does what the corresponding natural substance does. The essence of the issue is, however, that some major advances may not yet have a concrete use in medicine or agriculture or any other end use economic activity.

These R & D outputs, often the product of enormous R & D outlays, are more than basic research results but may not, without further R & D, result in something of immediate concrete value to mankind. Still, they may be sold in the marketplace, particularly to pharmaceutical firms. While an economist might say that whatever commands a price in the marketplace meets an economic utility test, a conventional legal view has been that something that is useful only in further research does not meet the statutory utility requirement.

For the purposes of emphasizing the factors at play it suffices to take just one hotly contested, indeed highly emotional, question now being fought out in the patent system. Suppose I use biotech methods to isolate not previously known partial complementary DNA sequences.[81] Yes, partial cDNA sequences may be patentable subject matter, but is the utility requirement met if we do not know for sure what they are useful for? Put in the language of the current debate, should we not wait until we at least know the function of these sequences? Or, to use the jargon of patent law, do the sequences have practical utility?[82] In short, do they provide "some immediate benefit to the public"?[83]

80. See, e.g., In re Vaeck, 947 F.2d 488 (Fed.Cir.1991). A recent statute extends biotech patent protection for processes by prohibiting obviousness rejections for biotech processes "using or resulting in a composition of matter" that is novel and nonobvious. P.L. 104–41 (1995).

81. A complementary DNA sequence is one derived from messenger RNA, which may be thought of as a half-way house between cellular DNA and the protein expressed by that DNA within the cell. For an explanation, see In re Deuel, 51 F.3d 1552, 1554 (1995).

82. On the patent law concept of utility, see Brenner v. Manson, 383 U.S. 519 (1966).

83. Nelson v. Bowler, 626 F.2d 853, 856 (CCPA 1980).

One answer is to say that we should just wait until we have something truly useful—of "immediate benefit to the public"— before granting a patent.[84] Under this view we should wait, for example, until we have isolated a useful protein using that cDNA sequence before considering patentability or until we have at least identified and located the cellular DNA or perhaps synthetically generated the full DNA sequences required to produce a protein. The essence of the policy argument for this wait-and-see approach is that issuing such cDNA patents would inhibit research leading to truly useful discoveries.[85]

The problem with this wait-and-see solution is twofold: First, given the progress in biotech methods, the method of identifying and locating the entire gene may be obvious from knowledge of the partial cDNA sequence. Second, the protein may be obvious from the gene or even from a complete cDNA sequence.[86] And so if there is no patent on the partial sequence, there may be no patent available at a later stage because of the nonobviousness requirement.

Would such an outcome serve the incentive function of the patent system? As already mentioned, it is well-known that pharmaceutical companies are reluctant to engage in R & D and unwilling to go through the expensive Federal Drug Administration clinical trial process on new drugs unless patent protection can be relatively assured because otherwise commercialization will not be financially feasible.[87] Of course, if the firm that discovers the partial sequence neither publishes it nor sells it publicly, then it may later be able to patent the full gene. The result would, however, be later disclosure to the public and to that extent, perversely, serve neither the incentive nor the access function.[88]

---

84. One can find an analogy in In re Joly, 376 F.2d 906 (CCPA 1967), which held that one cannot patent a chemical compound that is useful only because it is an intermediate in making another chemical compound in the absence of showing the utility of the latter compound.

85. Bernice Wuetherich, All Rights Reserved: How the Gene–Patenting Race is Affecting Science, 144 Science News 154 (Sept. 4, 1993), offers an example.

86. "Like mRNA [messenger RNA], cDNA contains only the protein-encoding regions of DNA. Thus, once a cDNA's nucleotide sequence is known, the amino acid sequence of the protein for which it codes may be predicted using the genetic code relationship between codons and amino acids." In re

Deuel, 51 F.3d 1552, 1554 (Fed.Cir. 1995).

87. Bernadine Healey, Special Report on Gene Patenting, 327 New England J. of Medicine 664, 667 (1992); Reid G. Adler, Genome Research: Fulfilling the Public's Expectations for Knowledge and Commercialization, 257 Science 908 (1992); Gerald G. Mossinghoff, Research–Based Pharmaceutical Companies: The Need for Improved Patent Protection Worldwide, 2 J. of Law & Tech. 307 (1987).

88. A recent development has been the effort of Merck to underwrite University laboratory sequencing of human cDNA followed by immediate deposit of the sequences in a public databank. This approach results in prompt disclosure to the public but also undercuts efforts by

No doubt recognizing this simple fact of business life, the Commissioner of Patents, reacting to criticism from the biotech industry, adopted guidelines in 1995 making clear that a patent examiner should not reject biotech applications where the asserted utility "would be considered credible by a person of ordinary skill."[89] Perhaps these guidelines will lead to patents being granted on cDNA sequences for their utility in construction of DNA probes or in new forensic applications or in tissue typing or in diagnostic applications.[90] Looking further ahead, cDNA sequences could be useful in some as yet unexploited ways based on the essential comparability of DNA in all of earth's creatures. Some of these utility theories, especially use in constructing cDNA probes to identify and locate the gene, have to confront the important principle of utility doctrine that frowns on any theory based on usefulness in further research.[91] This principle, which has its legal justification in the notion that an innovation useful only in further research is not of "immediate benefit to the public,"[92] is a somewhat dubious notion when biotech research itself has raised billions of dollars of capital from the public.

The legal memorandum accompanying the PTO's new utility guidelines casts doubt on the legal rationale for any research tool exception:

> Many research tools such as gas chromatographs, screening assays, and nucleotide sequencing techniques have a clear, specific and unquestionable utility (e.g., they are useful in analyzing compounds). An assessment that focuses on whether an invention is useful only in a research setting thus does not address whether the specific invention is in fact "useful" in a patent sense.[93]

other to patent such sequences. See Columbia Shuns Profits from Gene Fragments, 268 Science 487 (April 28, 1995). Since Merck is primarily a pharmaceutical rather than a biotech firm, the question of its motivation has arisen. Eliot Marshall, HGS Opens its Databanks— for a Price, 266 Science 25 (Oct. 7, 1994); and Jerry B. Bishop, Plan May Blow Lid Off Secret Gene Research, Wall St. J. B1 (Sept. 28, 1994).

89. 60 Fed. Reg. 97, 98 (1995), reprinted in BNA Patent, Trademark & Copyright Journal 234 (1995).

90. Rebecca S. Eisenberg, Genes, Patents, and Product Development, 257 Science 903 (1992); Eliot Marshall, The Company that Genome Researchers Love to Hate, 266 Science 1800 (Dec. 16, 1994); John Carey, Untangling the Legal Strands of DNA, Business Week 78 (May 8, 1995). For a critical review of these utility theories, see Stephen B. Mabius, Novel DNA Sequences and the Utility Requirement: The Human Genome Initiative, 34 J. Pat. and Trademark Off. Soc. 651 (1992).

91. See Burchfield, supra, at 57–59; and Rebecca S. Eisenberg, Symposium: A Technology Policy Perspective on the NIH Gene Patenting Controversy, 55 U. Pitt. L. Rev. 633, 645–647 (1994).

92. Nelson v. Bowler, 626 F.2d 853, 856 (CCPA 1980).

93. 50 BNA Patent, Trademark & Copyright J. 297, 298 (1995).

If this view is sustained by the courts, the incentive function will be preserved in the biotech industry. But what about access for future innovation? We must recognize that the fight over partial cDNA sequences arises from the fear in academia, and also in some portions of the pharmaceutical industry, that access to the basic biological building blocks of the human body will be preempted by patents.[94] Here again the solution to this burning biotech patent issue lies in a clear recognition and discussion of the balance between the incentive and access principles.

The foregoing discussion of the utility issue in biotechnology is not an attempt to lay down rules for its resolution in the manifold factual situations presented by the onrushing progress of the field but rather is simply an illustration of an economic approach to intellectual property law that is by no means limited to threshold issues of whether or not to protect a new technology. This economic approach throws light on nearly all of the technical issues of patent and copyright law.

---

94. On the possibility that the experimental use defense to patent infringement will satisfy the academic concerns, see Rebecca S. Eisenberg, Patents and the Progress of Science: Exclusive Rights and Experimental use, 56 U.Chi. L.Rev. 1017 (1989).

Study Questions:

1. People may reproduce short excerpts of copyrighted works under certain circumstances. For example, a book review may contain a few quotations of the book being reviewed. What is the economic explanation for this rule?

2. What is the relationship between intellectual property law and freedom of contract (Chapter 5)? Can intellectual property protections be created through contracts, or is there a problem of market failure?

3. Are the various copyright statutes likely to be efficient? Discuss them from a public choice perspective (Chapter 6)?

4. What is the economic explanation for the distinction between "ideas," which may not be copyrighted, and "expressions," which may?

5. Can you give economic content to the doctrines of novelty, nonobviousness, and utility in patent law?

8. Social Norms and Social Roles

Cass R. Sunstein[1]

I. Tales of Rationality and Choice

A. Ultimatums and Fairness[2]

Economists have invented a game: the ultimatum game. The people who run the game give some money, on a provisional basis, to two players. The first player is instructed to offer some part of the money to the second player. If the second player accepts that amount, he can keep what is offered, and the first player gets to keep the rest. But if the second player rejects the offer, neither player gets anything. Both players are informed that these are the rules. No bargaining is allowed. Using standard assumptions about rationality, self-interest, and choice, economists predict that the first player should offer a penny and the second player should accept.

This is not what happens. Offers usually average between 30% and 40% of the total. Offers of less than 20% are often rejected. Often there is a 50–50 division. These results cut across the level of the stakes and also across diverse cultures.

B. Littering

Why do people litter? Why do they throw things out instead? Social psychologist Robert Cialdini tried to find out.[3] He placed flyers under the windshield wipers of cars and waited to see what drivers would do with them. Cialdini made arrangements so that before reaching their cars, some people would see someone (a Cialdini associate) walk past them, pick up from the street a bag from a fast-food restaurant, and throw it in the trashcan. Of the group who both saw the responsible behavior and noticed the flyers, *almost none* threw them on the street. In the control experiment,

1. Karl N. Llewellyn Distinguished Service Professor, Law School and Department of Political Science, University of Chicago. This appeared in Cass R. Sunstein, Social Norms and Social Roles, 96 Colum. L. Rev. 903 (1996), and, in somewhat different form, in Cass R. Sunstein, Free Markets and Social Justice (Oxford University Press, 1997). This lecture was delivered in the autumn of 1995.

2. See C. Camerer and R. Thaler, Ultimatums, Dictators and Manners, 9 J. Econ. Perspectives 209 (1995); Handbook of Experimental Economics 270, 274–75 282–88, 296–302 (J. Kagel and A. Roth eds. 1995).

3. R. Cialdini, J. Cacioppo, R. Bassett, & J. Miller, Low–Ball Procedure for Producing Compliance: Commitment Then Cost, 36 J. Personality and Social Psychology 463 (1978).

with no one showing responsible behavior, over one-third of the drivers threw the flyers on the street.

Would it make sense to say that nearly all of the first set of drivers "had a preference for" throwing garbage in the trashcan, whereas merely two-thirds of the second set "had that preference"? This would not exactly be false, but it would not be very illuminating. Whether people put things in a trashcan, or litter instead, is partly a function of social norms and the observed behavior of other people.

C.   Smoking, Rationality, and Race

About 400,000 Americans die each year from smoking-related causes. Government has tried to reduce smoking through educational campaigns designed to inform people of the risks. Despite this fact, about one million Americans begin smoking each year, many of them teenagers, and people worry that educational campaigns will succeed, if at all, only with well-educated families. Indeed the government is now initiating a large-scale program to reduce smoking, especially among teenagers.

But consider this. Nationally, 22.9% of white teenagers smoked in 1993, a number that has been basically unchanged in the last decade. But in the same year, only about 4.4% of African–American teenagers smoked, a number that is *four times smaller* than the number a decade before.[4] What accounts for this difference? Part of the explanation appears to lie in differing understandings of what is fashionable. And part of that difference may lie in a private antismoking campaign in the African–American community, symbolized most dramatically by posters in Harlem subways showing a skeleton resembling the Marlboro man lighting a cigarette for a black child. The caption reads: "They used to make us pick it. Now they want us to smoke it."

D.   Recycling in the Hamptons

In East Hampton, New York—part of the famous and wealthy "Hamptons"—what used to be called the East Hampton Dump is now the East Hampton Recycling and Disposal Center. At the East Hampton Recycling and Disposal Center, there are separate bins for green glass, clear glass, newspapers, tin cans, paper other than newspaper, and more.

Almost every day in August, people at the Center can be found patiently separating their garbage for placement in the relevant bins. Sometimes this takes a long time. The people at the Center

---

4. American Lung Association, Summary of Trends in Cigarette Smoking (1995). It is notable that the reduction in current smoking among black teenagers was 51% between 1983 and 1994, whereas the reduction among black adults was 25.6%, a difference that suggests a substantial effect from social norms among teenagers.

tend to own expensive cars—Mercedes Benz, BMW's—that are parked near the bins. As they separate their garbage, they look happy.

E.   John Jones

John Jones lives in California. Here is a description of some aspects of his behavior.

1.   He buys smoke alarms and installs them in three rooms in his house.

2.   He loves chocolate and ice cream, and eats a lot of both. He also eats a fair amount of frozen foods; he makes sure that they are "lean" whenever he has a choice. According to his doctor, he is slightly over his ideal weight.

3.   On warm days, he likes to ride his bicycle to and from work, and he enjoys riding his bicycle on busy city streets, even though he has heard about a number of collisions there.

4.   He is happily married. He tries to share the work around the house, but he doesn't much like domestic labor. He does less than his share. He acknowledges that this is both true and unfair, and he supports many policies that are conventionally described as "feminist."

5.   He buckles his seatbelt whenever he is in a car. His own car is a Volvo, and he bought it partly because it is said to be an especially safe car.

6.   He is not worried about the risk of an earthquake in California. On some days, he says that he doesn't think that an earthquake is very likely; on other days, he claims to be "fatalistic about earthquakes."

7.   He does not recycle. He considers recycling a personal "irritation." He is mildly embarrassed about this, but he has not changed his behavior.

8.   He considers himself an environmentalist; his votes reflect his enthusiasm for environmentalism. He supports aggressive regulation designed to protect people from risks to their life and health. In fact he is in favor of mandatory recycling, notwithstanding his own failure to recycle.

9.   In his own mind, his resources fall in various mental "compartments." Some money is reserved for retirement; some money is saved for charitable donations. Some money is kept for vacation. Some money is for monthly bills. His forms of mental accounting are very diverse. He is fully aware of this.

Is Jones inconsistent? Is Jones risk-averse or risk-inclined? What is Jones' dollar valuation of a human life, or of his own life?

F.   The Point of this Essay

My goal in this essay is to challenge some widely held under-standings of rationality, choice, and freedom, and to use that challenge to develop some conclusions about human behavior and also the appropriate domain of law. I urge that behavior is perva-sively a function of norms; that human norms interact with human goods in surprising ways; that changes in norms might be the best way to improve social well-being; and that government deserves to have, and in any case inevitably does have, a large role in "norm management." Far too little attention has been paid to the place of norms in human behavior and to the control of norms as an instrument of legal policy.

Part of the motivation for this essay is practical. Consider the following table:[5]

Table 1
Preventable Risks of Death in the United States

Risk	Percent of Total Deaths	(Range)	Total Deaths/Year
Tobacco	19	14–19	400,000
Diet/Activity	14	14–27	300,000
Alcohol	5	3–10	100,000
Microbial	4	—	90,000
Toxic Agents	3	3–6	60,000
Firearms	2	—	35,000
Sexual Behavior	1	—	30,000
Motor Vehicles	1	—	25,000
Illicit Drugs	<1	—	20,000

What is notable is that these risks of death could be much reduced with different social norms. With respect to smoking, diet/activity, alcohol, firearms, sexual behavior, motor vehicles, and illicit drugs, current norms are a major problem in the sense that new norms could save lives.[6] A regulatory policy that targets social

5. McGinnis and Foege, Actual Causes of Death in the United States, 270, JAMA 2207 (1993).

6. Note in this regard dramatically shifting social norms with respect to bi-cycle helmets, as noted in Besides Sav-ing Lives, Wearing a Helmet When Cy-

norms may well be the most effective possible strategy. Social norms are also part and parcel of systems of race and sex equality; if norms would change, existing inequalities would be greatly reduced.[7] It is thus transparently important to see whether changes in social norms, brought about through law, might operate to save lives and otherwise improve human well-being.

But part of the motivation for this essay is theoretical; it involves a conceptual puzzle. In the last decade there has been an active debate about whether and to what extent law should respect "preferences." But the term "preferences" is highly ambiguous, and it is not clear what the participants in this debate are actually talking about when they say that "preferences" should or should not be respected by law. When the term is clarified, it becomes clear that the term "preference" can be understood in several different ways, and these differences are too often collapsed. When the idea of a "preference" is unpacked, it becomes clear that it may well be too ambiguous and too coarse-grained to be a foundation for normative or positive work.

More particularly, I aim to make a set of conceptual or descriptive points:

1. For many purposes, it would be best to dispense with the idea of "preferences," despite the pervasiveness of that idea in positive social science and in arguments about the appropriate domains of law and the state. In normative work, the idea elides important distinctions among the mental states of human agents. In positive work, the idea tends to disregard contextual factors that produce diverse choices in diverse settings.

2. Many well-known anomalies in choice behavior are best explained by reference to social norms and to the fact that people feel shame when they violate those norms. In fact money itself is not fungible, and this is because of social norms.[8]

3. There is no simple contrast between "rationality" and social norms. Individual rationality is a function of social norms. Many efforts to drive a wedge between the two rest on obscure "state of nature" thinking, that is, on efforts to discern what people would like or prefer if social norms did not exist. Those efforts are doomed to failure.[9]

cling Is Cool, The Wall Street Journal, 9/18/95, at B1.

7. For an especially illuminating discussion, see S. Okin, A Clash of Basic Rights? Women's Human Rights, Identity Formation and Cultural Difference (unpublished manuscript 1995). See also UNDP, Human Development Report.

8. See V. Zelizer, The Social Meaning of Money (1994).

9. A qualification is necessary if the definition of rationality is normative and defended as such. In that case it would be possible to say that a certain norm is irrational because (for example) it makes lives worse.

4. Social states are often more fragile than might be supposed, because they depend on social norms to which—and this is the key point—people may not have much allegiance. What I will call *norm entrepreneurs*—people interested in changing social norms—can exploit this fact; if successful, they produce what I will call *norm bandwagons* and *norm cascades*. Successful law and policy try to take advantage of learning about norms and norm change.

I also aim to make two claims about the appropriate domain of law. These claims have a great deal to do with law's *expressive function*—that is, the function of law in expressing social values and commitments, especially by moving norms in better directions.

1. Individual choices are a function of social norms, social meanings, and social roles, which individual agents may deplore, and over which individual agents have little or no control. Norms can tax or subsidize choice. Collective action—in the form of information campaigns, persuasion, economic incentives, or legal coercion—might be necessary to enable people to change norms that they do not like.

2. Some norms are obstacles to human autonomy and well-being. It is appropriate for law to alter norms if they diminish autonomy by, for example, discouraging people from becoming educated or exposed to diverse conceptions of the good. It is appropriate for law to alter norms if they diminish well-being by, for example, encouraging people to risk their lives by driving very fast, using firearms, or taking dangerous drugs.

G.   An Insufficiently Charted Domain

Libertarians, some economic analysts of law, and many liberals[10] give inadequate attention to the pervasive functions of social norms, social meanings, and social roles. Often it is said that in a free society, governments should respect both choices and preferences. But the case for respecting these things depends partly on their genesis, and as I have indicated, the determinants of choices, indeed the meaning of the term "preference," remain most obscure.[11] We should agree that social norms play a part in determining choices; that people's choices are a function of their particular social role; and that the social or expressive meaning of acts is an ingredient in choice.[12] We should try to see whether social norms,

10. The liberal tradition is very complex on this count, and I will not try to sort out its various strands here. I believe that all of the arguments made here fit well within central strands of that tradition.

11. Illuminating discussions include A. Sen, Behavior and the Concept of a Preference, in A. Sen, Choice, Welfare, and Measurement (1982); E. Anderson, Value in Ethics and Economics (1993).

12. See the especially instructive discussion in L. Lessig, The Regulation of Social Meaning, 62 U. Chi. L. Rev. 943 (1995); though I have referred to this

social roles, and social meaning can be obstacles to human well-being, and whether something might be done to change them, even if people are making "choices," even if there is neither force nor fraud, and whether or not there is "harm to others."

One of my central points here is that individual agents have little control over social norms, social meanings, and social roles, even when they wish these to be very different from what they are.[13] This is not an argument against norms, meanings and roles. Human beings can live, and human liberty can exist, only within a system of norms, meanings, and roles; but in any particular form, these things can impose severe restrictions on well-being and autonomy. Agents who seek to make changes face a collective action problem.

For example, it is impossible for an individual to say whether the act of smoking seems daring, or the act of recycling seems exotic, or the act of rejecting sexual harassment seems extreme and humorless. This is so even though the relevant norms greatly influence behavior. If, for example, smokers seem like pitiful dupes rather than exciting daredevils, the incidence of smoking will go down. If people who fail to recycle are seen as oddballs, more people will recycle. If the role of secretary is not connected with susceptibility to unwanted sexual attention, there will be less unwanted sexual attention. The point very much bears on current public disputes. If single parenthood is stigmatized, and if lesbian couples are treated just as "couples," social practices will change accordingly. Thus government might try to inculcate or to remove *shame*, fear of which can be a powerful deterrent to behavior.

Government cannot avoid affecting social norms. A market economy will, for example, have predictable effects on norms, and historically it has been justified on just this ground, as a way of softening social divisions by allowing people to interact with one another on a mutually beneficial basis.[14] A good deal of governmental action is designed to change norms, meanings, or roles, and in that way to increase the individual benefits or decrease the individual costs associated with certain acts. In fact social norms can operate as *taxes* on or as *subsidies* to behavior.

More particularly, I hope to draw attention to the fact that people's conception of appropriate action and even of their "interest" is very much a function of the particular social role in which they find themselves. This is true of (for example) judges, lawyers, doctors, parents, children, waiters, wives, husbands, colleagues,

paper at various points, my presentation here owes a general debt to Lessig's argument and in particular to his emphasis on the collective action problem presented by social meanings.

13. See id.

14. See A. Hirschman, Passions and Interests (1977).

friends, and law school deans. Attention to the place of social role shows that for many purposes, the contrast between "rationality" and social norms is unhelpful. What is rational for an agent is a function of, and mediated by, social roles and associated norms.[15] And when social norms appear not to be present, it is only because they are so taken for granted that they seem invisible.

At the same time, norms and roles—as taxes or subsidies—create a division between the judgments and desires that are displayed publicly and the judgments and desires that would be displayed without current norms and roles.[16] People's private judgments and desires diverge greatly from public appearances. For this reason current social states can be far more fragile than is generally thought—as small shocks to publicly endorsed norms and roles decrease the cost of displaying deviant norms, and rapidly bring about large-scale changes in publicly displayed judgments and desires. Hence societies experience *norm bandwagons* and *norm cascades*. Norm bandwagons occur when the lowered cost of expressing new norms encourages an ever-increasing number of people to reject previously popular norms, to a "tipping point" where it is adherence to the old norms that produces social disapproval. Norm cascades occur when societies are presented with rapid shifts toward new norms.[17] Something of this kind happened with the attack on apartheid in South Africa, the fall of Communism, the election of Ronald Reagan, the rise of the feminist movement, and the current assault on affirmative action.

To spell out the most general point emerging from the discussion: The notion of "a preference" can be deeply confusing and in many of its uses, it impairs both positive and normative analysis of law. In its standard form, a preference is supposed to be something that lies behind choices and that is more abstract and general than choices are.[18] But what lies behind choices is not a thing but an unruly amalgam of things[19]—aspirations, tastes, physical states, responses to existing roles and norms, values, judgments, emotions, drives, beliefs, whims—and the interaction of these forces will

---

15. See the discussion of conflicts between social norms and the purchase of life insurance in V. Zelizer, Morals and Markets: The Development of Life Insurance in the United States (1983).

16. See T. Kuran, Private Truths, Public Lies (1995).

17. Cf. S. Bikchandani et al., A Theory of Fads, Fashions, Custom, and Cultural Changes as Informational Cascades, 100 J. Polit. Econ. 992 (1992); V. Zelizer, Pricing the Priceless Child: The Changing Social Value of Children (1987).

18. This is the idea behind much of Gary Becker's work. See, e.g., G. Becker, A Treatise on the Family (2d ed. 1993). For Becker's most recent statement, see G. Becker, Accounting for Tastes (1996).

19. See G. Becker, The Economic Way of Looking at Life, University of Chicago, Law & Economics Working Paper No. 12, at 19 (1993): "An important step in extending the traditional analysis of individual rational choice is to incorporate into the theory a much richer class of attitudes, preferences, and calculations."

produce outcomes of a particular sort in accordance with the particular context. Hence we might say that *preferences are constructed, rather than elicited, by social situations,*[20] in the sense that they are very much a function of the setting and the prevailing norms.

I will be emphasizing the highly contextual nature of choice and hence the fine-grained nature of anything capable of being described as a person's "preferences." Some people think that the notion of "preference" can be identified with "rational self-interest" in a way that abstracts from social roles and norms. As the examples above suggest, the attempt at abstraction makes positive work treacherous; social norms are very much a part of what underlies choice. If preferences are understood to be bound up with social norms—with the wellsprings of shame and pride—positive analysis will be more accurate; but we will have to disaggregate the various wellsprings of choice. This point bears on the appropriate content of law and on the vexing question of paternalism; it also shows that important collective action problems, calling for a legal response, can appear in some unusual settings.

II. Definitions and Concepts

A. Norms

The term "social norms" might be understood in many different ways. For present purposes the differences among the possible definitions are not very important, and we can rely on conventional understandings. If a definition is thought necessary, we might, very roughly, understand "norms" to be social attitudes of approval and disapproval, specifying what ought to be done and what ought not to be done. There are social norms about littering, dating, smoking, singing, when to stand, when to sit, when to show anger, when, how, and with whom to express affection, when to talk, when to listen, when to discuss personal matters, when to use contractions. In fact there are social norms about nearly every aspect of human behavior.

"It isn't done" is a frequent reaction to certain conduct—even though the relevant "it" is indeed done. These attitudes span an exceptionally wide range. They may or may not begin or maintain themselves as a result of reflective judgments. Social norms may or may not promote liberty and well-being; they may or may not be easily malleable or go very deep into people's understandings. A

---

20. Cf. P. Slovic, The Construction of Preference, 50 Am. Psych. 364 (1995). I mean to use the idea of construction somewhat more broadly than does Slovic. Note in this connection the striking study by Ross and Samuels, showing that people cooperate when a certain game is denominated "Cooperation," but not when the same game is denominated, "Wall Street." See L. Ross & F. Samuels, The Predictive Power of Personal Reputation (unpublished manuscript 1993).

social norm can count as such whether or not people have thought deeply about whether it makes sense. Some norms set good manners, for example about how to hold one's fork; others reflect morally abhorrent views, as in the taboo on interracial relations; others reflect hard-won moral commitments, as in the taboo on racial epithets. Sometimes norms are codified in law.

Social norms are enforced through social sanctions; these sanctions create a range of unpleasant (but sometimes pleasant) emotional states in the minds of people who have violated them. If someone behaves in a way inconsistent with social norms, public disapproval may produce shame and a desire to hide. Sometimes the unpleasant feelings brought about by violations of social norms are intense, and the social consequences of these feelings, and of anticipating them, can be substantial.[21]

From these points we might conclude that choice among options is a function not only of (a) the intrinsic value of the option— a book, a job, a drink—but also of (b) the reputational benefit or cost of the choice and also of (c) the effects of the choice on one's self-conception. Someone may watch a television show on public broadcasting not only because it is enjoyable, but also because there are reputational advantages from doing so and advantages as well from the standpoint of promoting one's self-conception. Social norms are a key determinant in reputational benefit or cost. They can much affect self-conception as well. Hence changes in social norms can affect choices if intrinsic value is held constant, by altering the effects of reputational incentives and consequences for self-conception.

In a way social norms reduce freedom, understood very broadly as the power to do whatever one would like to do.[22] Certainly norms stop people from doing things that (if the norms were different) they would like to do, and certainly people would sometimes like the norms to change. But it would be quite ludicrous to deplore social norms, to see them only as constraints on freedom, or to wish them to disappear. In fact norms make freedom possible. Social life is not possible—not even imaginable—without them.[23] In the absence of social norms, we would be unable to understand one

---

21. The persistent urge to conform to social norms has been demonstrated in a good deal of work in social psychology. The classic study is Asch, Effects of Group Pressure upon the Modification and Distortion of Judgments, in Groups, Leadership, and Men (H. Guetzkow ed. 1963).

22. I do not mean to endorse this conception of freedom as a normative ideal. Many unobjectionable things—like speed limit laws or high prices—reduce freedom, thus understood. I seek only to draw attention to the fact that norms can constrain behavior and choice even though some or many people would like them to be otherwise.

23. This is a theme of J. Elster, The Cement of Society (1993).

another.[24] Social norms are thus facilitative as well as constraining. If everyone knows the norms concerning a raised voice, or wearing bluejeans, then people can raise their voices, or wear bluejeans, without having to decide what these actions mean.

There is a further and, for present purposes, an especially important point. Good social norms solve collective action problems, by encouraging people to do useful things that they would not do without the relevant norms.[25] Consider voting, littering, behaving courteously, keeping promises, cleaning up after one's dog, writing tenure letters, and doing one's share of administrative work. Without social norms, coercion or economic incentives—perhaps with large financial investments—would be required to ensure that collective action problems are solved. And when norms are inadequate, or start to disintegrate, society can encounter large difficulties and even collapse.

On the other hand, some people *like* to incur the disapproval that follows norm-violation, and hence some people like to "flout convention" by rejecting prevailing norms—by, for example, dating someone of another race, smoking, playing loud music in public, or wearing unusual clothes. Of course people who violate generally held social norms might be behaving consistently with particular norms in a relevant subculture. (Hence those who reject generally held norms may be the most committed of conformists.)

The fact that some people like to reject social norms is highly relevant to law. For example, a serious problem with legal efforts to inculcate social norms is that the source of the effort may be disqualifying. If Nancy Reagan tells teenagers to "just say no" to drugs, many teenagers may think that it is very good to say "yes." It is said that propaganda efforts in the former Soviet Union failed simply because the source of the propaganda was not trusted; hence the government's effort to inculcate norms of its choosing fell on deaf ears. These points bear on the regulation of risk, particularly in the areas of teenage smoking and potentially dangerous sexual activity. Efforts by private or public authorities to stigmatize certain acts may have the opposite effect.

24. Hence cross-cultural understandings are sometimes made difficult by the fact that social norms are different in different cultures, so that meanings have to be translated, and people may be unaware of that fact. Consider the example of whistling at sporting events.

25. See E. Ullmann–Margalit, The Emergence of Norms (1979). R. Ellickson, Order Without Law (1993), is an important discussion of how norms produce social order, and solve collective action problems, in the absence of legal constraints. But norm changes do not produce Pareto improvements; there are losers as well as winners. Moreover, there is a crucial question about which norms are taken as given, and which are put up for grabs, in the sort of analysis that celebrates certain norms as solving collective action problems.

The fact that norms are contested can lead to the creation of many diverse *norm communities*. People who are dissatisfied with prevailing norms can vote with their feet, using the power of "exit" to find groups built on more congenial norms. Many American high schools reflect this phenomenon, as students find groups that are defined in a relatively crisp way, and as groups intermingle only on occasion. On the other hand, it can be very costly to exit from the norm community in which one finds oneself, and the fact that one has been raised in that community may make other options seem unthinkable even though they might be much better.

Strange as it may seem, social norms mean that money itself is not fungible.[26] The uses of money, and the place of different "kinds" of money, are pervasively affected by social norms. People put money in different mental compartments and act accordingly. Some money is specially reserved for the support of children. Some money is for gifts; some is for one's own special fun. Some money is to be given to charities. Some money is for a rainy day. If you receive a fee for a lecture, or a small amount from the lottery, you may use it for a special dinner.

Social norms make for qualitative differences among human goods,[27] and these qualitative differences are matched by ingenious mental operations involving qualitative differences among different "kinds" of money. Thus a study of practices in Orange County, California, reports that residents keep "a variety of domestic 'cash stashes'—generally one in the billfold of each adult, children's allowances and piggy banks, a petty cash fund in a teapot-equivalent, a dish of change for parking meters or laundry—or 'banked stashes of money,' including Christmas club savings and accounts designated for special expenditures as property or other taxes, vacations, or home and car insurance payments."[28]

In short, there are complex procedures of "mental accounting" in which money that falls in certain compartments is assessed only in terms of its particular intended uses, and not compared with money that has been placed in different mental compartments.[29] We cannot understand the uses of money itself without understanding the role of social norms. Social theorists have often feared that the use of money would "flatten" social life, above all by erasing qualitative distinctions; but it would be more accurate to report that social life, pervaded as it is by social norms, has "unflattened"

---

26. See V. Zelizer, The Social Meaning of Money (1994).

27. See E. Anderson, Value in Ethics and Economics (1993).

28. Id. at 5, quoting Jean Lave, Cognition in Practice 132–33 (1988).

29. See R. Thaler, Mental Accounting Matters (unpublished manuscript, University of Chicago Business School 1995).

money, by insisting on and enforcing qualitative distinctions.[30] "There is no single, uniform, generalized money, but multiple monies: people earmark different currencies for many or perhaps all types of social interactions ... [a]nd people will in fact respond with anger, shock, or ridicule to the 'misuse' of monies for the wrong circumstances or social relations...."[31] Thus norms and law barring the use of money in certain contexts are complemented by norms barring the use of certain money (say, retirement money) for certain purposes (say, gambling or vacation).

B. Roles

1. *In General.* Many norms are intensely role-specific. Consider the following social roles: doctor, employee, waiter, law school dean, wife, friend, pet-owner, colleague, student. Each of these roles is accompanied by a remarkably complex network of appropriate norms. The network is not easily reduced to rules, but people know, often very well, what they are. If you are a waiter, and treat your restaurant's patrons the way you treat your friends, you will probably not be a waiter very long (except perhaps in California). If you are a student, and treat a teacher as if he were your employee at the local factory, you will be perceived as misbehaving very badly. If you treat a colleague in the way you treat your doctor, you will undoubtedly seem quite odd. If you treat a friend the way doctors treat patients, or lawyers treat clients, you probably won't have many friends. People rapidly internalize social norms about what their roles entail. Violations of role-specific norms can seem jarring and produce prompt social punishment (or reward).

Roles are accompanied by a wide range of included and excluded reasons for action. In your capacity as lawyer, you can act only on the basis of certain reasons. For example, you may reveal something told to you in confidence only to prevent a crime; you cannot breach a confidence on the ground that it would be economically profitable to do so. In your capacity as teacher of English, you may not rank students on the basis of family connections, looks, or athletic ability. In your capacity as judge, you may look only at a restricted set of considerations, a set far more restricted than those you may examine if you are a legislator. Confusion of role—is *X* speaking as a friend or as a colleague? is the judge a closet legislator? what exactly is my relationship to my employer?—can cause uncertainty, awkwardness, or much worse.

2. *Roles and Freedom.* Are social roles an obstacle to freedom? In a way the answer is yes, since people would often like to do things that their role forbids, and since people would often like to change the nature of their roles. But this would be a far too simple

---

30. See id. for an impressive argument to this effect.

31. Zelizer, supra, at 18–19.

conclusion. Without roles, life would be very hard to negotiate. Like social norms, social roles are facilitating as well as constraining.

Of course some of the norms associated with certain social roles are silly or even oppressive, and some people deplore them for this reason. What can they do? Large-scale changes in social roles normally require collective action, whether private or public—a point with considerable importance for those interested in the appropriate domain of law. But sometimes individual people act in ways inconsistent with their roles precisely in order to draw attention to their silly or oppressive character. Thus a slave in the pre-Civil War south might decide not to act deferentially; a student might raise his voice against an abusive teacher; a woman in an unequal society might insist that domestic labor should be shared; a homosexual man might "flaunt it"; a teacher in business school might wear bluejeans.

There are many possible reasons for rejecting prevailing norms with respect to role. Some people depart from the prevailing norm because of their *reflective judgments*. Such people think, on reflection, that the norm is too silly or too unworthy to affect behavior, or that relevant roles diminish autonomy or well-being. Marrying someone of a different race may reflect this judgment; sharing domestic labor on an equal basis almost certainly does.[32] In other cases, the departure simply *expresses defiance*, and the real desire is to flout convention, whatever the norm is. Many apparently odd practices involving dress and manners are rooted in this phenomenon; some people find defiance an intrinsic good, and what they are defying is more or less incidental. In still other cases, the departure is the expression of an individual *desire or taste*, which the person would pursue whether or not it is inconsistent with social roles and accompanying norms. Consider the view that Coca–Cola actually is better than all other drinks, a view that might be reflected in unconventional drink selections in many imaginable places.

3. *Roles and Law*. Prevailing roles and norms can be fortified by legal requirements; they may even owe their existence to law. Law is frequently an effort to prescribe roles. There are many specific legal provisions for people occupying different roles—parents, spouses, employers, employees, home-owners, nuclear power plant operators, animal owners, doctors, stock brokers, landlords, automobile sellers, and others. By prescribing appropriate behavior, law can help constitute the relevant social roles. Much of the law relating to families, employer-employee relations, and professional obligations has this feature. In fact many roles seem "natural" even though they owe their origin to social and even legal conventions.

32. See S. Okin, Justice, Gender, and the Family (1989).

Often law tries to redefine roles. In recent years, this has happened with respect to the roles of employee, husband, father, disabled person, and judge. Thus, for example, the law has said that husbands may not rape their wives; that absent fathers owe duties of support to their children; that disabled people have certain rights of access to the workplace.

Law's pervasive attention to role shows (yet again) the poverty of the familiar idea that "efficiency" and "distribution" exhaust the concerns of the state. Sometimes society and law revisit a currently conceived role for reasons that have nothing to do with either efficiency or distribution. People occupying a certain role may, for example, not be treated with appropriate respect; they may not receive love and affection; or they may not be targets of (deserved) shame.

4. *Citizens and Consumers.* Of course each of us occupies many different roles, and there is much to be said about the constraints imposed by these diverse roles. But for present purposes, an especially important and pervasive difference involves the relationship between *citizen* and *consumer*.

Return to John Jones in the fifth tale above. The example shows that in your capacity as a citizen, you might urge a result—with respect to, say, the duties of polluters or commercial broadcasters—that is quite different from what you seek through your market behavior in your capacity as a consumer. Acting as citizens, many people try to change social practices, and they often try to do this by changing social norms associated with a particular role. Sometimes these efforts are a function of the role of citizen and associated norms. In their private capacity—as consumers, employers, or family members—people may do what they know, on balance, to be unjust, and as citizens, they may support measures that better reflect their convictions. Sometimes efforts to change norms and roles reflect an understanding that human beings are selfish or have weakness of will, and that some measures should be taken to ensure behavior that, on reflection, we would like to follow.[33]

In addition, citizens do or say things just because of existing social norms, which impose sanctions on publicly expressed dissident behavior or judgments; in their private capacity, people may be freer to do or say as they wish. In all cases the difference is connected to the fact that a citizen is helping to make a judgment not simply for himself but for a collectivity. In this sense there are important contextual differences between market behavior and voting behavior. The former does not affect the collectivity in the

33. See J. Elster, Ulysses and the Sirens (1983); S. Holmes, Passions and Constraint (1995).

same way, and hence those concerned, for example, to protect the environment may believe that their own behavior is largely irrelevant, whereas laws can make a great deal of difference. Largely for this reason, the role of citizen is accompanied by norms that can discourage selfishness and encourage attention to the public good.[34]

In fact many efforts to change law are at least partly an outgrowth of the difference between citizens and consumers.[35] Consider laws outlawing sexual harassment, providing incentives to share domestic labor,[36] or granting workers a right to unionize. It should be clear that in such cases, there is no simple relationship among choices, preferences, norms, and roles. There may be conflict or tension between two or more of these.

C. Meaning

By "meaning," I refer to the expressive dimension of conduct (not excluding speech) in the relevant community.[37] The expressive dimension involves *the attitudes and commitments that the conduct signals.* A complex body of first amendment doctrine deals with the problem of "expressive conduct," that is, acts that carry an expressive purpose and effect, such as flag-burning, draftcard-burning, sleeping in parks. But most conduct has an expressive function— not in the sense that the actor necessarily intends to communicate a message, but in the sense that people will take the conduct to be expressing certain attitudes and commitments.

Consider some examples. If I light up a cigarette, I will, in certain parts of the United States, be signaling something relatively precise and very bad about myself, my self-conception, and my concern for others. In other parts of the United States, the signals are very different. In France, a smoker gives still different signals. If you fail to attend church—or if you do attend church, and tell everyone about it—your act will have particular meanings, and these have everything to do with the community in which you find yourself. If I decide not to get married, or not to have children, my act will convey a restricted range of possible meanings, and I will not have much control over those meanings. (If I were a woman, my decisions to this effect would have a quite different set of meanings. The meaning of a woman's not marrying or having children is quite different from a man's.)

Language also has social meanings, extending far beyond the words themselves and reflected in the attitudes and commitments

---

34. I am describing a possibility, not a certainty. Political behavior is very often selfish.

35. See A. Sen, Environmental Evaluation and Social Choice: Contingent Valuation and the Market Analogy, 46

Japanese Economic Review 23 (1995)(distinguishing consumer's willingness to pay from citizen judgments).

36. See Okin, supra, at 134–69.

37. See Lessig, supra.

signaled by how people talk. Context determines those meanings. The words, "You look great today," can have many different possible social meanings: consider their use from a mother to a fifteen year old daughter, from a male employer to a female employee, from a doctor to a convalescent patient, from a homosexual male student to a male classmate. If you refer to women as "ladies," you are also making (whatever your intentions) a certain set of statements about yourself and about your views on gender issues. A description of certain Americans as "blacks" will have a different meaning in 1996 (after the adoption of the term "African–American") from what it was in, say, 1976.

As with social norms and social roles, the social meanings of acts are something about which individuals can do relatively little (most of the time).[38] If a lawyer drives a Harley–Davidson motorcycle to Wall Street, his own attitude toward his act will have little relation to what other people take his act to mean. If a nonsmoker asks someone not to smoke, the social meaning of the act will be quite different in New York in 1995 from what it was in the same city in 1965, and different as well from what it is in Germany in 1995. This is a pervasive characteristic of social meanings. If you lived in a society of vegetarians, the act of eating meat—at, let us suppose, specially designated animal flesh restaurants—would be very different from what it is is a society of meat-eaters; and if you lived in a society of vegetarians, you might well choose not to eat meat. The meanings of actions are set by forces that are emphatically human but that are largely outside of the control of the individual agent.

On the other hand, there are contexts in which a person or a small group of people may make inroads on social meanings. In a household, a woman may be able to alter, a little or a lot, the social meaning to her family of her refusal to do dishes or to make dinner, or her decision to go out with colleagues at night. But the most entrenched social meanings are—by definition—not movable without concerted action on the part of many people. Hence private groups often attempt to bring about changes in meanings and the norms that produce them. Religious organizations, feminist groups, animal rights activists, groups challenging "political correctness," are prominent recent examples. Often they have been highly successful; sometimes they produce norm cascades.

Many roles are ascriptive and not chosen, even in postfeudal societies. We cannot fully control the roles in which we find ourselves. To be sure, people have power to assume or not to assume some roles. You can decide whether to be a spouse, a parent, a teacher, a dean, and so forth. And within limits, you can

38. See Lessig, supra, for discussion of the collective action problem.

decide what it means to be any of these things; people can certainly alter the roles associated with parent, wife, and husband, even if they cannot do a great deal about the meanings associated with their choices. But many roles are assigned rather than voluntarily assumed—child, man, African–American, old person, short person, and more. A role that is assigned might be described as a *status*, a distinctive kind of role that, if surrounded by objectionable norms, raises special problems (see the discussion of caste below). And many roles cannot easily be rejected in most societies—driver, employee, student, citizen, family member.

D.   Beliefs About Facts

Choices, meaning, role, and norms are commonly based on beliefs about relevant facts. In fact beliefs about facts help generate all of these things. Someone may believe, for example, that cigarette smoking is not dangerous, and he may smoke partly for that reason. If he really believed that smoking was dangerous, perhaps he would not smoke. Choices are pervasively a function of beliefs. The same is true for social norms. Consider the dramatic recent shifts with respect to social norms governing cigarette smoking. Such norms have a great deal to do with prevailing beliefs about whether smoking causes harm to nonsmokers. When the belief shifts, the norm shifts as well.

Norms about behavior are interpenetrated with beliefs about harm and risk. Thus many religiously-grounded norms about personal cleanliness and hygiene often owe their origins to beliefs about what is healthy; but the norms often outstrip the beliefs and receive a kind of moral grounding that is not simply reducible to an instrumental judgment about likely risks. When someone violates a norm relating to hygiene, people's reaction is different—more stern and more deeply moralized—than it would be if the reaction were based solely on the incremental increase in risk.

There are complex interactions between understandings of facts and social roles. Certainly beliefs about facts help generate roles. Thus beliefs about natural differences between men and women, or blacks and whites, affect social understandings about the appropriate roles of men and women or blacks and whites. When people see that apparent differences between social groups are not grounded in fact, the roles associated with group members may shift accordingly. Thus attacks on claimed natural differences have affected perceptions of appropriate role. But the converse is also true: Understandings of facts may be a function of roles and accompanying norms. There are complex scientific literatures on the differences between men and women; much of the relevant work, even in its most scientific forms, rests palpably on conceptions of roles and of surrounding norms.

Judgments about fact are similarly entangled with social norms. When most people smoke, it is hard for most people to believe that smoking is dangerous. The norm affects the belief, just as the belief affects the norm. In fact norms and judgments about risk are hard to separate.

E.   Divisions in the Self and Norm Bandwagons

I have noted that social norms can make people act and talk publicly in ways that are different from how they actually think, or from how they act and talk privately. People comply with norms that they wish were otherwise or even despise. Under the apartheid regime in South Africa, public criticism of apartheid—at least within South Africa—much understated private opposition to apartheid. The same is true for Communist regimes.[39] In a social group that punishes atheists or agnostics, few people may confess their uncertainty about whether God exists; in a group of atheists, few people may talk about their religious faith. Even in democracies, the deterrent effect of social norms on acts and beliefs creates a sharp disjunction between public acts (including speech) and private thought. Hence a state of affairs may persist even though there is widespread opposition to it. And eventually the norms may affect private thought itself.

Political actors might be able to exploit this disjunction in order to bring about large-scale social change. In fact many political participants can be described as *norm entrepreneurs.* Individuals who are in favor of changes in norms face a free rider problem. Political actors can exploit their dissatisfaction with existing norms by (a) signaling their own commitment to change, (b) creating coalitions, and (c) making defiance of the norms less costly. When the free rider problem begins to be solved, through reducing the cost of acting inconsistently with prevailing norms, the private thoughts will be stated publicly, and things can shift very quickly. Something of this sort happened in both South Africa and Eastern Europe, producing more rapid and more peaceful changes than anyone anticipated. Part of the reason is that hostility to the regimes was widespread and intense—but inconsistent with existing social norms and hence mostly invisible and thus much underestimated. When the norms began to collapse, the regimes collapsed too.

The point bears on norm bandwagons. People may publicly support an existing norm not because they are genuinely committed to it, but because they fear social sanctions. As I have said, there is a bandwagon effect when those sanctions diminish or disappear, as

39. See T. Kuran, supra, on which I draw for the discussion in this paragraph.

many people join the group opposing the existing norm and urging a new one. The result can be astonishingly rapid change.[40] An effect of this kind occurred with two opposing and recent movements— the feminist movement and the recent opposition to "political correctness" in the university.

III.   Choices and Preferences

If we attend to the functions of norms, meaning, and role, how will we understand the relationship between choices and preferences? An initial problem is that the notion of a "preference" is quite ambiguous. Suppose someone takes a job as a welder, recycles newspapers, or buys aspirin rather than chocolate bars. When we say that someone "prefers" to do as he chose, what exactly do we mean? There are two major possibilities. Attention to the place of norms, meanings, and roles complicates both of them.

A.   Preferences As Choices

The idea of a "preference" might be understood as simply a choice, as in the idea, influential within economics, of the "revealed preference." On this view, preferences *are* choices. This approach seems promising, because it makes it unnecessary to inquire into the mental states that accompany choices. Perhaps we can work from behavior alone. If, however, this is what we are doing, it is unnecessary and perhaps misleading to use the notion of a "preference," which seems to be intended to explain or to back something called choices. If we are really talking about choices, we can dispense with the idea of preferences entirely. We will have a list of choices and should speak only in terms of that list.

Perhaps this is merely a semantic quibble. Perhaps social theorists can work with the list for positive or normative purposes. But if they are really working just with choices, they will encounter many problems. Choices are inarticulate, and hence imperfect predictors of behavior, without an account of what lies behind them.[41] From the bare fact of (particular) choices, it is not always possible to make robust claims about future choices. Because of the function of norms, meanings, and role, even the weakest axioms of revealed preference theory can fail. John Jones, in the fifth tale above, presents an illustration; his particular choices do not allow observers to offer general predictions. But for the present let us take a simpler example. If Jones prefers X over Y, we might think that he will not prefer Y over X or Z; the introduction of the third

---

40. Id. at 288 ("A specific law, regulation, policy, norm, or custom can be abruptly abandoned when people who have helped sustain it suddenly discover a common desire for change.")

41. See A. Sen, Internal Consistency of Choice, 61 Econometrica 495 (1993); E. Aronson, The Social Animal (8th ed. 1995); A. Tversky & I. Simonson, Context–Dependent Preferences, 39 Management Science 1179 (1993).

alternative, Z, ought not to change Jones' preferences for X over Y. After all, Jones prefers X to Y, and he would have to be an odd person to prefer Y to X simply because of the introduction of Z.

But we can readily imagine cases in which the new alternative Z has precisely this effect. Jones might, for example, always select the second largest piece of cake, or he might want to be a person of relative moderation. Empirical work has encountered an effect called "extremeness aversion," in which people make choices that avoid the extremes.[42] Extremeness aversion is a product of social norms. People are generally taught to avoid extremes, and people who make extreme choices seem like malcontents, oddballs, or (never a word of praise) extremists. There are many examples. A voter might, for example, choose a Republican candidate over a Democratic candidate; but the introduction of some third candidate, say Ross Perot, may change the underlying choice, because it makes some new characteristic salient to voters,[43] or because it shifts the outcome produced by the decision, making it moderate where it would otherwise be extreme.

More broadly, choices are a function of prevailing social meanings and roles, which can bring into effect a wide range of relevant norms. If you are in a certain social group, you may well choose a drink of brandy or wine over Coca–Cola simply because of local practices. The choice of Coca–Cola may signal excessive informality, an unwillingness to unwind and enjoy oneself, or even disrespect. In a different group, your choice may be different (and all this regardless of what you would choose if you were in your house alone). You may purchase an American car, or display the flag on July 4, because of existing norms in your community. Perhaps your purchase of a non-American car would signal a lack of patriotism; perhaps your failure to display the flag would be taken as a political protest, whether or not you meant it that way. If you run a local television station, your decision whether to allow violent programming is very much a function of prevailing norms, even if such programming would attract a large audience.

These points suggest that to explain or predict behavior, it is important not only to know about choices but also to have some account of what underlies choices, or of what choices are *for*, and in this way to introduce an account of motivation.[44] Here social norms, meanings, and roles will be crucial. And if this is right, it is impossible to explain behavior by reference to choices, without

---

42. See Amos T. & I. Simonson, Context–Dependent Preferences, 39 Management Science 1179 (1993).

43. Cf. D. Leland, Generalized Similarity Judgments: An Alternative Explanation for Choice Anomalies, 9 J. Risk and Uncertainty 151 (1994). See also I. Simonson and A. Tversky, Choice in Context, 29 J. Marketing Research 281 (1992).

44. See A. Sen, Econometrica, supra.

using the very apparatus that the "revealed preference" idea was intended to eliminate. Normative arguments on the basis of choices alone[45] will also run into serious trouble. Choices do not suggest acontextual valuation of social goods, and thus even if we want to respect people's valuations, we will have to look not at but behind choices.

B.   Preferences Behind Choices

Let us turn, then, to another and more promising conception of a "preference." The term is often meant to refer not to choices themselves, but to something that lies behind and accounts for choices.[46] This idea has obvious advantages. It seeks to provide the motivational story on which choices are by themselves inarticulate, and if the motivational story is uncovered, positive work should be possible. And if we can identify what lies behind choices, perhaps we can get a sense of people's own conception of what promotes their well-being, and this is surely relevant for purposes of both ethics and politics.

But this idea introduces difficulties of its own—indeed, the difficulties that the "revealed preference" notion was intended to overcome. Recall John Jones, the protagonist of the fifth tale above. Can we provide an account of Jones' motivation or "preferences"? No simple answer would make sense. Several possibilities do present themselves. From the fact that Jones pays a certain premium for automobile safety, we might judge that he is risk-averse and we might even attempt to generate numbers capturing his own conception of the value of his life. But when it comes to bicycle-riding, Jones is somewhat reckless. And in his capacity as voter, Jones' valuations appear still more complex. To get an account of his motivation, we need to know many details—something like a personality profile.

The point raises some larger issues. If we think of a preference as something that lies behind choice, what is it exactly? Plainly it is a disposition or a mental state of some kind. And plainly people do have dispositions of various sorts. But internal mental states can be extraordinarily complex. People's decisions are based on a complex of whims, responses to norms, second-order preferences, aspirations, judgments, emotions, drives of various kinds, conceptions of role, and more, with all these producing particular results depending on the context. What lies behind a choice in one setting may be quite different from what lies behind a choice in a different time and place.

---

45. See W. Kip Viscusi, Fatal Trade-offs (1993).

46. See G. Stigler & G. Becker, De Gustibus Non Est Disputandum, 67 Am. Econ. Rev. 76 (1977).

In this light, it can be hard to make predictions about individuals or groups without knowing a great deal. Of course the value of positive work lies in what the evidence shows. Of course there are regularities in people's behavior, and these regularities can be connected to people's dispositions. But general dispositions of various kinds—to avoid extremes, to comply with norms, to drink beer rather than wine—manifest themselves in particular choices only in accordance with context. No simple thing called a "preference" accounts for choice. Preferences are not the building-blocks for a theory of decision; whatever we call a "preference" needs to be further unpacked.

Shifting from positive to normative, we can see that the complexity of mental states also makes it hard for governments to know how to respond to people's choices. Choices depend on norms that people may not endorse on reflection. Collective efforts to discourage damaging or risky behavior, or to encourage norms that promote well-being or solve collective action problems, might well be consistent with people's underlying aspirations and judgments.

C. Complex Preferences

From all this we might conclude that for many purposes, the whole idea of "a preference" is confused and misleading, because it is ambiguous between choices and underlying psychological forces, and because the mental operations that produce choices are a function of a great many factors. For many purposes, it might well be best to dispense altogether with the idea of preference and to work instead with choices on the one hand and with complex and somewhat unruly mental states on the other—or to relate choices to more concrete influences, such as norms, price changes, increases in leisure time, roles, and so forth. I believe that this point gives us reason to doubt the elaborate edifice of social science based on notions of "preference" or "metapreference" (though much of the edifice can remain if reconstructed on different foundations).

The next task is to separate positive, descriptive, and normative inquiries more sharply, and in the process to try to untangle relevant mental states and their influences. Of course it may the case that once we understand a person, or a group, very well, we will understand those mental states and their relation to external forces, and we may be able to make a wide range of predictions about how different forces will affect behavior.

IV. Anomalies

A. Willingness To Pay vs. Willingness To Accept: The Place of Shame

Recent empirical work suggests that many claims in economics[47] rest on an intriguingly false assumption, one that suggests

47. Including the Coase Theorem.

that it may sometimes be impossible for government to take preferences "as they are."[48] The basic finding is this: The initial grant of an entitlement of some good X to some person A can make A value X far more than he would if X had been initially allocated to B. (It also makes B value it less than he otherwise would.) The initial allocation—the legal rule saying who owns what, before people begin to contract with one another—serves to create, to legitimate, and to reinforce social understandings about presumptive rights of ownership. The effect of the initial allocation of a commodity or an entitlement is commonly described as the "endowment effect."[49]

This point has received considerable empirical confirmation, often in the context of environmental amenities. One study found that people would demand about five times as much to allow destruction of trees in a park as they would pay to prevent the destruction of those same trees.[50] When hunters were questioned about the potential destruction of a duck habitat, they said that they would be willing to pay an average of $247 to prevent the loss—but would demand no less than $1044 to accept it.[51] In another study, participants required payments to accept degradation of visibility ranging from 5 to more than 16 times higher than their valuations based on how much they were willing to pay to prevent the same degradation[52] A related experiment tried to ascertain the "existence value" of a houseplant that grows like a pine tree. The subjects were told that any trees not sold or kept would be killed at the end of the experiment. The mean willingness to pay (WTP) to avoid the "kill" option was $7.81. The mean willingness to accept (WTA) payment to allow a tree to be killed was $18.43.[53]

48. See R. Thaler, Quasi–Rational Economics (1993); see also Dubourg et al., Imprecise Preferences and the WTP–WTA Disparity, 9 Journal of Risk and Uncertainty 115 (1994).

49. It was first so-called in R. Thaler, Toward a Positive Theory of Consumer Choice, 1 J. Econ. Behavior and Org. 39 (1980). This essay, along with others of similar interest, can be found in R. Thaler, Quasi–Rational Economics (1990).

50. D. Brookshire and D. Coursey, Measuring the Value of a Public Good: An Empirical Comparison of Elicitation Procedures, 77 Am. Econ. Rev. 554 (1987).

51. J. Hammock and G. M. Brown, Waterfowl and Wetlands: Toward Bioeconomic Analysis (1974); R. Rowe et al., An Experiment on the Economic Value of Visibility, 7 J. Env. Ec. and Management 1 (1980).

52. R. Thaler, Toward a Positive Theory of Consumer Choice, 1 J. Econ. Behavior and Org. 39 (1980). A good overview is E. Hoffman and M. L. Spitzer, The Divergence Between Willingness-to-Pay and Willingness-to-Accept Measures of Value, Wash. U. L. Q. (1993).

53. See R. Boyce et al., An Experimental Examination of Intrinsic Values as a Source of the WTA–WTP Disparity, 82 Am. Econ. Rev. 1366 (1992).

In general, the range of the disparity appears to vary from slight disparities to a ratio of more than four to one, with WTA usually doubling WTP. In field studies, environmental goods tend to reflect a disparity of factors from two to over ten.[54] In some environmental experiments involving trees, the WTA/WTP ratio is extraordinarily high, ranging between 60/1 and 90/1.[55]

What explains this phenomenon? There are many possibilities, and none is likely to be exhaustive.[56] My suggestion is that some of the difference between WTP and WTA has a great deal to do with social norms and social meaning. If someone says that she is willing to accept $X to allow the expiration of a species, the meaning of her action is altogether different from what it is if she says that she is willing to pay $X (and no more) to prevent the extinction. Under prevailing social norms, one ought not to accept even a great deal of money to allow destruction of an environmental amenity—partly because the good at issue is collectively owned, partly because its loss may be irreversible, and partly because it is not thought to be commensurable with its cash equivalent (in the sense that it is not valued in the same way or along a single metric).

In these circumstances, people who announce their willingness to accept cash for the loss of a pond or a species feel *shame*. They believe that they are assuming responsibility for the destruction of something intrinsically valuable, not replaceable, and owned by many people. Because of the risk of shame, people will demand a great deal, and they may even refuse any amount is offered.[57] By contrast, those who refuse to pay an enormous or infinite amount to *save* an environmental amenity do not feel the same degree of shame (if they feel shame at all). They are confronted with a different set of social norms.

Take an analogy. If someone is asked how much she would be willing to accept to allow her dog's life to be shortened by six months—or how much she would be willing to accept to allow her dog to suffer severe pain for, say, one week—she might well say: "No amount is sufficient." The question is very different if a veterinarian is asking someone whether unusual and expensive medical procedures should be used to prolong a dog's life or reduce its pain. Here the answer need not be: "No amount is too high."

Some intriguing work suggests that the disparity between WTA and WTP is connected with the assignment of moral responsi-

---

54. See Boyce et al., supra, at 1366.

55. D. S. Brookshire and D. L. Coursey, Measuring the Value of a Public Good: An Empirical Comparison of Elicitation Procedures, 77 Am. Econ. Rev. 554 (1987).

56. See C. Sunstein, Endogenous Preferences, Environmental Law, 22 J. Legal Stud. 217 (1993).

57. Thus in surveys nearly 50% of people sometimes refuse to name any amount.

bility for the destruction of environmental assets, which are perceived as intrinsic goods. The WTA measure assigns responsibility to the individual. The WTP measure does so more ambiguously. These findings are consistent with the norm-based explanation I am offering here. People want to avoid or to minimize the feeling that they have been morally culpable for producing the loss of an environmental amenity.[58] Feelings of moral culpability are tightly connected with prevailing social norms.

B.   Shame, Altruism, and Free–Riding

The point relates to the first tale in Part I; we are now in a position to explain the apparent anomaly. When two people are to divide an amount given to them under the stated conditions, the offeror in the ultimatum game feels shame under prevailing norms—that he is demonstrating that he is a greedy and even horrible person—if he offers a penny or a dollar from a sum of (say) $200. If a sum is given to two people under the conditions of the game, good people share; they do not try to keep almost all of the money for themselves. For his part, the offeree feels mistreated—treated in a contemptuous way—if a small or token amount is suggested. The social meaning of the statement, "How about five cents for you?" is contempt; the social meaning of responding, "Great!" is a willingness to be dishonored.

Experimental work shows that people contribute to a shared good, and refuse to free ride, far more often than economists predict.[59] It also shows that agents are willing to cooperate, and hence to solve collective action problems without coercion, if most people are seen as cooperators; in such circumstances the social meaning of noncooperation is greed or selfishness. When a number of people free ride, and are seen to free ride, cooperation breaks down; in such circumstances the social meaning of cooperation is a willingness to be a "dupe" or a "sucker." The desire to contribute to a collective good is palpably a function of social norms. If social norms do not lead most people to contribute, contributions decrease steadily and dramatically. The second tale above should therefore be taken as a metaphor for many social outcomes.[60]

My suggestion, then, is that apparent puzzles of rationality are often a product of social norms and moral judgments that are

58.   See R. Boyce et al., An Experimental Examination of Intrinsic Values as a Source of the WTA–WTP Disparity, 82 Am. Econ. Rev. 1366 (1992).

59.   See Orbell et al., Explaining Discussion–Induced Cooperation, 54 J. of Personality and Social Psychology 811 (1988), Handbook of Experimental Economics 26–28, 141–69, 409–11 (J. Kagel and A. Roth eds. 1995). Note also that cooperation increases when people can talk with one another; discussion significantly raises contribution rates, perhaps because it increases empathy and the shame associated with noncooperation.

60.   See T. Kuran, Private Truths, Public Lies 48–49 (1995).

intertwined with those norms. Of course a full explanation would have to include an account of norms as well, and there is a risk that a reference to social norms will become a conclusory response to any anomalous results. But once we specify prevailing norms, we may be able to make robust predictions, and also to ask whether the anomalous behavior continues when it is not observed publicly.

These points suggest that it may well be impossible to distinguish between what is entitled by "rationality" and what is entailed by social norms. For the individual agent, rationality is a function of social norms. A norm-free conception of rationality would have to depend on a conception of what people's rational "interests" are in a social vacuum. Such a conception would not be very intelligible. It might seem natural to suppose that it is in people's interest not to pick up their garbage (see tale 2) and that social norms against littering add a kind of new or artificial factor to the individual calculus. But if we make this supposition, we are saying something about the individual's calculus without the anti-littering norm; and what is the basis for any particular conception of how calculus will come out? No such conception will be free of an array of ends, seen as such partly because of social influences, including social norms. Why, for example, is picking up garbage a cost rather than a benefit? An implicit (but undefended and obscure) state of nature theory seems to lie at the heart of many distinctions between social norms and rationality, or rational self-interest. To become separated from social norms, a conception of rationality must be frankly normative and defended as such.

VII. Government Action: On Autonomy and Tools

Sometimes it seems desirable to change choices. Government might attempt to change choices by changing social norms, social meaning, and social roles. In fact changes in norms may be the cheapest and most effective way to make things better, whatever are our criteria for assessing that matter. The relation between behavior and norms has yet to receive sustained attention; when we attend to that relation, we see that government has a policy instrument of great potential value.

To be sure, private power to create norm communities may make government action less necessary or less desirable. Often the best step is to allow those communities to be formed and to see how they work out. But sometimes it is too costly for individuals to create or join those communities, and sometimes the generally held norm is too damaging to human well-being. These issues cannot be solved in the abstract; the judgment depends on the details. But it is clear that norms can create problems of various sorts and that collective action may be required.

A.   Norms and Paternalism

Common objections to "paternalism" or "perfectionism" are not easy to sustain in such contexts. Recall that people usually do not choose norms, meaning, and roles; all of these are (within limits) imposed. As I have said, it would be ludicrous to deplore norms, meaning, and role; they make life possible and they much facilitate social engagement. They provide the context within which free interaction is possible. Nonetheless, some of them operate as severe limits on autonomy or well-being, and certainly they should not be treated as fixed or as given regardless of their content or consequences.

Private groups can test or even change norms. Indeed, the testing of current norms, meaning, and roles is a crucial function of groups intermediate between citizens and the state. Religious groups are in this sense norm entrepreneurs; the same is true for environmental and civil rights organizations. But sometimes private groups are unable to produce desirable change on their own. This is a point missed by the idea that the sole basis for government action is to avoid force, fraud, and "harm to others." Obstacles to autonomy and to good lives can also come from bad roles, norms, and meaning.

Often all or most people would on reflection like to see a change in a particular norm,[61] and they cannot bring the change about on their own, because in his individual capacity, each person has limited power to alter meaning, norms, or role. The case of mandatory helmets for hockey players is a familiar example.[62] Hockey players may prefer not to wear helmets if the meaning of helmet-wearing is cowardice; but their preferred solution, available only through a mandate, is a system in which all are required to wear helmets, and hence players wear helmets without signaling cowardice. Of course shifts in norms, meaning, and roles are pervasive. Consider, for example, changing norms with respect to smoking, littering, drug use, polluting, racial discrimination, sexual relations outside of marriage, the role of women and men, and interracial relationships.

In fact it is often hard to know what people would "like" or prefer, because their judgments and desires are entangled with norms, meaning, and role, and because once one or more of these is changed, they may be better off either objectively or subjectively. If government changes the social meaning of smoking (see the third tale above), has it acted illegitimately? What if most people, or most smokers, would, on reflection, want smoking to have a different

---

61. Their desire to this effect is likely to be a product of norms that are being held constant.

62. See Schelling, supra; Lessig, supra.

meaning? Or suppose that government tries to change an aspect of a certain social role, like that of unwed fathers, high school teachers, homosexuals, or workers. Surely the consequences of the change matter; surely it matters if the change is supported by (most or all) unwed fathers, high school teachers, homosexuals, or workers, and if members of each group face a collective action problem.

B.   Tools

Suppose that government is concerned to change norms, meaning, or roles. It has many different tools for doing so; some of these are mildly intrusive while others may foreclose choice. Government may restrict itself to *education,* understood as simple statements of fact. We have seen that norms, meaning, and role can be a function of beliefs, and beliefs are mutable. Perhaps prevailing beliefs are false and warrant correction. People may think that AIDS is a disease limited to homosexuals, that smoking does not hurt non-smokers, or that there is no relation between cholesterol and heart disease or between diet and cancer. Changing norms with respect to smoking are almost certainly a result—at least in part—of information from government about health risk. In principle, there should be no objection to governmental efforts to correct false beliefs, even if the correction affects norms, meaning, and role. In fact the change along this dimension may be the most important consequence of education, which may, for example, remove certain kinds of shame.

Government may also attempt to engage in *persuasion,* understood as a self-conscious effort to alter attitudes and choices rather than simply to offer information. Consider the third tale above; assume that some such advertisement had been issued by state officials. Perhaps it would have been effective (though its social meaning would have been altogether different if issued by officials rather than by members of the private African–American community). The "Just Say No" policy for drugs falls in the category of attempted persuasion; so too with efforts to control AIDS by strongly encouraging abstinence from sex or the use of condoms. Here government does not restrict itself to provision of information, but instead uses rhetoric and vivid images to change norms, meaning, or role, and in this way to persuade people to choose a certain course.

Some people think that although the provision of information can be justified, government may rarely or never attempt to persuade.[63] But if norms, roles, and meanings are beyond individual control, and sometimes bad, this thought is hard to sustain, at least if government is subject to democratic controls.

63. See Viscusi, supra.

Consider in this connection the problem of smoking and the lessons of the second tale above. Among blacks between 18 and 24, the rate has fallen from 37.1% in 1965, to 31.8% in 1979, to 20.4% in 1987, to 11.8% in 1991.[64] Among whites in the same age group, the rate fell from 38.4% in 1965 to 27.8% in 1987—but it has remained more or less constant since that time.[65] The change within black teenagers is universally described as a "public health success story," but one that government officials cannot explain. Though no one has a full account of this phenomenon, changing social norms appear to be playing a substantial role. Smoking does not have the same cachet in the African–American community that it has among whites. If government could bring about a general change in social norms—through, for example, attempts at persuasion—it is hardly clear that there would be a good objection to its behavior.

Government might also use economic instruments to *tax* or *subsidize* choices. Of course education is assisted publicly, as are day care, museums, and public broadcasting (at least as of this writing). Alcoholic drinks, tobacco products, generation of waste, and some polluting activities are met with taxes (though some of these are subsidized too). We can understand some economic incentives as efforts in part to counteract social meaning, social norms, or social roles with financial benefits or penalties designed to produce a good "equilibrium." A social meaning that is perceived to be bad might be "matched" with a financial incentive.

Government might also impose *time, place, and manner restrictions*. It might ban smoking in public places. It might say that television shows containing violence may be shown only in certain time slots. It might require government itself to choose low-polluting motor vehicles. It might ban affirmative action in the public sector but allow it in the private sector. Strategies of this kind might affect the social meaning of the relevant activity very generally. But they do not foreclose entirely choice; they channel it instead.

The most intrusive kind of government action is of course *straightforward coercion*. Thus government might prohibit the use of certain drugs; require everyone to recycle or buckle their seatbelts; or make education mandatory for people under a certain age.

VIII.   Government Action: Four Grounds

In this section I discuss several grounds for governmental efforts to change norms, meaning, and role. The unifying theme is *the expressive function of law*—the function of law in expressing

64. Statistical Abstract of the United   **65.** Id.
States at 143.

social values and in encouraging norms to move in particular directions. I do not discuss any of these grounds in detail; I offer instead a brief and far from definitive sketch of some possibilities.

A. Some Unusual Collective Action Problems

1. Standard Formulations and Conventional Accounts. In a standard formulation, many social practices would be inefficient if not for certain social norms; the norms solve a collective action problem. They do the work of law. They may provide conventions on which everyone voluntarily settles; table manners are examples. Or they may solve prisoner's dilemmas through social sanctions imposed on deviants; this is true of the idea that people should clean up after their dogs. And because of the absence of good norms, some existing practices are highly inefficient. Take the standard case of littering, captured in the second tale in Part I. Under conventional assumptions, each person may well litter—if the costs of throwing things in the garbage are wholly internalized, whereas the benefits of doing so are spread across a wide range of people. In the conventional account, "rational" individuals, acting in their "self-interest," will produce a great deal of litter, and perhaps so much that legal regulation is ultimately required. This idea helps explain legal responses to environmental degradation, as in the cases of mandatory recycling, taxes on or fees for polluting activity, and command and control regulation.

2. Puzzles. But many questions might be raised about the standard formulation and the conventional account. The relevant changes do not bring about Pareto improvements. Some people are losers; in fact many people may be losers, for example those who dislike helmets and seatbelts no matter the number of people who wear them. We should distinguish the simplest cases—in which all or nearly all people favor a change in norms—from cases in which there are bare majorities. If everyone would favor a situation in which people pick up after their dogs and this result cannot be brought about without government action, the case is easy: Government action should be initiated. But if 65% of people would favor the change, and 35% like the status quo, we have a harder case. To decide whether government action is appropriate, it is necessary to take a stand on a large question in political theory; the fact that norm-change is involved means that the setting is unusual, but not the basic analysis.

Even more fundamentally, the words "rational" and "self-interest" obscure a great deal, since they take so much for granted. There is no sharp dichotomy between rationality and social norms or between self-interest and social norms; what is rational and what is in an agent's self-interest are functions of social norms.[66]

---

66. A norm-free conception of interest would have to depend on a conception of what people's "interests" are in a social vacuum. Such a conception would not be very intelligible.

Return to our second story above and suppose that there is a social norm to the effect that everyone should pick up litter. If the norm is in place, people who act in their rational self-interest will not litter. In the second tale, were the nonlitterers or the control group acting in its rational self-interest? What is rational, and what promotes self-interest, depends on many exogenous factors, including existing norms.

There is a further point. Suppose that there is no norm against littering; that people think that there is too much litter; and that they would like to create a new, anti-littering norm. Would it be right to say that this is a case in which a collective action problem would be best served with the aid of social norms? The statement would not be false but it would be misleading and incomplete. *What makes the collective action problem is an array of individual judgments and desires that are themselves (in all likelihood) a function of social norms.* If people "want" a new norm, their desire probably stems from many other norms—such as norms favoring clean rather than dirty parks, norms in favor of shared rather than maldistributed burdens, norms in favor of solutions through norms rather than coercion or fines.

When a situation is supposed to create a prisoner's dilemma that would be satisfied by some norm Z, the situation presupposes a range of norms A through Y that are being held constant and not being put in contention. Then the question becomes: Why is it that norm Z (say, the norm with respect to littering) is put into question, rather than some other norm (say, the norm favoring clean parks)? This question has yet to be addressed in existing work on collective action and social norms. An answer might be found in one of two ways. We might put at issue those norms that are not part of the relevant agents' own deepest convictions and self-understandings. Typically the norms sought to solve collective action problems seem to be a form of "tinkering," encouraging conduct that preserves what people believe most deeply, have thought through, or most take for granted. Alternatively, we might not look to agents' convictions but venture instead an objective account of human needs and human interests. On such an approach, a collective action problem exists because if agents could agree on the norm in question, things would be better rather than worse. It is not clear, however, that this way of seeing things can coexist with ordinary understandings of collective action problems, which are rooted in subjective desires. A possible conclusion of what I have said thus far is that in the context of norms, the ordinary understandings face a conceptual problem.

3. Legal Responses. However rationality and self-interest are defined, a well-functioning society needs many norms that make it rational for people, acting in their self-interest, to solve collective action problems. When such problems exist, it is because of the social norms that make rational self-interest take a certain form. A large task is therefore to try to inculcate the relevant norms. Effective responses promote efficiency and simultaneously enhance a form of freedom, by producing outcomes that citizens reflectively judge best but cannot obtain on their own.

Much legal regulation has this goal. Such regulation might even consist of direct coercion, designed to generate good norms and to pick up the slack in their absence. There are laws designed to ensure that people pick up after their dogs; that people do not litter; that people do not smoke in certain places. These laws are rarely if ever enforced through criminal prosecutions. But they have an effect in shaping social norms and social meaning. They help to inculcate both shame and pride; they help define the appropriate sources of these things. They readjust the personal calculation, making what is rational, and what is in one's self-interest, different from what they were before.

The key point is that such a change may be supported by the reflective judgments of all or most people. When it is, there should be no objection in principle.[67] The point very much bears on the phenomenon of norm bandwagons. People may actually reject existing norms but fail to state their opposition publicly, and once public opposition becomes less costly, new norms may rapidly come into place.

B. Autonomy

Of course a liberal society might want to ensure that all of its citizens are autonomous. For the moment let us understand the notion in a way that leaves open many questions but that will be helpful for our limited purposes here. A citizen can be understood as autonomous insofar as she is able to choose among a set of reasonably good options and to be reflective and deliberative about her choice.[68] A society can be understood as self-governing, and as politically autonomous, to the extent that its citizens face a range of reasonably good options and exercise capacities of reflection and deliberation about their choice.

It should be clear that social norms, meanings, and roles may undermine individual autonomy. Above all this is because norms can compromise autonomy itself, by stigmatizing it. People may

---

67. Some cases can be imagined in which the response would be invasive of rights and therefore by hypothesis unacceptable.

68. Cf. E. Anderson, Value in Ethics and Economics (1993).

believe, on reflection, that the act of being well-educated should not be a source of shame; but in some communities, a good deal of education may be inconsistent with prevailing social norms. Or exposure to diverse options, and reflection about which is best, may seem inconsistent with existing norms. In such cases autonomy cannot exist without collective assistance; people are able to produce the norms, meanings, and roles that they reflectively endorse only with governmental involvement. Something must be done collectively if the situation is to be changed.

To promote autonomy, a society might seek to ensure that everyone has a minimal degree of education, a certain level of exposure to diverse conceptions of the good, and what might be considered the material bases of autonomy: food, shelter, and freedom from criminal violence. In modest forms this project is fully compatible with political liberalism; perfectionalist liberals might insist on a good deal in this vein in order to allow people to be (more or less) masters of the narratives of their own lives. In either case, social norms can undermine the liberal project, and government might try to alter them in order to promote autonomy. Prevailing norms and meanings may be adaptive to limits in existing opportunities;[69] but they are nonetheless an obstacle to autonomy.

A government that seeks to promote autonomy might well work against efforts by subcommunities to require conformity to a single defining creed. In fact conflicts between antidiscrimination principles and religious liberty have everything to do with perceived limits on governmental ability to change norms, meanings, and roles in subgroups that deny autonomy. These conflicts are generally resolved in favor of subgroups, especially in the area of sex equality. But if we attend to the autonomy-denying effects of norms and meaning, it might well make sense to resolve the conflicts against subgroups, even religious ones.

C. Caste

Many problems of discrimination actually raise issues of caste. We might say that we have a system with caste-like features when a highly visible and morally irrelevant factor is turned, by social and legal practices, into a systematic source of social disadvantage.[70] An important and disastrous feature of this situation is the *signaling effect* of the characteristic that is shared by lower caste

---

69. Cf. J. Elster, Sour Grapes (1983); A. Sen, Commodities and Capabilities (1985). Just as preferences can be adaptive to an unjust status quo, so can norms and meanings be a predictable outgrowth of limited autonomy or heteronomy.

70. See C. R. Sunstein, The Partial Constitution ch. 10 (1993); C. Sunstein, The Anticaste Principle, 92 Mich.L.Rev. 2410 (1994).

members. That characteristic promotes a certain social role for caste members, since it is associated with a range of undesirable or otherwise stigmatizing traits. Often an attack on a caste system amounts to an attack on that social role and its associated social norms—especially as a result of behavioral norms shared, or thought to be shared, by members of the lower caste.[71] For lower caste members, the problem is that the shared characteristic carries with it a meaning—stupidity, passivity, venality—that cannot be controlled by individual agents.

Suppose, for example, that it was thought important to alter social norms about gender relations. The social role of "being a woman" is associated with a wide range of social norms and social meanings. There are many examples from the present and recent past. Thus it may be that women do the majority of domestic labor. In these circumstances, a man who does most of the domestic labor might seem odd, or in some way woman-ish, and a woman who asks for something like equality in domestic labor might seem odd, selfish, or in some way man-ish. Or a woman in her fifties might be seen in a way fundamentally different from a man in his fifties, because of social norms associated with gender. Or a single woman might be stigmatized, or inquired about, in ways fundamentally different from what happens to a similarly situated man. Or a woman who complains about apparently mild forms of sexual harassment might seem to be a radical, a troublemaker, or someone without a sense of humor.

A wide range of "choices" might emerge from the underlying social norms. These choices might reflect adaptation by lower caste members to existing injustice; they might be a product of the social opprobrium attached to violation of social norms by lower caste members.[72] The choices might even be called "preferences"; certainly desires can be affected. But many women believe on reflection that the social meaning of being a woman is bad for them and that it should be changed. These women face a collective action problem that may be best solved with government action. In any case a caste system tends to deny autonomy to lower caste members.

This is simply a stylized discussion of the problems faced by people who live within a caste system,[73] and who might seek to

---

71. Note in this regard Richard Wright's suggestion that unlike most blacks in the south, he would "act straight and human." Wright says that most blacks, even those who felt great resentment, pretended to accept their inferior position. See R. Wright, Black Boy 253 (1945).

72. See the discussion of adaptation of preferences of lower caste members in India in T. Kuran, Private Truths, Public Lies 196–204 (1995).

73. See Kuran, supra, at 134 ("Because society will generally ostracize anyone who abandons the caste system, the potential member of an anticaste

enlist the law to make things better. Such people face a free rider problem that pervasively undermines reform efforts.

D.   Expressive Action

Many laws have an expressive function. They "make a statement" about how much, and how, a good or bad should be valued. They are an effort to constitute and to affect social meanings, social norms, and social roles.

Of course human goods are valued in different ways; people have a wide variety of evaluative stances toward relationships and goods. Laws with expressive functions are often designed to promote a certain way of valuing certain goods. Many such laws are intended to say that specified goods should be valued in a way that deters thinking of them as mere objects for use. Laws forbidding the purchase and sale of certain goods can be so understood. A ban on the sale of children is designed (among other things) to say that children should be valued in a way that forbids the acceptance of cash as a reason for taking them out of parental care. A ban on vote-selling can be viewed similarly. We might understand such a law as an effort to make a certain statement about the pricelessness—not the infinite value—of the right to vote. In the environmental area, debates over market valuation are partly debates over this question.[74]

Laws with expressive justifications may or may not be designed to have social consequences. Some such laws might be defended on the ground that they will affect social norms and move them in appropriate directions. At this stage there are empirical questions: Do laws affect social norms and social meanings? Under what conditions? But laws with expressive justifications might be defended for the statement they make, quite independently of consequences. Certainly this is true for individual behavior. People may avoid a certain course of action because of the meaning of that course, apart from consequences.

VIII.   Blocked Grounds

What I have suggested here should unsettle some common understandings about government "paternalism" and "meddling." If private choices are a function of roles, norms, and meanings over which private people have no sovereignty, many imaginable initiatives are consistent with individual autonomy, rightly conceived. But this conclusion ought not to suggest that government should be licensed to do however it wishes.

colony is likely to withhold his participation until it appears likely to succeed. With other potential members reasoning likewise, the colony will remain unformed.").

74. See S. Kelman, What Price Incentives? (1983).

Often government action should be rejected on simple pragmatic grounds—because, for example, it is likely to be futile or counterproductive. The "just say no" campaign with respect to drug use probably falls in this category. Or perhaps government has mistakenly concluded that there is a collective action problem calling for governmental response. Perhaps most people are happy that littering is not stigmatized; perhaps efforts to stigmatize teenage smoking will backfire and make smoking seem bold or glamorous. If government action would be ineffective or counterproductive, it should not go forward.

It is also true that government interference with norms, role, or meaning might be confused or otherwise wrong. Government might compound a collective action problem, respond to well-organized private groups promoting unjust goals, or aggravate a caste-like situation. Imagine an effort to promote the use of cigarettes, alcohol, or drugs, or to discourage the buckling of seatbelts, or to increase the opprobrium associated with the role of being a homosexual. Nothing I have said suggests that government is not properly criticized when it engages in activity of this sort. But any such criticism should be on the merits, not on the ground that government may not interfere with private preferences or choices.

There is a final point. A liberal society limits the permissible bases for governmental action. It might well describe the limits as "rights." A full account of these limits would be far too ambitious for an essay of this sort; but a few notes will be helpful.

Some government action designed to change norms, meaning, and role might be based on religious grounds; these should be banned as reasons for public action. At least in the American constitutional system, for example, it is unacceptable for government to attempt to legislate on the ground that the divinity of Jesus Christ requires a certain state of affairs. So too, it would be unacceptable to base government action on grounds that deny the basic equality of human beings—as in efforts to encourage norms that treat members of racial minorities as second-class citizens.

In any case some human interests are properly denominated rights, and efforts to change norms, meanings, and role should not be allowed to invade rights.[75] Many imaginable efforts ought to be rejected because of this risk. Consider, for example, a suggestion that the meaning of refusing government officials into your home is now "personal courage and independence"—accompanied by the not implausible thought that things would be better if the meaning were "unpatriotic unwillingness to cooperate with the crime-fighting effort," culminating in a proposal that everyone should be required to open their homes to the government. There is a

---

75. I do not mean to say anything here about the status or basis of rights.

collective action problem here. But if it is believed that people should have a right to keep government officials from their homes, this proposal should be rejected.

Political liberals go further and urge rejection of any ground for action that is based on a "comprehensive view."[76] Of course there are many complexities in this claim. What is important for present purposes is that on any sound view of liberalism, there is no *general* basis, in principle, for objection to proposals of the sort I have suggested. Political liberals ought to acknowledge, for example, that social roles and social meanings may undermine the equality and liberty of citizens and that changes require collective action. The constraints imposed by political liberalism impose no bans on those changes.

Conclusion

Many claims about the appropriate limits of law are insufficiently attentive to the pervasive effects of social norms, social meanings, and social roles. In fact these effects have yet to receive much attention.[77] But the behavioral effects of law are an important matter for lawmakers to understand, and those effects have everything to do with social norms. An understanding of norms will therefore bear a great deal on effective regulatory policy. Many of the most dramatic gains in health and safety policy are a product of changes in norms, meanings, and role.

Norms relate to some broader issues as well. Often it is said that the common law, and a liberal regime dedicated to freedom, take "preferences" as they are and do not seek to change them. But the term "preferences" is highly ambiguous. If the term is meant to refer to "choices," it should be understood that choices are very much a function of context, including governing norms, meanings, and roles. Certainly the particular choices made by people in markets—in their capacity as consumers or laborers—do not suggest global or acontextual valuations of relevant goods. If the term "preferences" is meant to refer not to choices but to the mental states behind choices, it is important to recognize that those mental states include assessments of social norms, the expressive meaning of acts, and the expectations associated with a dazzling variety of social roles. Norms and roles affect both public action and public talk, in ways that can much disguise how people think privately. This point has large implications. In many settings, it would be best to dispense with the idea of "preferences." Moreover, norms can be far more fragile than they appear; hence "norm entrepreneurs" can

---

76. See J. Rawls, Political Liberalism (1993); C. Larmore, Patterns of Moral Complexity (1988).

77. The principal contributions are Lessig, supra, and from a different direction, Ellickson, supra.

help solve collective action problems, and hence "norm bandwagons" are common.

While social life would be impossible without norms, meanings, and roles, individual people have little control over these things. The result can be severe limits on human well-being. Certainly there is a problem with existing norms when all or almost all people would seek a change and when existing norms deny people the preconditions for autonomy. In fact lives are shortened and unjustified inequalities are perpetuated by the existence of many current norms. People need collective help if they want to change norms, meaning, or roles. Collective help may be futile or counterproductive; it may be illegitimately motivated. But these matters require an inquiry into context. The issue should not be foreclosed by resort to confusing claims about the need to respect private choice.

Study Questions:

1. Consider the following argument:

    Currently, there is a social norm against buying and selling body parts, like kidneys and eyeballs. If such a norm did not exist, wealthy people with health problems would pay a lot of money to poor people for body parts. Both sides of the bargain would be better off: the buyers would have better health, and the sellers would have more money. What blocks these exchanges is the social norm. Therefore, the government should take steps to change this social norm.

    Evaluate this argument in light of Sunstein's lecture.

2. Can the economic defense of expectation damages (see Chapter 3) be criticized for ignoring the effect of promise violations on the social norm of keeping one's promises?

3. How might social norms explain some of the regulations of financial institutions described by Geoffrey Miller (Chapter 4)?

4. How might social norms explain rent control laws, minimum wage laws, and laws against usury? Does a "social norm" explanation justify these laws?

5. Many vigorous political debates concern laws that seem largely symbolic. Consider flag desecration laws, the public display of crèches and other religious objects, and the propriety of displaying Confederate flags on public buildings. How might these debates be explained in light of Sunstein's lecture?

9. Transaction Costs and Property Rights: Or Do Good Fences Make Good Neighbors?

Richard A. Epstein[1]

The selection of the title for my Coase lecture was in part an act of trepidation and in part an act of literary license, which fits in with the distinctive stylistic excellence in Ronald Coase's work. This quarter I have taught two property-based courses: property itself and a seminar on the Federal Communications Commission, a subject on which Coase wrote with such perspicacity nearly 40 years ago (when he was younger than I am today).[2] So the metaphor of the fence came naturally to me as the sign of property rights. But I put it in the form of a question to communicate the uneasiness that one has about fences, and by implication about boundaries. And I am not alone in that pursuit. Susan Gzech not only teaches immigration law—a subject in which boundaries are of no little importance—but she also memorized poems in third grade. So she reminded me (with verse recited from memory) that Robert Frost's poem, *Mending Wall*, achieved its greatness precisely because its long dialogue showed a deep ambiguity about fences, and perhaps about the boundaries that these were designed to protect.

The ambiguity is captured in the passage that supplies the title for this section:

There where it is we do not need the wall:

He is all pine and I am apple orchard.

My apple trees will never get across

And eat the cones under his pines, I tell him.

He only says, "Good fences make good neighbors."

And note this irony: the author says that we do not need fences (a cost) because there are no boundary crossings that they need to deter, given the fixed positions of pines and apple trees. He does not say that boundaries require fences under other circumstances; much less does he say that boundaries are not important as between neighbors. Yet I shall not dwell at length on this passage, let alone this poem, for we have miles to go before I earn my keep.

---

1. James Parker Hall Distinguished Service Professor. This lecture was delivered in February 1996.

2. Ronald Coase, The Federal Communication Commission, 2 J.L. & Econ. 1 (1959).

The poet is often thought to be not the precursor, but the antagonist to the law and economics scholar, in which capacity I come to this speech today, but I think that the message Robert Frost has offered us is a good one: good fences are not necessarily the right way to create good neighbors, nor even to demarcate boundary lines between neighbors. By the same token, we should not want to say that bad fences make good neighbors, or indicate that boundaries are themselves unimportant in how individuals structure their relationships with each other. We should simply realize, as the poet points out, that it is costly to build the wall. The best way to understand the boundary is to presume its validity, and then to find the set of circumstances in which those boundary conditions could be relaxed to the mutual advantage of the parties on both sides of the line. Even people who do not like fences often like the privacy that they can foster.

One simple way to make this basic point is to ask what the world would be like if we did not have boundaries along which we could build fences. At this point we would have a world that would allow individuals to have some interest in all land, or perhaps no individual to have any interest in any land. But once these individuals lack any separate property of their own, then they will have to develop some governance mechanism to structure their interactions in the never-ending commons—not an easy task to do. The preferences for certain kinds of behaviors and hence certain kinds of rules may have a grim level of predictability across individuals. But with the increasing rise of diversity in tastes and temperaments, we can be sure that a continuous ongoing deliberation about the nature of the common good is sure to be contentious, placing an enormous stress on the collective decision procedures needed to manage the common resources on which everyone depends for sustenance. A little community and a little participation might be good things; and so might a little bit of commonly-owned property. But too much of a good thing turns out to be a bad thing, and the simple and most profound influence that drives us towards private property is the sense that we would prefer to have more neighbors and fewer partners in this world, and that only by drawing boundaries and creating separate spaces is this possible.

This does not mean that we have discarded deliberation and common property. The existence of common areas in condominiums and apartment houses shows that the equilibrium, even when privately generated, does not make all space private. Rather, the hope is that separating individuals into smaller groups can introduce a greater measure of agreement into the deliberations that remain: it is easier for each family or sub-group to make decisions on its side of the boundary than under a common property regime. The simple act of division reduces the stress on the decisionmaking procedures, and this breakdown of vast collective decisions gives private property its origins—and its limits. Clearly, separation has some gains that can be captured by entrepreneurs on both sides of the line. We can see the power of boundaries by noting that they are created by agreement and conveyance when none existed before. The question is how to best understand the uses and limitations of such boundaries.

Given what we have said, the creation of boundaries has both benefits for those who are given the right to exclude, and costs for those who are excluded. To simply compare the gains and losses in any individual trespassory encounter is quite beside the point; the question is whether or not we can find some systematic advantage to a rule that treats the boundary as irrelevant in all cases, and we cannot. The ability to plant and to plan depends on secure property rights that allow one to reap what one sows, and the classical writers (which cover both Blackstone and Bentham, for all their apparent differences) were correct to assume that labor on property would cease if the return from that labor could be routinely captured by another. I sow and you reap, I work and you collect, are the first and most powerful indications of a mismatch between labor and reward. The person who has internalized the labor should, as a first approximation, be allowed to internalize the gain. That statement becomes an exaggeration with intellectual property, but it is a powerful instinct with land, where only one person will ever be in that position to internalize the gain in question—no matter how hard one labors he cannot "copy" the crops. So the boundary has a powerful initial validity. But what kinds of complications does the boundary introduce?

To see how the simplest model works, let us start by focusing our attention on land, which is assumed to be owned indefinitely, and ask about the potential conflicts between neighbors and how these might be resolved. Here I can think of at least four situations where the limited relaxation of the boundary works to the benefit of both neighbors, not perfectly, but with enough rough generality and predictability to be the basis of a rule of law.

The first is a simple agricultural practice. In medieval times, when fields were plowed, a nonproductive space at the end of the field was needed for the plow to turn around. Simply stating the proposition in this fashion shows the incentives to having long thin strips, so that the ratio of unusable to usable land can be reduced. But that solution does not depend in whole or in part on cooperation between neighbors, and the question is whether those neighbors can do better by agreement (or by custom) if they deviate from an exclusive property rights regime. And it turns out that they can. By having a common area (just for two) for turning the plow at the end of each strip of land, the two parties can reduce the level of wasted space by 50 percent. There is, of course, a question of where the common strip would be placed. At first blush, there seems no reason not to place it all on the land of one party and have both use it. But the distributional consequences would not come out evenly between the parties, and the designated loser might forego the inconvenience, since he receives nothing in return. Therefore, under these circumstances, the tendency is to split the turning strip equally between the two neighbors' land, so that each gains half of the surplus, or if the situation does not quite permit that, one can imagine some possible side-payment between the parties to equalize the division of economic surplus from an uneven physical division.

In this situation, never let anyone think that simple equity is at stake. A rule that divides the surplus reduces the possibility of unilateral defection from that common solution. And the clear point of reference—even division at the margin—facilities the emergence of a broad custom that allows people to reach this solution without having to figure out time and time again that sharing at the border is consistent with the joint maximization of wealth. To be sure, the solution will not work everywhere: fences are needed for cattle and other animals unless the parties think that one large meadow is better than two small ones (which is often the case). Yet here too the poet is the equal to the challenge, and anticipates the major findings of the law and economics movement:

If I could put a notion in his head:

<u>Why</u> do they make good neighbours? Isn't it

Where there are cows? But here there are no cows.

Before I build a wall I'd ask to know

What I was walling in or walling out.

The boundary solution for turns in open fields, moreover, has a direct parallel in the public law of takings and eminent domain. Oftentimes, one of the critical issues in a farming community was the location of a road to take goods to market. If placed along the boundary line between two neighbors, each can have access to it. Yet here the situation is such that all other persons can access it as well, so that typically the cost of construction and maintenance does not fall on the original landowners. But a rule that says that they contribute the land evenly, without compensation, leaves them the net winners when the values of the retained lands are increased due to their greater access to markets. And the principle of even division of contributed land (or side payments in lieu of land) has the same virtues of stabilization noted above. It reduces the incentive for parties to push the land over to the neighbor.

In other cases, the deviation from strict land borders exhibits a similar logic of mutual advantage. It is evident to all observers that the law of trespass has a harder edge (at the boundary quality) than the law of nuisance.[3] And it is important to understand why: with invasions that do not involve actual entry, there are opportunities for gains at the margin by relaxing either the rule that all invasions are wrong, or the rule that all noninvasions are completely permissible. I first worked on these cases in the 1970s when I was trying to see what was wrong with some of the work that I had done on the strong boundary principle in the law of torts.[4] And I discovered that Ronald Coase was not the first Englishman who had focused on the role of transactions costs in softening up situations at the boundary.

The most famous illustration of this principle is the so-called rule of "live and let live at the boundary," which says that each individual must tolerate a certain amount of noise and interference from his neighbors, on condition that they do the same with him. The explanation for this result was put forward in unmistakable terms by Baron Bramwell in Bamford v. Turnley:[5]

> There is an obvious necessity for such a principle as I have mentioned. It is as much for the advantage of one owner as of another for the very nuisance the one complains of, as the result of the ordinary use of his neighbour's land, he himself will create in the ordinary use of his own, and the reciprocal nuisances are of a comparatively trifling character. The convenience of such a rule may be indicated by calling it a rule of give and take, live and let live....

> The public consists of all the individuals of it, and a thing is only for the public benefit when it is productive of good to those individuals on the balance of loss and gain to all. <u>So that if all the loss and all the gain were borne and received by one individual, he on the whole would be the gainer.</u> But whenever this is the case,—whenever a thing is for the public benefit, properly understood,—the loss to the individuals of the public who lose will bear compensation out of the gains of those who gain. It is for the public benefit there should be railways, but it would not be unless the gain of having the railway was sufficient to compensate the loss occasioned by the use of the land required for its site; and accordingly no one thinks it would be right to take an individual's land without compensation to make a railway.

3. See Thomas W. Merrill, Trespass, Nuisance, and the Costs of Determining Property Rights, 14 J. Legal Stud. 13 (1985).

4. Richard A. Epstein, Nuisance Law: Corrective Justice and Its Utilitari-an Constraints, 8 J. Legal Stud. 49 (1979).

5. 122 Eng. Rep. 27, 32 (Ex. 1863). (emphasis added).

It is odd perhaps to think that some obscure nuisance decision involving reciprocal injuries at the boundary has made the following modest contributions. First, its clear and powerful statement of methodological individualism as the way to proceed to particular results (i.e., there is no public interest as such, only a set of private interests from which net gains and losses are aggregated to find the correct social result); second, the importance of the Paretian criterion of social welfare based on the improvements for all individuals in the social system; and third, its intimate connection to the principles of eminent domain: no compensation in cash is needed when compensation is provided in kind, but the opposite result is reached when all the damage by way of invasion falls on one party to the transaction (as with the railroad and the sparks).

Bramwell has therefore identified those situations between neighbors where the relaxation of the strict boundary conditions is likely to yield mutual advantage. Once again a set of customary practices paves the way to the legal rule, but here, unlike the cases of plowing at the boundary lines, we cannot be so confident that the parties will generate the best solutions if left to their own consensual devices. The temptation to act unreasonably, to demand compensation, or to seek injunctions for trivial losses may prove too great when individuals can insist that any invasion of their space, however minute or indirect, is subject to legal sanction. And even in the best of worlds, it costs money and imposes impediments and encumbrances on legal title to negotiate the thousands of transactions needed to reach the position that the live and let live rule gives us in the first place. In this situation, the relaxation of this boundary makes perfectly good sense. And for persons who derive title from a common owner, for whom the live-and-let-live rule provides too much noise at the boundary or too little, it is possible to create by private covenants a distinctive environment that suits the tastes of the members of that community even if it suits none other.

The argument also works in reverse with respect to the easement of lateral support. Once again, it was nineteenth century English judges, this time, Jessel, M.R., who stated the rule clearly and forcefully.[6] If a neighbor digs out to the boundary, the land next door will fall. If each restrains that behavior, then both will benefit. It would be a mistake to allow people to build first and claim the easement of support thereafter, so the obligation was wisely confined to support the land in its natural state. For the support of preexisting structures, however, an obligation was imposed, but it was to *notify* the other owner with a view toward allowing him to shore up his own structures, or to negotiate with the neighbor for rights of support before the neighbor commenced

6. Corporation of Birmingham v. Allen, L. R. 6 Ch.D. 284 (C.A. 1877).

construction. The alternative rule would have bad consequences. One party's unilateral action should never be allowed to transfer rights from another. Although building a structure on one's own land is noninvasive and surely legal, if the development rights on the other side are compromised, then such actions can be taken for strategic advantage, actions that would not be taken if a single owner had possession of both plots of land.

It may seem to be a long march from the law of lateral support to the law of privacy with respect to eavesdropping and spying, both in the public and the private context. However, the movement principle involved here is really quite small—a nice result if we wish to develop a unified approach to all legal problems. Let us assume that we had a rule allowing all individuals to eavesdrop at their pleasure so long as they did not trespass on the land of another. To keep conversations private, one would need to erect various devices to block the overhearing. The traditional law of trespass would, of course, offer landowners some protection for their privacy. They could hide behind their walls or congregate in the center of their property in order to reduce the chances that others would eavesdrop.

Yet we can do better, and in the process free up land for more useful pursuits. If one could establish that each person values his right to privacy more than his right to snoop, then a social norm against eavesdropping could be adopted to the mutual advantage of both sides. The next question is how to determine whether that norm is in effect. We can once again look to consensual commons and consider the applicable rule in restaurants or clubs. The no-overhearing rule is in strong effect, and informal sanctions, such as ostracism, are imposed on those who snoop. The development of these rules in a consensual setting is a good reason to adopt them as a matter of public law to govern relations between strangers, especially when it appears that the values attached to the various activities throughout society do not differ unduly from those found in restaurants and clubs. And that norm has powerful enforcement in the modern law of privacy.[7]

As with other rules, what begins as a private rule between consenting parties ends up ordering relationships between the individual and the state. The erstwhile government position that snooping by electronic devices is not wrongful because it is not trespassory is falsified by the prior developments in the common law of privacy. The question of whether electronic wiretapping by law enforcement officials is a search and seizure under the Fourth Amendment has a long and tortuous history, but receives a clear answer. The practice is covered by the Fourth Amendment, so that

7. Roach v. Harper, 105 S.E.2d 546 (W.Va. 1958).

the government can wiretap, but only with the appropriate safe-guards.

The Supreme Court has reached that position[8] but with too great a reliance on some undifferentiated notion of reasonable expectations. It is all too easy to say that one is entitled to privacy because one has the expectation of getting it. But the focus on the subjective expectations of one party to the transaction cannot explain or justify any legal rule. Should the result change if the state routinely practices snooping, so that no one has any reason-able (read, predictive) expectation that his conversations will go undetected? It is dangerous, to say the least, to allow a succession of government wrongs to ripen into a prescriptive right of sorts. That unfortunate conclusion is avoided by stressing the social optimality that comes from adopting a rule that extends protection against certain forms of nontrespassory conduct, for once the optimality of the rule is established, then its frequent violation by government is no longer viewed as framing expectations but as violating rights.

The last of the relaxations of the boundary conditions is not so simple because it involves the integration of the temporal and the spatial domains, which was hinted at in the discussion of lateral support. When Ronald Coase wrote about the problem of social cost,[9] he illustrated much of the difficulty with the well-known case of Sturges v. Bridgman,[10] which involved a boundary dispute be-tween a physician and a druggist. The druggist had long made up his compounds in the back of his shop without inconveniencing anyone. But when the physician decided to construct a new examin-ing room near the back of his premises, the noise that had been harmlessly dissipated now became, in the standard sense of the term, a nuisance to the new neighbor who had just arrived on the scene. The question was whether the physician could recover for his damages and obtain an injunction against a continuation of the druggist's prior practice. Coase used this case to illustrate that no matter which way the original right was assigned, the imbalance could be corrected (at least if transactions cost were zero) so that the more valuable use would continue and the other would be modified, with appropriate side payments between the parties, whose direction and amount depended on the specification of the original set of rights.

The case has continued to exert a fancy over legal imagina-tions, and just recently Brian Simpson (who taught me property at

8. Katz v. United States, 389 U.S. 347 (1967).

9. Ronald H. Coase, The Problem of Social Cost, 3 J.L. & Econ. 1 (1960).

10. [1879] 11 Ch.D. 852

Oxford) has written,[11] subject to a pungent reply by Coase himself,[12] an extended essay on the social history of the case that reveals the pattern of broken negotiations and disappointed maneuvers that dogged this unhappy lawsuit to its conclusion. But our fascination with the complexities of this situation should not allow us to deviate from our appointed goal, which is to understand something about the role of boundaries in disputes between neighbors.

The easiest way to organize the case is by asking whether the plaintiff has made out a prima facie case of nuisance. Recall that for the better peace between neighbors, the presumptive definition of a nuisance is a nontrespassory invasion that results in visible inconvenience to the affairs of a neighbor. The question of time does not yet enter into the equation, and it seems clear that the physician thus far has the upper hand in the negotiations. But for every good prima facie case, we can find some affirmative defense, and on this occasion the plaintiff may have assumed the risk of the injury because he came to the nuisance. While it would be easy if the plaintiff trespassed on the defendant's land, the case is difficult precisely because the plaintiff had remained a good neighbor by not crossing over.

The usual case law on this point is in accord with the result of this drama—it allows the plaintiff to win, and thus the defendant has the obligation to purchase any needed property interest needed to continue with his business. But why should this be the case? To answer this question, it is necessary to think back to an earlier point in time to explore the options available to the physician, or his predecessor in title, the moment the druggist started his business. If he knew that down the road, the druggist's original activities could ripen into an easement to continue, then it is clear that the plaintiff-physician is in a worse position if he does nothing rather than immediately bringing a legal action to protect his property rights. After all, by hypothesis if the two activities started simultaneously, the physician could have prevailed in his action for injunction and damages. So the only way that he could stop the creation by prescription of an easement to cause damages is to sue promptly. Thinking about that suit raises the following question: cui bono? It hardly helps the physician to have to act early to protect his rights. And it certainly does not help the druggist to be shut down before an actual injury occurs. Why precipitate a conflict over future legal rights when there is no present interference, even

11. A.W. Brian Simpson, "Coase v. Pigou Revisited," 25 J. Legal. Stud. 53 (1996).

12. Coase, "Law and Economics and A.W. Brian Simpson," 25 J. Legal Stud. 103 (1996).

though there is an admitted transmission of these noises over the boundary line? So we clearly want to avoid the suit.

One way to achieve this result is to have the two parties negotiate some sort of a stand-still agreement. But that option is costly and holds open the possibility that the physician might demand an amount significantly greater than his expected harm in order to resolve this dispute. And the problems become more intractable if a defendant's activity extends noise and vibration across the unoccupied lands of many individuals. So the law has created a bargain of its own. The plaintiff is told that he cannot sue today, and the defendant is told that he cannot plead the statute of limitations tomorrow by claiming in retrospect that the harm really started when the defendant commenced his operations. So there is a forced exchange of sorts between the two parties that looks to make things better off for both.

But one can only judge the success of this engineered deal in the fullness of time. As matters go on, the result opted for here could prove triumphant if the actual conflict never occurs. The physician never builds the examining room close to the party wall, or the druggist sells out to a new developer who abandons the older noisy practice when the neighborhood becomes more fashionable. At this point, the postponement of the legal dispute works its magic at both the front and the back end, and as a guess one would say that for either or both of the reasons just mentioned, just this outcome is likely to occur.

But in some scenarios the outcomes are less happy. The conflict is postponed but not avoided altogether. Now the physician exercises his right to build the examining room. Looking at this transaction as a one period problem, we might be tempted to say that the party who is last to arrive is the one who stirs up the conflict, and thus create a kind of prescriptive right for the druggist. But once we recall the structure of the legal agreement imposed at an earlier time, we cannot have so limited a perspective on the problem. Instead, it looks as though we are in payback time. The physician can exercise his right and the druggist has to give way. The only help that he is given is some time to get his belongings in order, and normally that will be demanded before the conflict arises. There are some cases that deviate from this pattern, and some academic commentary that does not take this line. But the overall sense of the deal should be clear enough. It is possible to reconcile time and space, although not perhaps in exactly the same sense that Immanual Kant would have asked for us. And once again, the analysis of the private law question gives us guidance in public law areas: when the state shuts down the piggery to protect nearby development, it need not compensate its owner, but can stand in the shoes of the neighbor whom it protects.[13] The analysis is the same as above.

This discussion of space and time affords a convenient transition to our next question, involving boundaries in time between different parties. This problem is ordinarily obscured to common understanding because the ownership in land and in chattels is normally regarded to last forever, at least in the sense that one person has no definite limitations over the period of ownership, and can consume, sell or dispose of property just as if he were to live forever. But there are, or at least have been, situations where temporal boundaries between individuals have been created, such as in leases and life estates, so that now the law must police the boundaries between the two successive generations of holders. This sort of boundary creates a different set of neighbors from those in the spatial conflicts (with and without a temporal dimension) that we have just had the opportunity to witness.

The key point is that these temporal divisions contain no element of reciprocity of the sort that governed all the cases to date. No longer can we talk about the sharing of common spaces, or reciprocal easements of support. Here there is one party that possesses the property and the other who is entitled to take it at some future time. By definition, the party who is out of possession can do little to harm the party who is in possession, but the converse arrangement is surely not true. The party in possession understands the maxim that possession is nine points of the law, and is able to do grave harm to the holder of the next generation. Just as we can consume our seed corn, there is a greater temptation to consume the seed corn of another. So the creation of the temporal boundary gives the regrettable opportunity for another forbidden boundary crossing. Property that has an expected value and use past the present term or the present life can be mined, cut, or harvested so that the remainder is but a mere hulk with the value sucked out of it. And here the common law action of waste is offered as a counterweight to the premature destruction of assets by the present tenant in possession.

But exactly what is expected of that tenant in possession? It is hard to give any categorical answer, for so much depends on the nature of the resource in question. It will not do for the tenant in possession to cut down an entire forest, but if a mine is already open it is far from clear that he should stop extraction altogether and thus make a gift, of sorts, to the remainderman of the premises. So the best that one can say in the abstract is that the patterns of utilization by the present tenant should be roughly those that would be followed by an individual with successive interests in the

---

13. See Hadacheck v. Sebastian, 239 U.S. 394 (1915).

property, that is, if he acted as a prudent fee simple owner of the estate. That position is not perfect because if one could show that the prudent owner would engage in a process of dramatic extraction and consumption, it would be an open question as to whether that pattern of behavior was desired by the grantor who created the division of interests. Was there some intention to create a transfer that provided benefits to the next generation?

In a sense, that is precisely the point. Now that the boundaries are unclear and the obligations are no longer reciprocal, it is very difficult for the law to fashion an ideal set of rules that keeps the two interests on a strict sequential course. So here the legal norm falls, but the consensual solution rises in importance—the inverse pattern from the live-let-live-situation where regularities between neighbors are more easily observed. In waste cases we say that the grantor of the two interests (or the one if one is retained and the other is transferred out) can usually specify with greater detail exactly what can be done with the property and by whom and at what time, and if that direction is spelled out with specificity, then we might allow the boundary crossings to take place with relative impunity. The owner of a life estate in a grand mansion may be allowed to renovate or rip it down if that is allowed by the original deal. The life tenant of a mine may be able to speed up production. And a tenant in possession of real estate may be forced to surrender the leasehold improvements at the end of the lease, but usually for a cash settlement that compensates him for any unrecovered investment in the original structure, either by a predetermined formula or by a fresh appraisal when the lease terminates. So here again the rules are default rules, but typically they are not as robust as the default rules between neighbors. The fit between law and intentions is not strong enough to cover the immense kind of variation in transactions of this sort.

It is perhaps too much to go on discussing the importance of boundaries, save one—the boundary between law and economics. Here I think that the disciplines are to some extent different. The lawyer seeks to delineate the rights and duties of citizens and to work transactions within that framework. The economist seeks to understand the logic of the rules and the consequences that they generate. But in this case, at least, I would emphasize more the common mission and less the boundaries between the two. I think that Ronald Coase made his great contributions because he was able to use simple cases to illustrate important economic principles. I believe that other areas could benefit from the kinds of arguments I have made today about the use and limitations of boundaries in ordering human affairs. Intellectual property is surely one; and the study of the spectrum and the Federal Communications Commission, alluded to above, is yet another. In fact, I think that too much of economics today is driven by the desire to obtain mathematical sophistication even at the cost of institutional mastery. Subtle insights are often celebrated while important institutional arrangements are often overlooked because they are too obvious for serious theorists to dwell upon. Perhaps that is the observation of someone for whom economics is a tool that helps explain how legal rules emerged and why they are sound. But even if this study is not the only way to look at the interaction between law and economics, it is surely one of the most fruitful ways to use the study of each to enrich the understanding of the other.

The reorientation of law and economics offers a response to some of the challenges that are found in Frost's Mending Wall. The poem concludes with the poet's protagonist unbowed:

> He will not go behind his father's saying,
>
> And he likes having thought of it so well
>
> He says again, "Good fences make good neighbours."

One sees in this passage some of the recurrent themes in the traditional defense of private property and industry custom. "He will not go beyond his father's saying," makes it appear as though his thoughts are just handed down from generation to generation, and perhaps, just perhaps, are not capable of any rational defense in the here and now. And the reappearance of the punch line "Good fences make good neighbours" could lead one to believe that simple repetition of this saying is tantamount to a rational argument in its defense. At one level I sympathize with the protagonist's attitude because it is all too clear that the nineteenth judges who did best by economics did so in advance of the theoretical developments of the field that gave voice to the concerns they were addressing. Yet once we can marry the newer insights to the older rules we can perhaps do better than simple repetition. We can gain some understanding as to why older principles served us well, and why modern judicial efforts to accommodate the expansion of state power have unanticipated consequences in at least two dimensions. They both lead to inferior social institutional arrangements, and they stand at odds with any coherent and systematic development of general legal theory.

Study Questions:

1. What are the boundaries drawn around intellectual property rights (see Chapter 7)—for example, my right to benefit from my computer program? How would Epstein analyze this problem?

2. The speaker in the poem seems to be offended by the neighbor's construction of a wall. Why? (See Chapter 8.)

3. One lesson often taken from the Coase theorem is that property rights should be as clear as possible. Epstein seems to agree. What is the basis of this view? Is it correct?

4. Another lesson of the Coase theorem is that if the cost of transacting is low or zero, it does not matter who gets the property right. For example, it does not matter whether the property right is given to the physician or the druggist in Sturges v. Physician. What is the explanation for this view? Is it correct?

5. The lengthy quotation from Baron Bramwell includes a description of what is today called the "collective action problem." What is this problem? What does it have to do with property rights?

10. Values and Consequences: An Introduction to Economic Analysis of Law

Richard A. Posner[1]

I am going to give a very brief, thumbnail sketch of economic analysis of law, and then focus on just two uses of the analysis, and in doing so try to give you a bit of its flavor. The first use is to make law simpler to understand and evaluate; and the second is to press you to defend your values.

That there is a relation between economics and law has been known for an awfully long time, at least since Hobbes's discussion of property in the seventeenth century. But until very recently, the relation received focused attention only in relation to a handful of legal fields, mainly antitrust and public utility regulation, that dealt explicitly with competition and monopoly, which as early as the 1930s were receiving the sustained and sophisticated attention of leading English and American economists. (Competition and monopoly had received the attention of economists since Adam Smith; hence the qualification "sustained and sophisticated.")

In retrospect, an economic literature dealing with other fields of law, notably Robert Hale's work on contract law, which also dates from the 1930s, can be identified. But even after the *Journal of Law and Economics* commenced publication—at this law school, naturally—in 1958, the "law and economics" movement, if discernible at all, would have been associated primarily with problems of competition and monopoly, although occasional forays had been made into taxation (Henry Simons) and corporations (Henry Manne), even patents (Arnold Plant), and if one went back to the eighteenth century there was Bentham's largely forgotten utilitarian—essentially, economic—analysis of crime and punishment. It was not until 1961, when Ronald Coase's article "The Problem of Social Cost" was published,[2] and at about the same time Guido Calabresi's first article on torts,[3] that an economic theory of the

1. Chief Judge, United States Court of Appeals for the Seventh Circuit; Senior Lecturer, University of Chicago Law School. This is the text of a Coase Lecture given at the University of Chicago Law School on January 6, 1998.

2. 3 *Journal of Law and Economics* 1 (1960 [but actually published in 1961]).

3. Guido Calabresi, "Some Thoughts on Risk Distribution and the Law of Torts," 70 *Yale Law Journal* 499 (1961).

common law could be glimpsed. When Gary Becker published his article "Crime and Punishment: An Economic Approach,"[4] reviving and refining Bentham, it began to seem that perhaps no field of law could not be placed under the lens of economics with illuminating results. And within a few years, sure enough, papers on the economics of contract law, civil and criminal procedure, property, consumer protection, and other areas new to economists had appeared and the rough shape of the mature field was discernible. Later, books and articles would extend the economic analysis of law into such fields as employment, admiralty, intellectual property, family law, legislation, environmental law, administrative law, conflict of laws, and judicial behavior; and this is only a partial list. The field has developed to the point where the dean of the Yale Law School, a critic of the field, said recently: "The law and economics movement was and continues to be an enormous enlivening force in American legal thought and, I would say, today continues and remains the single most influential jurisprudential school in this country."[5]

The economic analysis of law, as it now exists not only in the United States but also in Europe, which has its own flourishing law and economics association, has both positive (that is, descriptive) and normative aspects. It tries to explain and predict the behavior of participants in and persons regulated by the law. It also tries to improve law by pointing out respects in which existing or proposed laws have unintended or undesirable consequences, whether on economic efficiency, or the distribution of income and wealth, or other values. It is not merely an ivory-tower enterprise, at least in the United States, where the law and economics movement is understood to have influenced legal reform in a number of important areas. These areas include antitrust, the regulation of public utilities and common carriers, environmental regulation, the computation of damages in personal injury suits, the regulation of the securities markets, the federal sentencing guidelines, the division of property and the calculation of alimony in divorce cases, and the law governing investment by pension funds and other trustees, and to have been a significant factor in the deregulation movement and in free-market ideology generally. Most major and many minor law schools have one or two full-time economists on their faculty; a number of law professors have Ph.D.'s in economics; there are six scholarly journals devoted to economic analysis of law, with a seventh on the way; the use of economists as expert witnesses has become conventional in a range of important fields; judicial opin-

---

4. 76 *Journal of Political Economy* 169 (1968).

5. Remarks of Anthony T. Kronman, *The Second Driker Forum for Excellence* in the Law, 42 *Wayne Law Review* 115, 160 (1995).

ions refer to economic concepts and cite economic books and articles; and a number of federal judges, including a Justice of the Supreme Court (Stephen Breyer), are alumni of the law and economics movement. Economic analysis of law is generally considered the most significant development in legal thought in the United States since legal realism petered out a half century ago.

Noneconomists often associate economics with money, capitalism, selfishness—with a reductive, unrealistic conception of human motivation and behavior, a formidable mathematical apparatus, and a penchant for cynical, pessimistic, and conservative conclusions. It earned the sobriquet of "the dismal science" because of Thomas Malthus's thesis that famine, war, and sexual abstinence were the only ways in which population and food supply could be equilibrated. The essence of economics is none of these things, however. The essence is extremely simple, although the simplicity is deceptive; the simple can be subtle, can be counterintuitive; its antithesis is "complicated," not "difficult."

Most economic analysis consists of tracing out the consequences of assuming that people are more or less rational in their social interactions. In the case of the activities that interest the law, these people may be criminals or prosecutors or parties to accidents or taxpayers or tax collectors or striking workers—or even law students. Students treat grades as prices, so that unless the university administration intervenes, unpopular professors, in order to keep up their enrollments, will sometimes compensate students for the low perceived value of the course by giving them higher grades, that is, by raising the price that the professor pays for the student.

I said that the tracing out of consequences is subtle as well as simple, and here is an example. Have you heard of the spendthrift trust? That is a trust, very common, indeed standard, in which the trustee is forbidden to pay out any of the money or other property in the trust to the creditors of the trust's beneficiaries. The law will enforce such a restriction, yet it has seemed to many students of the law a fraud on creditors; for the trust beneficiary, assuming that his whole wealth is in the spendthrift trust, can borrow all he wants, spend what he borrows, and not be forced to repay the lenders. But if you think about this for a moment, you'll be driven to the opposite conclusion—that, provided the provision preventing creditors from reaching into the trust is not concealed, a spendthrift trust *limits* borrowing by the trust beneficiary, because he can't offer security to the lender. And the next step in the analysis is to see how increasing the rights of debtors in bankruptcy, far from causing an avalanche of reckless borrowing, could reduce the amount of borrowing, and so the incidence of bankruptcy, by causing lenders to make smaller loans to risky borrowers. So lenders may oppose easy bankruptcy not because they fear there will be more defaults, but because they fear a reduction in the volume of loans. To see this, imagine how many, or rather how few, loans there would be if borrowers had no obligation to repay. Notice also how creditors are as hurt by excessively stringent as by excessively lenient bankruptcy rules: if creditors had the legal right, as under ancient Roman law, to carve up a defaulting borrower into as many pieces as there were creditors, most people would be afraid to borrow. Can you see now why loan sharks in Chicago break the legs of defaulting borrowers, but do not kill them?

Rationality implies decision making, and people often have to make decisions under conditions of profound uncertainty; fortunately, economists have devoted a good deal of attention to decision under uncertainty. A simple but important example of a law-related decision under uncertainty is the decision as to how much care to take to avoid an accident. The accident will occur with probability P, and let us assume that if it does occur it will impose a cost that I'll call L, for loss; and assume further that eliminating the possibility of such an accident would impose on the potential injurer a cost, which I'll call B (for burden). Then it is easily seen that the cost of avoiding the accident will be less than the expected accident cost (or benefit of avoiding the accident) if B is smaller than L discounted (multiplied) by P, or $B < PL$, and if this condition is satisfied then the potential injurer can be said to be negligent if he fails to take the precaution. This is the negligence formula of Judge Learned Hand, announced in a judicial opinion in 1947[6] but not recognized as economic formula for negligence until many years later. It is a simple formula but its elaboration and application to specific doctrines in the law of torts have generated an immense and illuminating literature.

By glancing at the Hand Formula you can see how an injurer could be deemed negligent even if the probability of an accident were very low (because B might be low or L very high), or even if the cost of avoiding the injury were very high (because P and/or L might be very high). You can put a minus sign before B, and thus model the case in which the injurer would incur a cost saving by not injuring: the case, in short, of deliberate injury; and you would see how in that case the injury is never cost-justified. Or you can think of B not as the cost of taking a precaution, but as the cost of reducing the output or other activity of the potential injurer, since that's another way of avoiding injuring people. And that will give you a clue to the role, or a role, of strict liability in the law. Suppose you kept a tiger in your backyard for self-defense, and the tiger got out and bit a neighbor's head off. It would be a case of high P and high L, and maybe high B in the sense that you couldn't have been

---

6. United States v. Carroll Towing Co., 159 F.2d 169 (2d Cir.1947).

more careful than you were to keep the tiger in your yard; but B might have been low if viewed as the cost of not having a tiger at all, of substituting another method of self-protection; and in fact this is a case where strict liability is imposed.

Well, I could go on and on with these examples, moving from one tort doctrine to another through the whole field of torts and then to contracts and property and so on throughout the legal system. But time does not permit that and if you want a fuller sketch of the field today, I suggest you take a look at my book *Economic Analysis of Law*, a new edition of which has just appeared.[7] I want to move on to the two specific uses of economic analysis that I said I'd concentrate on—making law simpler and challenging you to defend your values. I shall begin with a case that the Supreme Court decided in 1911, an antitrust case called *Dr. Miles*.[8] The issue was the legality under the Sherman Act of a contract that a supplier of patent medicines entered into with his dealers forbidding them to charge a price for his medicines lower than the retail price that he fixed; this is the practice known as resale price maintenance. The Supreme Court, holding the practice illegal, noted that it had the same effect as would an agreement among the dealers to fix the price at which they would sell Dr. Miles's medicines: a dealers' cartel. But the Court overlooked another effect. If dealers cannot compete in price, yet would make money if they could sell more, they will compete in nonprice dimensions of competition, such as stocking more inventory or having better-informed salespeople. If these services are important to the manufacturer's marketing strategy, he can use resale price maintenance to evoke them. For by setting the minimum resale price above the dealer's barebones cost of sale, dealers will vie to get additional sales by offering customers more service, until eventually they bid away the profit built into the minimum resale price, which is just what the manufacturer wants.

A dealers' cartel would have this effect too; members of the cartel, each of whom would like to increase his sales at the cartel price because it's above cost, will try to attract customers away from other dealers by offering better service. The difference is that the dealer may be providing more service than the customer wants, in the sense that the customer might prefer a lower price with less service. If that is what the customer prefers,[9] the supplier, if he is doing the price-fixing, will give it to him; for otherwise the supplier will lose business and profits to a competitor. But if the customers want a lower price and less service, competition will force the

---

7. Richard A. Posner, *Economic Analysis of Law* (5th ed. 1998).

8. Dr. Miles Medical Co. v. John D. Park & Sons Co., 220 U.S. 373 (1911).

9. More precisely, the marginal customer, but I will not pursue that refinement. See Posner, note 7 above, at 321.

supplier to give them that, provided the dealers aren't allowed to collude.

I now skip to what may seem an unrelated topic. Critics of the deregulation of the airline industry have pointed out that airline service is in some respects inferior to what it was in the days when it was a regulated industry. Planes are more crowded, there is less legroom, and the food is poorer. Gone are the piano bars from American Airlines' 747s. This is what economics predicted. The regulated airline industry was a government enforced cartel. Prices were kept high and as a result the industry was deflected into nonprice competition. When the airlines had finally competed away all their cartel profits in the form of service competition, the industry was ripe for deregulation. And when it was finally deregulated, price fell and with it the level of service, because this was what the consuming public wanted, as we can infer from the enormous growth in air travel since deregulation.

So we see, and this is the point of the discussion, that resale price maintenance of patent medicines and the deregulation of airline transportation raise the same economic issue, that of the relation between price and nonprice competition, even though one involves goods and the other services, one is old and one is recent, and one involves the judicial interpretation of the antitrust laws and the other legislative reform of common carrier regulation. And this is the sort of thing we encounter all the time in the economic analysis of law. Practices, institutions, bodies of law that seem wholly disparate from the standpoint of orthodox legal analysis are seen to involve the identical economic issue. Whole fields of law are interchangeable when viewed through the lens of economics. When I was a law student, the law seemed an assemblage of completely unrelated rules, procedures, and institutions. Economics reveals a "deep structure" of law that exhibits considerable coherence.

Consider the famous tort case of *Eckert v. Long Island R.R.*[10] A man saw a child on the railroad tracks. A train that was being operated negligently (that's crucial, as you'll see in a moment) was bearing down. The man dashed forward, scooped up the child, tossed the child to safety, but was himself killed. Should the railroad be held liable to the rescuer for its negligence? Or should he be held to have assumed the risk? The issue is one of tort law but a helpful way to approach it is in terms of contract. Ask the question this way: if transaction costs, that is, the costs of negotiating a contract between the railroad and potential rescuers, had been low, rather than prohibitive because the potential rescuers were not identified, would the railroad have negotiated a contract whereby a rescuer of a person endangered by the railroad's negli-

---

10.　43 N.Y. 502 (1871).

gence would be compensated if the rescuer was killed or injured in the rescue attempt, provided he was acting reasonably? The answer is probably yes, the railroad would make such a contract. Here's why. The railroad would be liable under tort law to the person saved if he weren't saved. And so the rescuer would be conferring an expected benefit on the railroad for which the railroad would be happy to pay provided the expected cost of the rescue to the railroad was less. In *Eckert* the rescue was successful. Suppose the child's life was worth as much as the rescuer's, say $X; and suppose further that the rescuer had only a 10 percent chance of being killed in the course of the rescue (and a zero chance if the rescue was unsuccessful). Then, ex ante, which is to say before the outcome of the rescue attempt was known, the railroad would have been eager to make the contract I have described. For the expected benefit to it would have been $.9X, since in nine cases out of ten it would save the full $X damages judgment.

While you ponder that example, let me move on to the second use of economics in law, what I have called challenging your values. I'll use as my opening text a short article by the well-known Harvard political theorist Michael Sandel in a recent issue of the *New Republic*.[11] The article surprisingly conjoins approval of baby selling with condemnation of contracts of surrogate motherhood. A doctor named Hicks, practicing medicine in the rural South during the 1950s and 1960s, "had a secret business selling babies on the side." He was also an abortionist, and "sometimes he persuaded young women seeking abortions to carry their babies to term, thus creating the supply that met the demand of his childless customers." Sandel believes that the doctor's "black market in babies" had morally redeeming features, thus unconsciously echoing a position that an economist and I took in an article published twenty years ago,[12] but he thinks that surrogate motherhood has no morally redeeming features.

Sandel's attempt to distinguish the practices reveals an ignorance of basic economic principles. To begin with, he points out that compared to Dr. Hicks's "homespun enterprise, commercial surrogacy, a $40 million industry, is big business." But Sandel is comparing one seller in a market to an entire market, and moreover one seller in an illegal market, where sellers conceal themselves, to an entire legal market. With more than a million abortions a year, the potential for "baby selling," if legalized, to eclipse commercial surrogacy is manifest.

11. Michael Sandel, "The Baby Bazaar," *New Republic*, Oct. 20, 1997, p. 25.

12. Elisabeth M. Landes and Richard A. Posner, "The Economics of the Baby Shortage," 7 *Journal of Legal Studies* 323 (1978).

Sandel's principal ground of distinction between baby selling and surrogate motherhood is different; it is that commercial surrogacy, unlike what Dr. Hicks did, encourages what Sandel, using a Marxist term, calls commodification, but which just means commercialization. "Dr. Hicks's black market in babies responded to a problem that arose independent of market considerations. He did not encourage the unwed mothers whose babies he sold to become pregnant in the first place." He did not have to. Demand evokes supply. Women who knew there was a market for their baby if they did not want to keep it would tend to use less care to avoid becoming pregnant. No doubt fewer women knew there was a market than would if it were a legal market rather than a black market. But Sandel does not suggest that Dr. Hicks's practice is redeemed by having been illegal!

I do not suggest that on the basis of my economic analysis those of you who are opposed to surrogate motherhood should give up your opposition. I don't believe that economics (or any other body of thought, for that matter) can compel a moral judgment. But those of you who are opposed to surrogate motherhood may feel pressed by my analysis to reconsider your opposition. Maybe you agree with Sandel that what Dr. Hicks did was not immoral even though it was illegal, and maybe you agree with me that Sandel has committed an economic error in thinking that what Hicks did was different from what the commercial surrogacy industry is doing and that it makes a difference that he was just one person and the commercial surrogacy industry consists of a number of persons.

Here is a different and (though I promised you simplicity) somewhat more complex example.[13] The federal pension law, ERISA, provides that if an employer establishes a defined-benefits pension plan—he doesn't have to establish any pension plan, let alone a defined-benefits plan, but if he does—it has to provide for the vesting of the employee's rights under the plan after five years. The purpose is to correct an abuse consisting of establishing a nonvesting pension plan and then firing an employee on the eve of his retirement.

The economist asked to evaluate this provision in ERISA would want to consider first how common this nonvesting scam would be in the absence of the law and whether forbidding it might have bad effects, in particular on the intended beneficiaries, the employees. Before the law was passed (in 1974), depending on the rules of vesting and of crediting years of service adopted by the particular plan a worker who left before retirement age might find himself

13. The discussion that follows is   374.
based on Posner, note 7 above, at 371–

with a pension benefit worth much less than his contributions and perhaps worth nothing at all. So he had a strong incentive to remain with the same company until he reached retirement age. And the employer had the power to expropriate employees' firm-specific human capital—which is to say the earning power an employee has that is tied to his working for this particular firm, so that he would earn less working for any other firm—by threatening to fire them before their pension rights vested if they insisted on a salary commensurate with their value to the company. One could imagine an employer reducing the employee's wage to a point at which the wage and the pension benefit together would just exceed the employee's wage in his next best job. So the year before the employee retired and became eligible for the pension the wage might be zero or even negative; the employee would pay to be allowed to work long enough to become entitled to his pension.

I may seem to have just made a strong economic case for ERISA's vesting provision. Yet empirical study has shown that employer pension practices were rarely exploitative before ERISA, and that the law was mainly motivated by abuses associated with multiemployer pension plans administered by the teamsters and other unions. The reason the companies' pension practices were not exploitative was first of all that the terms of retirement, including pension rights, are a matter of contractual negotiation between employer and prospective employee, not a unilateral imposition. Even if a particular employer refused to negotiate separately with each employee but offered terms of employment on a take-it-or-leave-it basis, competition among employers would give prospective employees a choice between different wage-benefit packages. The packages offered by some employers would emphasize good retirement or other benefits at the cost of lower wages, while those offered by other employers would emphasize high wages at the cost of less generous or secure retirement or other benefits. Employees would tend to be sorted to employers according to the individual employee's preferences regarding risk and the allocation of consumption over the life cycle.

As for incomplete vesting, by making pension benefits contingent on the employee's remaining with the firm and performing satisfactorily it facilitated the recovery by employers of their investment in their employees' firm-specific human capital. This would be expected to lead to more investment and higher wages. Incomplete vesting also solved the problem of the employee who being about to retire no longer has an incentive to work hard. It solved this problem, what economists call the "last-period problem," not only with the stick (the threat of discharge before pension rights vested) but also with the carrot, since pension benefits are usually heavily weighted in favor of the employee's wage in his last years of employment.

The employer's incentive to abuse the power that incomplete vesting conferred on him by reneging on his unwritten contract to deal fairly with his employees was held in check by his concern with preserving a reputation for fair dealing (if he lost that, he would have to pay new employees higher wages) and by the bargaining power that the possession of firm-specific human capital confers on a worker. (If he quit in anger or disgust, or was fired to eliminate his pension benefits, the firm would have to invest in training a green employee to replace him.) In fact, as I have said, before ERISA opportunistic discharges of workers covered by a pension plan were rare; and the statute has had no detectable impact on discharges of covered workers.

But by limiting incomplete vesting, the Act has tended to reduce the control of employers over their older employees. Such a loss of control would be expected to have two bad effects on the employees themselves. The first would be to lead employers to invest less in the employees' firm-specific human capital, and so the employee's productivity and hence wage will be lower. Second, because employers would have a smaller investment in the employees to protect and the employees would have less incentive to perform well (not being faced with a substantial loss of pension benefits if they were fired), employers would be expected to resort more frequently to an explicit or implicit threat of discharge in order to maintain discipline. And third, anything, legal or otherwise, that adds to the cost of employing a worker will cause employers to employ fewer workers or to pay them lower wages or both.

Even if you agree with my economic analysis, you may feel that on balance it is more important for workers to have secure pension rights or greater autonomy from their employers. But, once again, you will be forced to ask yourself whether your feeling is strong enough to offset the consequences brought out by economic analysis, including adverse consequences on the workers themselves, in the form of lower wages—or even, ironically, *less* secure employment.

I've given two examples of what might be called the "conservative" bias of economics. But actually economics is pretty value-neutral, or at least aspires to be value neutral, and there are many liberal practitioners of economic analysis of law, such as Guido Calabresi of Yale and now of the Second Circuit and John Donohue of Stanford. And so I'll close with an example of how economics can throw some cold water on a policy that conservatives favor.[14]

14. The discussion that follows is based on id. at 66–67; Daniel A. Farber, "Economic Analysis and Just Compensa- tion," 12 *International Review of Law and Economics* 125, 131–132 (1992).

Consider statutes that empower the government to designate a building's façade as a landmark; upon designation, the owner cannot alter the façade. An alternative to designation would be the purchase (possibly backed up by the threat of condemnation, subject to payment of just compensation) by the government of an easement in the façade. This is favored by most conservatives. They believe that the government should not be permitted to get things for nothing and in the process impose heavy costs on the owners of property. And so they urge that the principle of just compensation be given maximum play. They would be inclined to argue, these conservatives, that landmark-preservation statutes lead the government to designate too many landmarks compared to a regime in which the government must pay the owner of the landmark for the reduction in his property values as a result of his not being allowed to alter the façade.

Actually, it is unclear that there would be fewer landmarks designated under the payment approach. The very fact that there is no compensation under the typical landmark-preservation statute means that landmark owners will resist designation by complaining to their congressmen, bringing other pressure to bear on the designating authority, hiring lawyers to find loopholes in the statute, even organizing the defeat or repeal of the legislation. The resistance of taxpayers to paying the taxes necessary to finance a program of buying landmark easements might be less. Government tax and spend programs (agricultural subsidies, for example) are often as socially costly as regulatory programs, the costs being spread so thinly over the taxpaying public that few taxpayers squawk.

Might the government, however, because it isn't putting its money where its mouth is, designate the "wrong" landmarks, that is, property that would be worth a lot more in an altered state? Possibly not, since the greater the alternative value the stronger the resistance to the designation. There is, to be sure, a danger of reducing the supply of landmarks under the designation approach; building owners may rush to demolish potential landmark façades in advance of designation. But that is not the nature of the conservatives' objection.

The basic problem with that objection is its implicit assumption that the government is an ordinary purchaser and so responds to financial incentives just as a private purchaser would. The government is not an ordinary purchaser, and in fact it is meaningless to speak of *making* the government pay for the things it wants just like everybody else, when the government *must* resort to coercion to obtain the money it uses to pay for the things it wants. To pay just compensation for a taking, or even to make a voluntary arms' length purchase without any implicit threat of resorting to condemnation if the seller refuses to sell, the government must first take, without any compensation, the necessary funds from the taxpayer. Just compensation entails an anterior act of expropriation.

So, once again, given the practical consequences illuminated by economics of substituting a payment scheme for the present landmark designation statutes, those of you who support the just compensation principle on moral or political grounds will have to consider how much you're willing to pay for the principle, for it may turn out that government may take more resources out of the private sector and freeze more landmarks if it is forced to the just compensation route rather than the landmark designation route.

As these examples illustrate, the role of economics in moral and political debate is to draw attention to consequences or implications that people ignorant of economics commonly overlooked. What you do with those consequences is your business. The basic job of the economist is to remind us of the consequences, often though not always adverse or at least costly, of acts or practices that we might otherwise think clearly good or clearly bad.

Study Questions:

1. What is the difference between "positive" and "normative" analysis of the law?

2. What is the relationship between Sandel's concern about surrogacy and Sunstein's lecture (Chapter 8) on social norms?

3. What would be Epstein's (Chapter 9) view of the statutes that enable governments to designate facades as landmarks? Would he agree with Posner?

4. What is the economic explanation for resale price maintenance? What was the error in *Dr. Miles*?

5. If lenders and borrowers prefer bankruptcy laws that are neither too strict (one must repay under any condition) nor too lax (one does not have to repay at all), why is it necessary for the government to mandate a particular bankruptcy system? Why not allow lenders and borrowers to make their own arrangements by contract?

*

11. Carrots and Torts

Saul Levmore[1]

I.   Positive and Negative Incentives in Private and Public Law

The study and practice of law begins with legal rules but turns
rather quickly to the ability of parties to bargain around rules.
Rules are sometimes little more than starting points for bargains.
And to the extent that "thinking like a lawyer" has come to mean
designing bargains around rules, the clever lawyer and lawmaker
see that nearly every rule and bargain have a mirror image. This
lecture is about the choice between these images. In most cases the
choice is between positive and negative incentives.

The easiest place to consider this relationship among rules,
bargains, and mirror images is where simple torts are concerned.
Imagine that A does a variety of things that annoy B. The rules of a
legal system will tell us which of these annoyances create claims
that B might usefully pursue against A through the court system.
A's actions may all burden B, but only some of these give B the
right to collect from A. These rights are normally associated with
legal doctrines, and these doctrines—along with the ability to use
them imaginatively—keep most lawyers busy.

The leap from rules to bargains is often associated with law
and economics because that methodology has drawn attention to
the counterintuitive and remarkable possibility that these rules
may not much matter. Even where B can collect from A, A might
often avoid liability by bargaining in advance with B for the right to
do as A pleases. To the extent that B's initial claim against A arises
in tort, we might say that the tort suggests a carrot. In this case
the law offers a legal remedy to the harmed party, but the very
shadow of that remedy suggests to the potential injurer that the
legal rule might in some sense be purchased by the private offering
of an inducement to the party who might otherwise seek a legal
remedy against the injurer. Thus, by bargaining in advance with B,
A can acquire an easement in order to avoid what might otherwise
be regarded as a trespass, allowing B to collect damages from A.
Indeed, virtually any nascent tort by A against B can be trans-

1. William B. Graham Professor of
Law, University of Chicago. This lecture
was delivered in the autumn of 1998.

formed into a transaction in which A pays B to turn the other cheek or to avoid injury by taking some precaution.[2]

One generalization is that many legal rules are nothing more than starting points because affected parties can often bargain around rules. A related idea is that legal constraints are sometimes nothing more than prices; A can sometimes behave as she pleases and simply pay B according to the legal rule or some other amount to which B agrees.[3] But even where this is not the case, because repeated "violations" will incur prohibitive costs in the form of more serious legal remedies, it is sometimes the case that A may do as she likes if she secures B's permission (or property) in advance. Conversely, A may alter her behavior because the law insists on it, because the law makes such behavior modification worthwhile, or because B makes it worthwhile.

Tort law emphasizes cases where the law offers a kind of negative incentive, in the form of liability for the failure to take precautions, and where private bargains may in the law's shadow offer positive incentives. But of course law itself can choose between positive and negative incentives, and the larger point is that for every penalty designed to affect behavior there is a corresponding reward—and for every reward, a corresponding penalty. In the public sphere it is now commonplace to observe that every tax suggests a corresponding subsidy. A government that wishes to encourage fuel-efficient vehicles can, among other things, tax heavy, gas guzzling vehicles but it might instead subsidize fuel efficient vehicles. And a federal government that seeks to direct the activities of its states can threaten dire consequences to those that decline to follow central commands or, alternatively, it can offer conditional grants to those states that conform to the central government's wishes. Much as good lawyers have learned through a combination of theory and practice that many paths can lead to the same result,[4] policymakers have also learned to substitute back and

---

2. There are circumstances where A must gain B's consent–and where A even contracts for payment *from* B–or A's behavior is tortious, as when A plans to perform a medical procedure on B. But my focus is on payments from A to B in order to establish the normal substitution between positive and negative inducements.

3. A well known article on the subject is Robert Cooter, Prices and Sanctions, 84 Colum. L. Rev. 1523 (1984).

4. Ironically, it is sometimes easier to see the penalty-reward equivalence, or substitution, where bargaining is difficult and where institutional design seems more relevant than the Coase Theorem. Thus, where A is inclined to pollute less because A's neighbor B can collect damages, many lawyers have trouble seeing that in the absence of such a legal remedy B might buy A's property or induce A to reduce the pollution. Similarly, where A would like to pollute as before and, if necessary, simply pay B the damages allowed by law, many lawyers have trouble seeing that a legal rule in B's favor might well not generate a decrease in pollution. In contrast, virtually all citizens see that the government can reduce smoking by taxing tobacco or subsidizing its curtailment. Note, in passing, that equivalent

forth between positive and negative inducements.[5]

From the lawmaker's perspective, an important and omnipresent question in many situations is therefore whether to try to influence behavior with positive or negative incentives. When the answer is positive there is then the secondary question of how to finance the incentive, and when a negative incentive is preferred there is the question of who benefits from liability payments or a fine (or how to finance enforcement or a costly negative incentive such as incarceration). These secondary questions might determine the correct answer to the primary question (of positive versus negative incentives), although it is rare for the debate to go this deep.

Some of the examples already used, and more to come, point to the literature on framing effects. Analytically equivalent rewards and penalties might produce very different reactions because most of us do not process information as automatons. In some settings we might be more receptive to positive inducements than to painful blows to our egos. This may be because of a kind of loss aversion or because we are "fooled" by rhetoric, or the style of the incentives. In a variety of settings the very choice between penalties and rewards seems to convey a message that influences the recipient. At the personal level, what qualifies as polite behavior in a given culture often proves to be useful behavior as well. And at the international level, nations are careful in choosing whether to offer carrots or to threaten sticks. One rarely threatens allies, but one is also careful not to offer carrots where it might look as if evil had been rewarded and therefore ultimately encouraged. We would not have paid South Africa to end apartheid, even if boycotts seemed ineffective.

For the most part, I will try to set these things aside or to imagine that these convictions about moral distinctions might themselves be the products of other differences. One reason for this limiting move is that I hope to show that a law-and-economics approach illuminates the choice between carrots and sticks in ways that are useful even to those who normally look to other disciplines

results sometimes entail very different incidence of costs. But inasmuch as it is hard to generalize about the distributional effects of positive versus negative incentives, these are generally treated as beyond the reach of this essay.

5. I do not mean to imply that law and economics deserves sole credit for this analytic advance. The reward-penalty equivalence arises in many settings and is the stuff of predictable fads. Thus, one generation of parents might

be encouraged to discipline children who misbehave while the next is encouraged to shower praise on children when they are good. Grade inflation in higher education might be understood in a similar vein. High grades for achievers are now the fashion, where low and even failing grades for modest underachievers was once the norm. From parenting to managing business employees to grading, sticks are currently in disfavor and carrots are in vogue.

for insights about behavior and the design of legal rules. Another reason is that much as human psychology might suggest the advantages of sweet carrots, these positive incentives are often costly—and there are other powerful aversions to higher taxes and other sources of financing for these incentives. Put in positive terms, there is no shortage of sticks in the world of law. Tort law and various regulations and sanctions are everywhere. Even if it is generally true that private parties prefer bonuses and other carrots rather than sticks, our governments do not spare us their rods in favor of rewards when it comes to such things as pollution control and a host of other social problems. One purpose of this exercise is to understand why this is so.[6]

To summarize, law and economics teaches us to hold up rules and provisions to a special kind of mirror, looking for a carrot equivalent for each stick and vice versa. This is indeed an important insight. But there are reasons sometimes to prefer one or the other, which is to say that sticks and carrots are not perfect substitutes. It is to these reasons that I now turn.

II.   Imprecision and Moral Hazards

Consider first the fairly simple public policy goal of encouraging motorists and other occupants of vehicles to wear seat belts. About one-third of motorists do not wear them. A legal system might apply penalties or threats of liability (or the threat of a contributory negligence rule) to those who do not fasten their seat belts. Alternatively, the system can offer rewards to those who conform with the same safety rules. Minor penalties for the failure to buckle up are common, although various localities have tried mirror-image rewards. Indeed, there is even the possibility of public or private rewards to randomly selected motorists who are found to be wearing seat belts. But such rewards, or carrots, are unusual. A fairly conventional reaction to the preference for sticks over carrots in this setting is to say that since there are twice as many seat belt wearers as non-wearers it is easier to aim sticks at the smaller group than to offer carrots to the larger group. This reaction represents a kind of raw transaction costs approach to the choice between positive inducements and negative threats. The basic strategy is to compare the cost of administering rewards to one group with that of leveling penalties on another, and in most cases this amounts to looking for the smaller of the groups and directing the

---

6. One obvious reason for fewer sticks in the private sphere is that there is less of a captive audience. The government can usually choose between carrots and sticks but if a private party tries to influence customers or businesses it must generally offer a benefit. It has no right to "tax" other private parties until they agree to be, or are somehow locked into being, part of its schemes. But even here, framing issues are omnipresent and I mean to hold them constant rather than to dismiss them.

incentives at that group. Put differently, one can normally reward or penalize every member of a target group or a randomly selected subset of that group. In most cases, the smaller the number of subjects, the more the reward or penalty is multiplied. Thus, a speeding driver who is apprehended might be subject to a significant fine, and this fine might be increased as the probability of detection drops.

But where detection is fairly easy, it is both sensible and politically expedient to have a policy that both avoids the unnecessary introduction of chance and minimizes administrative costs, and this is normally done by rewarding or penalizing all members of the target group. In the university setting, for example, incentives are sought to encourage the timely payment of tuition. The university might reward those who are timely or penalize those who are tardy. All members of these groups are easy to identify, and this ease of detection enables precision. Administrative costs are then minimized by focusing on the smaller group, consisting of those who are late with their payments. Somewhat similarly, and on a national scale, everyone who files a late income tax return is penalized, and almost everyone who files a tax return and has a minor child receives an exemption, and so forth. We prefer exactness rather than lotteries, and sometimes the choice between carrots and sticks is made on the basis of which provides for less costly exactness. There are many explanations for this taste for (easy) precision, including risk attitudes, fear of uneven enforcement, and chilling effects, but I think we can simply proceed with the observation that where detection and administration are relatively easy, the preference for precision makes the method of regulation fairly obvious. In other cases, as we will see, there are secondary effects, or costs, that are serious enough to drive the preferred method away from that suggested by merely comparing the sizes of the groups that can be encouraged or discouraged.

In any event, there are many settings where we cannot possibly expect to reward all who are well behaved or to penalize all who violate a rule. In these cases precision is costly or even impossible and it is often not obvious how much weight to attach to first-level, or administrative, costs which will still normally be lower if incentives are aimed at the smaller group. In the seat belt case for, example, we can identify some random set of those drivers without seatbelts, and then raise the penalty to make its expected value appropriate. Alternatively, we can find some random set of belted drivers, and then treat them to appropriately enlarged rewards. The penalty might need greater enlargement than the reward because there are more drivers who wear belts than drivers who do not. But once we are in the game of multiplying penalties or rewards, and doing expected value calculations, there is something of a new degree of freedom in fashioning tools of social control. Once we abandon precision as too costly, there seems to be little opposition to yet further reductions in precision.

Second-level costs are often more obvious where some imprecision is an accepted part of the landscape. We can compensate for inexactness or underenforcement by randomly stopping some drivers and then either giving large rewards to those who have fastened their seatbelts or placing large penalties on those who have not. But if we give large rewards to occasionally selected seat belt wearers, there is the danger that car owners will start cruising in their vehicles (with seat belts fastened, of course) not so much for transportation purposes but in order to earn the reward! We may even perversely increase the number of accidents by offering these carrots, in which case the reward system can be characterized as a moral hazard.

To be sure, penalties for non-belt-wearers will also require augmentation in order to compensate for the inability to detect every violation. Fortunately, this large penalty will not symmetrically cause risk averse persons to avoid driving (even where it is efficient to drive) because they can avoid the stick by wearing a seat belt. In short, substantial rewards may induce more driving, and inefficient driving at that, but it is unlikely that substantial penalties will discourage much efficient driving. We might, I suppose, try a system in which drivers received rewards if they wore seat belts and could show that they were engaging in useful driving, but this seems very difficult to administer.

In sum, there will surely be cases where the second-level effects of penalties may be as troublesome as those associated with rewards, or more so, but the main point here is that it is to these second level effects that we must normally look in order to see the nonequivalence of penalties and rewards. Put somewhat differently, these secondary affects suggest that there is more to carrots and sticks than mere choices as to framing.

If we carry the analysis over to excessively fast driving, other secondary effects further complicate the matter. Again, speeding drivers could be deterred by fines or through the prospect of private tort claims. Alternatively, rewards could be offered to those drivers who do not speed, or more realistically to some modest fraction of these model drivers. But, again, these rewards might generate additional, socially inefficient driving. The tort form of the penalty has the advantage of offering some compensation directly to those who lose the most from excessive driving speeds and it has the advantage of stimulating a private enforcement mechanism. The tort remedy is most attractive when it provides optimal deterrence, as it might if the only harm caused by speeding is accidents, and if all these accidents generate tort claims. If, on the other hand, there is underdeterrence, then the system might work with enlarged recoveries or use some public enforcement or remedy alongside private tort suits. The former can create a moral hazard if would-be victims are able to put themselves at risk. The latter raises the possibility that private parties will settle on the side (at too low a price) in order to diminish the payments otherwise collected for the public coffers.

The preceding discussion offers a glimpse of the problem with public enforcement quite generally. If well behaved drivers earn rewards, then there is the problem of corruption in identifying those who get these rewards. The rewards might go to those who bargain with the police (or other authority entrusted with enforcement) rather than to those who actually drive properly. It might seem that the same problem appears when penalties are used. Someone who speeds and is required to pay the victim and the state, or someone who through police enforcement is required to pay a large fine, might succeed in bargaining with this private or public enforcer by paying a side amount rather than the legislated amount. But this is not necessarily destructive, because there remains a powerful incentive to drive safely. Very serious corruption might well do the system in; if, for example, the enforcement authorities threaten drivers with fines regardless of whether they are actually speeding, then the problem is truly serious. Still, the penalty system is probably superior to the reward system because it is a bit easier to monitor the corruption accompanying the penalty system.[7] But assuming some personal or evidentiary integrity to the system, the secondary effects here suggest that torts or other sticks are probably superior to carrots. It is this sort of logic that explains, I think, our preference for sticks rather than carrots in combating speeding and the like.

III. Secondary and Tertiary Effects

Similar secondary effects dominate other incentive schemes where the prospect of rewards seems less fanciful. Consider a (purely hypothetical) proposal to encourage, for better or worse, a parent to stay home with young children. For every positive incentive, a negative counterpart comes to mind. That is, after all, one familiar lesson drawn from the basic insight about bargaining around rules. Moreover, where family membership or other easily confirmed matters are concerned, the tax system offers an ongoing

---

7. Unjustly levied penalties can be uncovered by spot checks of the underlying behavior. If another citizen or officer observes the same driving behavior and finds it unobjectionable, then suspicion will fall on an enforcer who levied a penalty with respect to the same behavior. In contrast, an enforcer who colludes in favoring some drivers with rewards will be harder to unmask because the underlying driving behavior may be perfectly good.

reporting vehicle that makes positive and negative incentives comparable in terms of administrative and enforcement costs.[8] But the tax system need not be the delivery vehicle. Roughly speaking, one can design tax and non-tax versions of both reward and penalty schemes. In the case of incentives for parents to stay home with young children, for example, the government could pay parents who stay home or it could offer a tax deduction or credit to such parents. On the penalty side, the government could charge parents who do not stay home (an option that seems a bit excessive for any current tastes), or it could tax dual career couples heavily (through progressive rates, perhaps) in order to discourage decisions to work out of the house and to out-source child care. The government could also increase its regulation of for-profit child care and in this manner raise its price. Every carrot seems to have a corresponding stick,[9] and most of these positive and negative incentive schemes come in tax and non-tax versions. In most cases the administrative, or first level transaction, costs, of the alternative systems do not differ in ways that explain the likely choice among policy tools.

The important differences, once again, are found in the secondary effects. If there is a reward attached to staying home with children, then, on the margin, responsive parents might not only stay home but also have more children. And a penalty in the form of a tax or regulatory cost for those who have children but do not stay home might have the secondary effect of a lower birth rate.[10] These secondary effects might be welcome news to some citizens and interest groups, while they might deter others from supporting the penalty or reward they otherwise favored in the interest of the stay-at-home goal, but the point is that these secondary effects undo the penalty-reward equivalence. A political coalition in favor of encouraging parents to stay home with children may be unable to agree on a means to this end because members of the coalition

---

8. Drivers might self-report the number of miles they drive, as they often do to their insurers or state tax assessors, because there is some prospect of spot checks of odometers and the like. It would be more difficult to design a workable system in which drivers reported (and were rewarded or penalized accordingly) their seat-belt usage or excessive driving behavior. In the example that follows in the text, taxpayers report facts that are fairly easily observed long after filing, such as the birth or presence of a child.

9. There is no need to pause and define "corresponding" or the "mirror image" expression used earlier. The basic idea remains that of identifying a behavioral aim and seeing that if one can get there with a penalty (reward) incentive, then one can usually get to the same place with a reward (penalty) scheme.

10. There is the possibility of a penalty for those who leave home or a reward for those who stay home regardless of the presence of children, and it is even possible that these incentives could be calibrated to achieve (or maintain) the desired birth rate. But the efficiency costs of such schemes are likely to be prohibitive because the assumption is that the lawmakers have no interest in discouraging out of house work on the part of those who do not have children at home.

disagree on the question of whether to encourage higher or lower birth rates. It may be difficult to affect the child-care decision while leaving birth rates unchanged.

There is also a kind of tertiary effect, as is generally the case when a proposal is not revenue neutral. If, for example, we pay those who stay home with children, then the likely source of financing is a tax increase on some or all of those who work. And if the higher tax rates encourage work over leisure, this could lead to yet more work, fewer rather than more stay-at-homers, and finally a lower birth rate.[11] On the other hand, higher tax rates might on the margin encourage substitution away from work and to untaxed leisure or home-staying. These tertiary effects are surely small and unlikely to offset the secondary effects. But, again, various members of a political coalition in favor of the original policy of encouraging parental child care might prefer the reward or penalty strategy–or no strategy—because of these secondary and tertiary effects.

It is important to see that these various complications do not simply offset one another or add a layer of complexity that changes nothing. In some cases, and perhaps more often than not, a reward will produce hazardous secondary effects that can defeat the primary goal for which the reward was designed; meanwhile, the corresponding penalty may avoid defeating the primary goal because the penalized behavior can be specified sufficiently to reduce undesirable effects. Furthermore, where this contrast between rewards and penalties has a relationship to the size of the groups in need of rewarding or penalizing, the size differential is itself likely to reinforce the choice between penalties and rewards suggested by first-level transaction costs. These rather non-intuitive, abstract claims are easiest to see with concrete illustrations.

Consider, for instance, the seat belt example, where rewards might encourage inefficient driving and penalties might chill efficient driving. The latter problem seems modest because the penalty (however magnified to take account of inexactness and underenforcement) is easily avoided by wearing one's belt. Inasmuch as this is easier to monitor than is the question of whether a given car trip is efficient or motivated by the reward, the penalty appears superior. This superiority can be traced to a number of things. First, it is a function of "technology" in the sense that it is easy to observe a fastened seat belt and difficult to observe a "good" car trip or a trip that should have been taken but was not. That fastened belts can

11. Note that the effect on birth rates might be dampened by announcing that the incentives only apply to those who already have children. But taxpayers will know that the same plan might be used in the future. And even if taxpayers are unsure whether future programs will use rewards or penalties, there is likely to be some effect on birth rates.

easily be observed is not of itself important; it makes both penalties and rewards easy to assign. But the ease of observation means that drivers need not be chilled from efficient driving. If we could easily observe and distinguish good from bad car trips, we could protect against excessive driving caused by rewards; a secondary rule would simply limit the rewards to seat belts worn on "good" trips or would impose penalties on inefficient trips. And even if the primary behavior is not easily observed, we could protect against the undesirable chilling by penalizing some inefficient driving. In sum, the combination of easily monitored primary behavior (seat belt wearing) and less easily monitored secondary behavior (good trips and bad) creates circumstances where a penalty is superior to a reward.

Note that a policy maker can be fairly flexible with these tools. One can begin with rewards for seat belt wearing and then check to see whether there appears to be an increase in miles driven by all drivers. Gasoline sales might provide an indicator of mileage. If the reward does appear to have created a hazard, then it is appropriate to reduce the reward or try an offsetting penalty and so forth. Similarly, one can try a penalty and observe evidence of car usage. If this usage drops, then there is room to adjust to the apparent chilling effect that has reduced efficient driving.

If the setting is one where there are many more seat belt wearers than not, there is reason to think that the penalty is to be preferred over the reward. First-level transaction costs suggest that it might be easier to work on the smaller group, and in this case that consists of those who did not wear belts and might be penalized. At the level of secondary effects the slightly more subtle point is that those who did not wear belts have revealed themselves as both less likely to react to a reward by driving more and more likely to react to a penalty by driving less. Correspondingly, those who wore belts do not seem to mind doing so, as it were, and might therefore be more likely to cruise around in search of new rewards but not to cease driving because of any penalty. Put differently, if a reward generates a marked increase in driving, one might reasonably guess that the incremental driving was coming disproportionately from those who drove with belts before the reward.

All this suggests that where group C conforms to what the law desires and group D does not, and C is larger than D, there is reason to choose a penalty for the failure to conform. And this is especially the case where it is easy to observe the behavior sought by the law. Where it is easy to observe the secondary behavior, penalty-reward equivalence is reasserted.

There are other complexities to be noted here. There will be cases where the social costs associated with chilling are much greater (or less) than those associated with the extra behavior induced by rewards. In these cases the size of the groups will matter though obviously in a different way. Second, there is the problem of evaluating the law's aim in the first place. Seat belt wearing, for example, is not an end in itself but is a useful tool in a world in which it is difficult to undertake cost-benefit calculations particular to every driver and trip. Much was made of the ease of observing fastened seat belts, but the matter might have looked different if we compared the rewarding of "safely undertaken" trips to the penalizing of unsafe trips.

It is also useful to see that the significance of secondary effects has little to do with whether the system is exact or whether it places rewards and penalties on randomly chosen subsets of actors. In most of tort law, moral hazard problems arise where damages are multiplied. The more damages can be kept to a compensatory level, the more it will be true that all parties will avoid rather than encourage accidents. In the seat belt case, however, rewards are almost necessarily supercompensatory for many drivers. It is difficult to know each driver's reservation price, so that many will be paid more than necessary, and rewards are wasted on drivers who would have fastened their seat belts even in the absence of rewards.

This framework might explain why we rarely find mixed systems of rewards and penalties, a topic returned to below. Such mixed systems would seem like a clever solution to the problems caused by secondary effects because chills might be offset by rewards which encouraged the very same activity. There is, for example, the familiar idea that if rescues are discouraged (secondarily) by penalties, because potential rescuers might then avoid locations or activities where they could effect rescues—but might also be found to have wrongfully failed to rescue—then a coexisting reward for successful rescues (with a penalty for fraudulent behavior) might create a good package of incentives.[12] Somewhat similarly, the law might penalize the failure to wear seatbelts, but then try to compensate for the chilling effect on efficient driving, if any, by rewarding some drivers found with their seatbelts fastened. In theory, the potential reward could offset the chill associated with the penalty. The problem, however, is that drivers value these things disparately. A reward that offsets the chill on average (or for some drivers) will simply create a moral hazard for others who do not object to wearing seatbelts and who will be encouraged by the reward to undertake excessive driving.

---

12. William Landes & Richard Posner, Salvors, Finders, Good Samaritans, and Other Rescuers: An Economic Study of Law and Altruism, 7 J. Legal Stud. 83 (1978); Saul Levmore, Waiting for Rescue: An Essay on the Evolution and Incentive Structure of the Law of Affirmative Obligations, 72 Va. L. Rev. 879 (1986).

In some settings, the law might use categories to separate out areas where chilling effects or moral hazards are most troublesome. In rescue law, for example, the law might impose penalties for nonrescue, but decline to do so for the failure to rescue at a beach. The idea is to sort out circumstances where the chilling problem is most likely. It is arguable that admiralty law uses categories in just this way; it imposes penalties for some failures to rescue while land-based law does not.[13]

In some settings, however, it is difficult to separate out the secondary effects of penalties and rewards. Thus, if former employers or teachers who provide references are liable in the event that they negligently confuse two students, and then say something unsupportive about (the wrong) one, then these sources of information might simply decline to provide references. Potential beneficiaries can be seen as agreeing to a regime in which they ask for a recommendation and promise to hold all but bad-faith actors harmless. Note that in this setting we do have an absence of sticks where we fear the avoidance of rescue spots, in a sense. Moreover, the law does not combat the chilling effect by allowing sticks for negligent references but bundling them with carrots for decent references. It seems likely that such carrots would do more harm than good, as recommenders themselves might become less reliable as they competed for business.

By and large secondary effects play a more important role in illuminating the law's use of positive or negative inducements than in understanding private contracting. This is because private parties care less about some secondary effects and can use others to their benefit. Thus, where the government offers carrots for at-home childcare, there is the secondary effect on birth-rates. But when the employer puts in an inducement for course-taking, the secondary effect is that a job applicant who identifies as a likely course-taker might gravitate to that employer. If an employer paid a bonus to an employee who stayed home with a new baby for six months or penalized you if you give birth and come to work and do not stay home, there would also be secondary effects—but of course in most private cases there is either no such trigger event or at least none that the incentive designer dislikes. To the extent that employees self-select among employers, this is probably welcomed by the employer who wishes to encourage behavior such as course-taking. Indeed, an employer might offer an incentive plan for taking courses precisely in order to attract the sort of person who sees herself as one who self-improves. This is a secondary effect but from the employer's point of view it is entirely desirable.

13. See Levmore, supra, at 909–13.

These observations about secondary effects as the keys to understanding the choice between positive and negative incentives extend far into law's past. There are rules in Hammurabi's Code penalizing those who do not maintain irrigation systems properly.[14] Maintenance might have been encouraged by carrots as well. But unless these carrots are perfectly calibrated there is the danger that opportunistic persons will create leaks in order to repair them and the problem of distorting locational decisions because of the prospect of these carrots. Here, too, sticks seem superior to carrots where there is little uncertainty as to compliance with the rule, or standard of maintenance. Interestingly, Hammurabi's Code offers a mixture of incentives to surgeons; a reward for success and a penalty for failure.[15] I return to such mixtures below.

IV. Discontinuities

A. Contractual Carrots and Sticks

Secondary effects explain primary tools in private arrangements much as they do in regulatory decisions. Consider an employer who wants to encourage employees to take courses outside of the workplace in order to develop employees' skills. Carrots are conventional; employers often subsidize tuitions, offer release time, or promise higher pay to those employees who acquire the extra education. But there is, as always, a corresponding stick. The same employers might begin with a higher wage scale but threaten reduced compensation for those who do not take specified courses. Carrots are sweeter than switches, of course, and employers have no interest in paying a higher price to get the same result, but this begs the question of why our taste buds perform that way in the first place. It cannot simply be that most of us always hate to lose something rather than not to gain, because there is no shortage of sticks around. Contracts regularly contain penalties or damages, and salespeople are accustomed to bonuses for high sales but reductions in pay—and even loss of employment—for subpar results. In this tuition example, it happens that there is a handy tax explanation for the common use of rewards rather than penalties. The employer can deduct the expenses paid directly or indirectly for employee training, and employees are not taxed on the tuitions they receive. If instead compensation is raised and employees are penalized if they fail to take courses, then most employees will be unable to deduct the full cost of the courses and they will have higher income to report.

---

14. Saul Levmore, Rethinking Comparative Law: Variety and Uniformity in Ancient and Modern Tort Law, 31 Tulane L. Rev. 235, 258–60 (1986).

15. Id. at 261–65.

Consider next a typical automobile dealership that encourages its sales force by offering bonuses to its top two salespeople out of a staff of fifteen. The employer uses carrots for performance but could, of course, raise base compensation and levy penalties on the thirteen poorest performers. Even tournament theory with respect to compensation could be inverted.[16] Tournament theory suggests a grand prize for the best salesperson and lesser prizes for a few runner-ups. But tournament theory could just as well have generated a scheme with higher base pay and then no penalties for the best performer, substantial penalties for a few salespeople, and even greater penalties for the large majority.

These last examples suggest the presence of a cultural or expressive element. They may also reflect non-smooth utility functions, such that people are willing to trade small losses for the chance of a large life-changing gain. Many people buy lottery tickets or participate in betting pools in apparent quest of such a gain. It would be most surprising to find a thriving betting pool for a sports event requiring each entrant to put up $X with the promise of a loss of $X for the entrant who most mis-predicts the outcome of that event and a gain of a few dollars for all other participants. Betting pools, lotteries, and poker games are played for the chance of a big win and not for the chance to profit a small bit from a very few persons' large losses. Similar observations might explain typical bonuses to salespeople and the more general use of carrots rather than sticks in some settings.

B. Penalty Damages

The sometime equivalence of carrots and sticks plays an important role in the design and enforcement of contractual incentives. A might offer B, a building contractor, some positive inducement to complete a construction project according to some deadline. Alternatively, A might offer a higher base price for the project but stipulate that B will owe A certain liquidated damages if B fails to meet the deadline. Such damages present well-known problems of enforcement because courts will sometimes rule these incentives to be unenforceable "penalty damages."[17] One who breaches a contract pays damages based on what the breacher should have expected the other party to lose, and while customizing a contract is one way of changing the other party's expectations, courts are disinclined to enforce damage clauses if the damages seem like penalties rather than reasonable measures of the losses from breach. If S calls a taxi for a trip to the airport, and S informs the dispatcher on the telephone that "if I miss my plane I will forfeit a $250 gain I

16. Tournament theory suggests that it is sometimes wise to motivate a group with substantial prizes for top finishers.

17. E. Alan Farnsworth, Contracts 895–904 (1982).

expect to earn at my destination, and I will hold you responsible," then a court may refuse S's $250 claim even if the reason S misses his plane is that the taxi is late for the pick up, and surely if the reason is that the taxi has a flat tire on the way to the airport.[18] Academic commentary has been hostile to this unwillingness of courts to abide by an apparent bargain and by the logic of contract damages' information-forcing rules.[19]

The apparent equivalence of carrots and sticks raises the question of why these court decisions make any real difference. If penalty damages are scorned, then the drafter ought to use significant bonuses. Instead of a $30 fare for a taxi ride with $250 of specified damages, S might offer $280 if the taxi company is timely. If S is so cautious as to be concerned about the taxi not appearing on the appointed day, S might enter into the agreement a day in advance and say to the taxi company "pay me $250 today, and then tomorrow come take me to the airport and in the event of a timely arrival I'll pay $280 for the trip and nothing otherwise." Assuming that S is reliable, or that S's own promise can be bonded in some manner, the law's disinclination to respect penalty clauses (as well as the academic literature's distaste for this law) seems relatively unimportant—although it should be noted that it would not be shocking for a court to refuse to enforce a large bonus on grounds that it reflected a (disfavored) kind of gambling agreement. Indeed, the carrots-and-sticks scheme is surprisingly useful here; the insight that associates every carrot with a corresponding stick can be put to good use by the practicing lawyer who learns, in some cases subconsciously, to draft contracts with rewards rather than penalties. At the same time, it is noteworthy that there is little to gain by focusing on secondary effects. As a practical matter, if contracts with large bonuses were common, we would find contractors and taxi companies that expected to perform in timely fashion to be (mostly) indifferent between carrots and their correspondingly drawn sticks.

The choice between carrots and sticks is usefully viewed through the lens offered by the obvious question of why the law is indeed hostile to penalty damages in contract. There is, perhaps, the danger that serious "discontinuities," as I will call them, might encourage opportunistic behavior that would, in turn, be expensive for courts to sort out. If A contracts with B for the latter to complete a building project, with a large penalty due A if B finishes the work more than one week late, there is the danger that when A

---

18. The example may be especially interesting, or misleading, because regulated rates may prevent the taxi company from charging a premium in return for its exposure to high damages.

19. See Charles Goetz & Robert E. Scott, Liquidated Damages, Penalties and the Just Compensation Principle, 77 Colum. L. Rev. 554 (1977) (finding the traditional penalty rule anachronistic).

observes B close to meeting the contractual deadline, A may profit by sabotaging B's schedule in order to make B eight days late—and in order to allow A to collect from B more that A actually loses from the delay. To be sure, B might anticipate this hazard in advance, in which case B will hesitate to agree to penalties that are large enough to create this hazard. But B may have insufficient information in this regard. B might also agree only to a penalty after specifying reasons for delay that do and do not trigger the penalty clause. But this sort of approach is likely to generate a good deal of litigation, and courts may avoid this litigation by discouraging the trigger in the first place. Put simply, the discontinuity in the contract between A and B, as reflected in the liquidated penalty damage clause that is triggered by a certain amount of lateness, might lead to opportunistic behavior and litigation.

If it is true that courts will discourage discontinuities (such as serious penalties attached to work that is eight days rather than seven days late, because the discontinuity generates opportunities or sabotage, and so forth) then it follows that courts will be more accepting of continuous penalties. Thus, A might contract for a penalty of $x for each day that B is late. The continuous penalty is less likely to cause opportunistic behavior on A's part. Put differently, excessive damages will encourage opportunism by A but, holding that variable constant, a discontinuous term or trigger will further encourage opportunistic behavior by A.

In short, it is possible that the traditional doctrinal claim about penalty damages may camouflage the fact that the real target of judicial hostility is the prospect of opportunistic behavior by the party who hopes to collect damages. This behavior is more likely the more difficult it is to monitor and the more the damages exceed the real losses that are suffered. This behavior is also more likely where there are discontinuities in contractual terms because these discontinuities can make small opportunistic acts quite profitable. We might expect law to discourage these discontinuities in order to discourage opportunistic behavior and unnecessary litigation about such behavior.

One problem with this association of antipathy to penalty damages with the opportunism that discontinuous contractual terms can generate, is that positive inducements can also be discontinuous. D might offer E a carrot for timely performance that is far greater than D's true gain from timeliness. And D might then sabotage E's performance in order to avoid paying the carrot. Presumably, the carrot is attached to a lower base rate of compensation than would be found without the special inducement, so that D stands to gain from paying a lower price for a near-completed contract. This sort of strategic behavior by D works only if E does not anticipate this danger when entering into the original contract with its positive, discontinuous inducement. Similarly, opportunism is a significant factor with negative inducements only if the performer does not anticipate the danger of sabotage. My sense is that as a matter of practice carrots are more often structured in continuous fashion than are sticks. If so, it is easy to see why there would be more cases striking down penalty damages than windfall rewards. But the more general point does not depend on any intuition about where discontinuities are found. It is simply that, under contract law, breaches normally generate expectancy damages—and these are generally a smooth function of nonperformance. The idea is that discontinuities breed opportunism, and that it is therefore interesting that contract law often appears to abhor discontinuities in inducements.

C. Employment at Will

Employment at will is perhaps an important exception or counter-example to this observation about law's aversion to discontinuities that can breed opportunism. Under this well-known common law doctrine an employer can fire an employee at the former's "will" much as an employee can always quit, unless there is some particular contractual provision to the contrary. I regard this as a kind of exception to the point about discontinuities because an employee is likely to suffer some serious loss when fired, and in turn the employer does enjoy some opportunities for strategic behavior. Courts do hear cases of this sort of course, sometimes protecting employees who have invested in a job specific skill or location. But the legal response has not been to declare at will employment contracts meaningless, so as to discourage these contracts and resulting opportunism in the first place. It may be that this sort of "solution" is too expensive, whereas the aversion to penalty damages imposes fewer costs on contracting parties. Nor do I wish to claim that it is only with respect to employment at will contracts that the law tolerates and even constructs discontinuities that breed opportunistic behavior. Criminal law obviously thrives on discontinuities, and tort law sometimes does as well.[20] But I

---

20. In tort law discontinuities can be both useful and troubling. See, e.g., John E. Calfee & Richard Craswell, Some effects of Uncertainty on Compliance with Legal Standards, 70 Va. L. Rev. 965 (1984). Tort law is also a place where the carrot-stick substitution can be useful in encouraging honest claims. Consider, for example, a discussion drawn from the literature on property rules and liability rules. Imagine that A pollutes and B seeks to stop A. The law might offer A the opportunity to choose to stop and then to collect from B that amount which B claims he would gain if A stopped. See Saul Levmore, Unifying Remedies: Property Rules, Liability Rules, and Startling Rules, 106 Yale Law Journal 2149 (1997). This asks for the maximum amount B would pay to get A to stop while an alternative, somewhat more familiar rule (B stops A but pays A's relocation costs) asks for the minimum A would require. But the threat of the maximum amount encourages B not to exaggerate his costs from A's operation. But put in terms of negative and positive inducements, the point is that one of these rules taxes A while the other subsidizes A's precaution-taking.

leave the more general question of when law does and should use discontinuities to its advantage for another day.

Still, in the employment-at-will area, the identification of an avoidable discontinuity does not dispose of the matter. Consider, for example, an employer, E, who offers a huge end-of-year bonus but only if the employee, F, remains at the firm and is there on December 31. Here we have a discontinuous carrot that can generate opportunistic behavior—and some protection by courts. If E fires F on December 30, on the eve of the announced bonus, F has a reasonable chance of securing the bonus, because despite the at-will relationship and the explicit condition attached by E to the bonus payment, a court will feel free to intervene, effectively protecting E against the opportunism that was generated by the discontinuous carrot. If E does not fire F, but E simply declines to pay the bonus despite F's continued employment through December 31, it would be most unlikely for a court to side with E. Penalty damages might be voided even when there is no evidence of opportunistic behavior, but analogous, discontinuous carrots bring on a kind of invalidation (in the form of forcing their payment by ignoring an attached condition), only when there is reason to fear that opportunistic behavior has in fact taken place. Note that this asymmetry between discontinuous sticks and carrots is not explained through the observation that allowing E to treat the discontinuous inducement as void would reward the (potentially) opportunistic party, E. After all, had the employee, F, quit in December for a perfectly innocent reason, there is little reason to think that E would then be required to pay the bonus. In the absence of opportunism by F, there appears to be no legal hostility to the discontinuous carrot. In contrast, imagine that the original employment contract had taken the form of a stick rather than a carrot, providing for higher compensation for F but a $25,000 penalty if F is not at this job on December 31. If E fires F for no good reason, there is no reason to expect that F will be made to suffer the contractual penalty. But even if the employee, F, quits to pursue educational opportunities or to tend to a family responsibility, I think there is now some likelihood of the penalty clause being struck down in F's favor even though there is no evidence of opportunism on E's part. In short, the discontinuity idea may improve our understanding of these issues and the relevant case law on penalty damages, but it does not explain the likely results all on its own. If my intuition about the likely judicial decisions is correct, then there remains room for a cultural or behavioral explanation of the asymmetry between carrots and sticks.

D. Mixed Systems

The discussion thus far has explored sticks and carrots as (sometimes imperfect) substitutes, but they can of course also be used in tandem around some baseline. Thus, automobile dealers may encourage a salesperson by announcing a target for monthly sales and offering a reward for sales above this target as well as a penalty for shortfalls. Indeed, most such reward structures have implicit accompanying penalties in the form of dismissal for very poor performers. In these settings it is often the case that the mixture of carrots and sticks serves to eliminate discontinuities. The smoothness that is produced by this mixture helps to avoid opportunism. The same can be true in public law; we might offer welfare payments to low income citizens and then gradually reduce these payments and (eventually) increase taxes as income rises with an eye toward encouraging work effort and avoiding discontinuities that encourage undesirable behavior.

But in most of public law it is rare to find mixtures of rewards and penalties. It may be quite unusual to reward those who abide by highway speed limits, but it is even less likely that we find a legal system penalizing speeders *and* rewarding nonspeeders. This might be explained with the observation that the system avoids the carrots or the sticks because of their secondary effects and using both only exacerbates or maintains the original problem of secondary effects. In sum, mixed systems can produce desirable smoothness but sometimes this advantage is overcome by the cost of introducing undesirable secondary effects.

There are times however when the mixture is beneficial. We have already seen such a mix in rescue law, where carrots might offset the chilling effect of sticks. And if these carrots generate moral hazards, then sticks can also be used to dissuade those who might be tempted to create accidents, as opportunities to effect rescues. This sort of mixture is obviously complex and it is perhaps no surprise that something of a social norm in the form of optional carrots and social sticks does the job instead. Thus, there is a serious social stigma attached to a failure to rescue (as was attached to gentlemen who survived the Titanic's voyage), and communities or rescued persons often choose to reward and exalt rescuers. It goes almost without saying that rewards would be withheld if there was suspicion that the putative hero had caused the danger in the first place.[21]

Comparable complexity might be introduced in other contexts. With regard to the earlier example of encouraging at-home childcare, the government could provide a penalty tax on those who do

21. This is probably true even where the rescuer created the danger by accident and without apparent intention to rescue. If so, the social norm is remarkably similar to the likely legal treatment of the employer, discussed above, who designs an employment contract with a substantial discontinuity.

not stay home with children but at the same time increase the per-child exemption in order to leave the birth-rate constant. This mixture might generate a magnified secondary effect, in the form of encouraging childbirth by those persons who expect to stay home, because they now get double payment so to speak, but this may not be politically troubling.

Conclusion

I have suggested here that there are multiple levels of analyzing the choice between positive and negative inducements. The first step is to see that carrots ad sticks are normally substitutes. If there is legal or practical hurdle to fashioning a positive (or negative) inducement, then it is useful to think about the acceptability of its mirror image. This substitution between carrots and sticks is an important step in the study of law, and it is related to many of the central insights of law and economics.

A second step is to appreciate that secondary effects often make carrots and sticks something other than perfect substitutes. These secondary effects can lead to a preference for either carrots or sticks depending on the context. A fair amount of law (and private arrangements) can be explained or justified this way.

The final step adds in the problems created by discontinuous inducements. There is much more to be said about discontinuities, but it is likely that the dangers associated with discontinuous carrots and sticks play an important role in understanding the law's use of carrots, torts, and other sticks more fully.

Study Questions:

1. Are you persuaded by Levmore's explanation of the penalty doctrine? Is there a market failure here (see Chapter 5)? What about his discussion of employment at will?

2. Suppose that you would like to hire a contractor to build a bridge but you are worried that the contractor, which has a reputation for lateness, will not finish by the completion date of July 1. Every day late will cost you $1000, so you would like to have a liquidated damages clause that says that the contractor must pay you $1000 for every day late. The contractor would agree to this, but your lawyer advises you that a court might strike down the liquidated damages clause if a dispute arises. Is it possible to design a contract that would have the same behavioral effects but that would not be struck down by the court? If so, what would it say?

3. Why aren't carrots used in the criminal law—for example, a reward if you have not been convicted of a crime over the last year?

4. What are the carrots and sticks in intellectual property law (Chapter 7)?

5. What are the carrots and sticks in the regulation of corporate finance (Chapter 4)?

*

12. Agency Models in Law and Economics

Eric A. Posner[1]

I. The Basic Theory

This lecture is about agency models and agency relationships. An agency relationship, in its simplest version, is a relationship in which one person, the "principal," benefits when another person, the "agent" performs some task with care or effort. I will start with an example, then discuss the theory, and then talk about legal applications.

Suppose that you want to sell your house. You have no experience selling houses, and you don't have the right contacts, so you hire a real estate agent. You want the agent to use as much care or effort as possible to sell your house. You want her to show the house to as many potential buyers as possible, to lavish it with praise, to prod buyers to make generous bids, to display its charms while minimizing its defects. But you know that the agent might not want to work as hard as you want her to work. She might prefer working 9 to 5, when in fact the best time to contact potential buyers is in the evening when their defenses are down. But the agent is tired in the evening, and would rather play with her kids than call buyers. She might want to take frequent breaks during working hours; she might avoid your house because it is a little farther away than the other houses that she sells; she might be lazy, as far as you know. Maybe, she has a side business—an internet startup, no doubt—on which she would rather spend her time. Your problem, then, is to figure out a way to get the real estate agent to work hard for you, when she might prefer to do other things, and do the bare minimum for you.

Now, one possibility is to monitor the agent and fire her if she does not do a good enough job. But how exactly would you monitor her? You have work to do, and can't follow her around to make sure that she is showing your house to her clients. If you are devious, you might set up a voice-activated tape recorder in your house, so at least you can determine, when you get home from work, whether

1. Professor of Law, University of Chicago. I thank the John M. Olin Fund, the Sarah Scaife Foundation Fund, and the Ameritech Fund in Law and Economics for generous financial support. Thanks to Jack Goldsmith, Kate Kraus, Saul Levmore, George Triantis, and Adrian Vermeule for comments. This lecture was delivered in January 2000.

the agent ever stopped by, and whether she does a good job of praising your house. But suppose you find out that she has stopped by only once the day before, you confront her, and she responds that her clients on that day all preferred to see a less expensive house. How do you know whether she is lying or telling the truth?

Another possible solution to this problem—which is generally called an agency problem—is to wait a while and see if the house is sold, and fire the agent if it is not sold. But suppose you wait a month and the house is not sold. You ask the agent why, and she says that currently the market is down, but it may come alive again at any moment. She knows that some people would buy your house at a low price, but she is confident that if she waits a little longer, she will be able to find someone who will pay you more. Again, unless you are an expert about the housing market, it will be difficult for you to evaluate the agent's claims. The problem, as before, is that you cannot directly observe the agent's efforts, and you cannot infer them from the outcome of her work—the sale or non-sale of your house within a certain time—because you do not know the influence of luck and other extraneous factors on the sale of your house.

There is a solution to this problem, or at least a partial solution, and that is to design a contract that gives the agent the right incentives to use effort in selling your house. What should this contract look like?

To keep the example clear, let's make some simplifying assumptions. First, let's assume that the agent can take two levels of effort—high or low. The agent prefers to take the low level of effort, everything else equal. And let's assume that the house will be sold either for a high amount (say, $200,000) or a low amount (say, $100,000). If the agent engages in a high level of effort, the house will more likely (say 90%) be sold for the high amount; and if the agent engages in a low level of effort, the house will more likely (say 90%) be sold for the low amount. But the key fact is that some luck is involved, so a high-effort agent might sell the house for $100,000 because of low demand (with 10% probability), and the low-effort agent might sell the house for $200,000 because of high demand (with 10% probability)—and demand is not observable by you, the seller, who is known as the "principal" in the model we are discussing.

Second, let's assume that the agent is risk-averse. This means that the agent prefers, say, $100 to a 50–50 chance of receiving a payoff of $200 or 0. This is a reasonable assumption. The real estate agent owns her own home, and has to make mortgage payments on it. She needs food for her children. If in a particular month, she does not receive any income, she will default on her mortgage, lose her house, and so on. So she would be willing to give up a little money in order to ensure a relatively steady stream of income over time. She would rather earn $3000 every month than $3100 on average every month where some months she receives much more and some months she receives much less.

Finally, let's add some nonessential structure to the problem. Let's assume that your house will definitely be sold one month after you put it on the market—either at the high price or the low price. You can hire one real estate agent, and can design any contract you want. If you don't hire an agent, you sell the house by yourself, and because you have no idea how to do this, you would net only about $80,000. The agent must be paid some minimum amount; otherwise, she will look for some other job. Let's say this minimum amount is $3000 for a month of work, assuming that she gets that amount with certainty and does engage in high effort. If she engages in low effort, $2000 will be adequate compensation. If there is some risk that she will get less than that amount, she will demand a larger amount in expected value terms. And let's assume that you, the principal, are risk-neutral.

Given these assumptions, how should you design your contract with the agent?

A nice way to answer the question is to produce a baseline contract that assumes away all of our agency problems, then relax those assumptions. In other words, suppose that you have perfect information about what the agent does, so you know exactly how much effort she takes. Then the optimal contract is this: $3000 for the agent if she uses high effort, and $0 otherwise.

Why is this the optimal contract? First, you pay the agent the least amount of money that you can get away with, namely $3000. Second, you ensure that she will engage in high effort. She prefers $3000 with high effort, to $0 with low effort, so she will work in order to get paid. Third, you ensure that she will accept this contract rather than going elsewhere for work. We assumed that the agent does better by receiving $3000 with high effort, than by getting whatever she can get elsewhere. And we don't have to worry about her risk aversion: she knows that if she engages in high effort, she will be paid $3000 with certainty. While you can't be sure that your house will be sold at the high price—remember that luck can't be eliminated entirely—you do ensure, at least cost, the highest probability that your house will be sold at that high price.

But this optimal contract can only be taken as a baseline, because it wouldn't work in the real world, where you can't directly observe the effort level of the agent. You wouldn't be able to say to her, "I'll pay you only if you engage in high effort," because she would reply, "how would you know whether I engaged in high effort?" So let's consider some alternatives.

The flat-rate contract. One possibility is to pay the agent a flat rate. You might, for example, promise to pay the agent $50 per hour. An alternative is to pay the agent $3000 when the house is sold. Let's stick to the last possibility. Is this a good idea?

The answer is no. The agent knows that she will receive $3000 regardless of whether the house is sold for the high price or the low price. Thus, the amount of effort she uses will have no influence on the amount of compensation she receives. But we know that she prefers to engage in low effort, rather than high effort, so we know that she will choose to engage in low effort. But you want her to engage in high effort, so you should consider an alternative contract.

The high-power incentive contract. Another possibility is to pay the agent an amount that increases with the sale price. A simple example would be: pay the agent $3000 if the house is sold for a high price and $0 if the house is sold for a low price. (Notice the difference between this contract and the baseline, full-information contract of $3000 if the agent uses high *effort*, and $0 otherwise.)

This contract would give the agent an incentive to engage in high effort. If she does not, she most likely receives 0, which we assume does not compensate her even for low effort. More precisely, as long as the agent prefers a 90% chance of $3000 (given high effort) to a 10% chance of $3000 (given low effort), she will engage in high effort. But we face two further problems. First, remember that the agent needs to get $3000 if she puts in a high level of effort. But there is a chance that even with a high level of effort, the house will fetch a low price. You need to give her at least $3000 in expected terms. So if there is a 10% chance that a high level of effort will result in a low price, you need to pay the agent at least $3333 if the house is sold at the high price.

Second, and more important, remember that the agent is risk-averse, and would accept $3000 only if she can expect it with certainty. But the current contract, while giving her $3000 in expected terms, forces her to bear the 10% risk of receiving no payment, that is, when the house is sold at the low price. She would not agree to such a contract unless you paid her much more than $3000 in expected terms. Maybe, you would have to pay her $4000 if she sells the house at a high price, in which case her expected payoff would be $3600.

In sum, under the high-power contract you pay the agent a lot of money—$4000—with 90% probability, so you expect to pay her $3600. She engages in high effort, so you maximize the likelihood that your house will be sold for a high price. But can you do better?

The mixed contract. The final possibility is to give the agent both incentives to engage in high effort and insurance against a bad outcome—what I will call a "mixed contract." The contract might say: pay the agent $3400 if the house sells for a high price, and pay the agent $1000 if the house sells for a low price. Although the numbers are arbitrary, as they depend on unspecified parameters such as the degree of risk-aversion on the part of the agent, they illustrate the basic point. By making the compensation higher when the good outcome occurs, you give the agent an incentive to engage in high effort. By giving the agent some money even if the bad outcome occurs, you give the agent some insurance against bad luck. Because she receives some money in the bad state of the world, she will feel secure against her fear of missing a mortgage payment, and so won't demand quite as much money in the good state of world, where she is able to sell the house at a high price. You get high effort from her, but because you agree to bear some of the risk, you don't have to pay her as much as under the high-power contract ($3160 rather than $3600 in expected terms).[2]

Actual real estate agents usually earn a percentage commission, like 6%, on the sale. This contract is similar to what the agency model predicts, but not exactly. Note that there is an incentive to work hard, because the agent's compensation increases with sale price. And there is some insurance: the agent receives something as long as the house is sold. But when effort is continuous and there is a chance of no sale, as is the case with the real world, one would predict something else. One would expect the percentage to increase with the sale price. If it takes a tremendous amount of effort to sell your lousy house for more than $200,000, then it makes sense to give the agent a higher percentage of the surplus over that amount. And if there is a chance of no sale, then it might make sense to give the risk-averse agent a small base fee (like $500 per month) and percentages above that depending on the sale price. But we do not observe these contracts, and the reason is that the agency model so far described is too simple.[3]

II.   Some General Observations and Some Complications

Now let's pull back a bit and look at what we've learned. Then we'll talk about some complications—or reasons why you should take this model with a grain of salt.

2. If the agent is risk neutral, then the optimal contract will pay her $13,-000 if the house sells for a high price; and *she* will pay the *principal* $87,000 if the house is sold for the low price! To see why, note that the principal would be happy to sell the house to the agent for its expected value given high effort, while compensating her for that effort: so $190,000—$3,000 = $187,000. The agent will use high effort, and net $13,-000 with 90% probability ($200,000—$187,000); and lose $87,000 with 10% probability ($100,000—$187,000). In expected terms, the agent receives $3000. This is the same as the contract described at the beginning of this footnote.

3. See Karen Eggleston, Eric A. Posner, and Richard Zeckhauser, Simplicity and Complexity in Contracts (manuscript, University of Chicago Law School, 2000).

An agency relationship is a relationship between two people, one of whom (the "principal") benefits when the other (the "agent") performs some task. The principal benefits more when the agent takes care or uses effort when performing the task, than when the agent fails to take care or use effort. The agent, however, would rather not go to the effort unless she is compensated for that effort. If the principal can observe the agent's level of effort, then the principal will pay the agent to engage in the proper level of effort, and if the payment is large enough, the agent will engage in the proper level of effort. But if the principal cannot directly observe the agent's level of effort, we have what is called an agency problem. The agent might engage in low effort, or what is often called "moral hazard." The agent might promise to use effort, but unless the principal can observe the level of effort, the agent's promise is not enforceable, so the principal has no reason to believe the agent's promise.[4]

Although there is a tension between the principal's and the agent's goals, this should not be exaggerated. The agent will work if paid enough; and the principal may benefit enough by the agent's work that he would be willing to pay the agent enough. Even if the agent is highly risk-averse, and monitoring is very costly, the parties will be able to make a deal, as long as the gains from trade are high enough that they can compensate each party for his or her costs.

We've learned that in any agency relationship, the basic problem is that the principal wants the agent to work hard, but the agent doesn't want to work hard, and because information problems are ubiquitous, the principal cannot directly reward the agent who works hard and penalize the agent who does not work hard. If the principal pays a flat amount under these conditions, the agent will engage in little effort. Compared to the baseline hypothetical contract—where the principal compensates the agent for engaging in the right amount of effort—there is an efficiency loss, which is called the "agency cost." If there were no agency costs, the efficient or first-best outcome can be obtained; because of agency costs, it cannot. But if we figure out ways to reduce agency costs, we increase efficiency.

Principals want to minimize agency costs (and the agent wants the principal to minimize agency costs, to the extent that she will share the savings). There are two main ways of doing this. The first is what we've been discussing: design a contract that makes compensation depend on the output of the agent. As output rises, so

---

4. The clearest sophisticated treatment of the agency model that I have seen is David M. Kreps, A Course in Microeconomic Theory ch. 16 (1990), which also contains a bibliography of the economic literature on the subject. See also Bernard Salanié, The Economics of Contracts: A Primer (1997).

should compensation. Notice that the principal does not need to know the actual level of effort; he simply looks at the amount of output, which should be easily verifiable. The problem is that if the agent is risk-averse—and this will almost always be the case—the agent will demand insurance against unlucky outcomes. So the principal might offer a mixed contract containing both insurance and incentives.

The second way of reducing agency costs is to invest in monitoring. Employers do this all the time. They buy computer programs that count the number of keystrokes made by secretaries. They videotape cashiers. They listen in on telephone operators. They put bumper stickers on company trucks asking drivers to call in if the truck is being driven carelessly. But all of these things are expensive, so there is a limit on how much monitoring will be profitable.

Now here are the complications. First, in our model the agent has one task. Usually, agents will have more than one task, or more complex tasks than the one described in the model. Consider a different agency relationship, where an employer hires a salesman to travel around selling the employer's products. In the simple model, we might conclude that the employer should pay the salesman on commission, so that more sales mean higher pay. The employee engages in the high-effort hard sell, rather than a more comfortable and friendly, but less remunerative, "soft sell." But in a more complex model, we might have doubts. The hard sell yields high sales in the short term, but in the long term offended and humiliated customers go elsewhere—but long after the salesman has left the company. The soft sell yields medium-level sales in the short term, but in the long term customers stay with the employer. The employer wants the salesman to be nice and polite, but if he uses the commission system the salesman has the wrong incentives. He'll engage in the hard sell, because he gets more pay in the short term, and in the long term he'll either be gone or he'll share the general decline in sales with other employees rather than incurring the entire cost of his behavior by himself. It is possible that the employer should pay the salesman a flat fee, in the hope that if he prefers nice and polite to the hard sell, his actions will align more closely to the employer's interests.[5]

The second complication is that while our model has only one agent, often a principal will have several agents. An employer usually has many employees, not just one. This fact can have various implications. On the one hand, when there are many

---

5. See Bengt Holmstrom and Paul Milgrom, Multitask Principal–Agent Analyses: Incentive Contracts, Asset Ownership and Job Design, 7 J. Law, Econ. & Org. 24 (1991).

agents, the principal may have an easier time determining whether a particular agent shirked or was the victim of chance. If all of the salesmen had poor sales, then one is more confident that market conditions are responsible than if only one salesman had poor sales. Moreover, it may be possible to design incentive schemes that exploit large numbers: for example, giving a bonus to the salesman with the most sales might produce incentives that track level of effort. On the other hand, when tasks require cooperation among multiple agents, but agents are paid only on the basis of independent work, they will shirk on cooperative tasks. For example, piece rate workers will work very fast on the assembly line but they will not take the time to train newcomers.[6]

The third complication is that we assumed only one principal, when in many cases a single agent will have multiple principals. A good example is the CEO of a corporation, who is responsible to hundreds or thousands of shareholders. When these shareholders' interests are aligned, we need not worry about the multiple principal problem. But in small corporations with few shareholders, different shareholders might have difference risk tolerances and different interests. What is the optimal contract for the CEO? Also think about real estate agents, who usually represent multiple seller/principals rather than a single one. One implication of this is that their contracts might not need a lot of insurance built into them, because as long as one's luck for each sale is independent of the other sales, the large numbers will provide some insurance. If the agent has trouble selling one house because no one likes it, she may have at the same time no trouble selling another house which happens to catch the eye of an eccentric millionaire.

The fourth complication is that often both parties in a contract will have agent-like and principal-like qualities. Imagine that two lawyers set up a partnership. Who is the principal and who is the agent? The answer is that both are both. Each lawyer benefits if the other lawyer uses high effort, because they share all profits. So they are both principles. Each lawyer has an incentive to shirk on his own side, because he must pay some of his returns to the other lawyer; and neither lawyer will find it easy to monitor the work of the other.[7] Even in a more typical agency relationship, the agent might depend on the principal's engaging in the right conduct. A real estate agent wants the owner of the house to keep it clean; if the agent obtains all the profit from the sale, the principal will lose the incentive to keep the house clean, making the agent's job

---

6. See, e.g., D. Mookherjee, Optimal Incentive Schemes with Many Agents, 51 Rev. Econ. Stud. 433 (1984).

7. See, e.g., Bengt Holmstrom, Moral Hazard in Teams, 13 Bell J. Econ. 324 (1982).

harder. As a result, the optimal contract might split the profits between the two parties.[8]

One could go on for a long time, spinning out more complications. But even as we take into account the complications, the basic lessons of the model hold. In any agency relationship there will be potential agency costs, which can be minimized through clever monitoring and clever design of the contract that trades off incentives, on the one hand, and insurance, on the other.

III. Applications to the World

Agency relationships are ubiquitous, and so are agency problems. Agency problems arise whenever one individual (the agent) can benefit another individual (the principal) by taking a certain action, but the latter cannot directly monitor the first and pay him for doing the right thing. Usually, the agent has some expertise or other advantage that the principal lacks, and the principal benefits enough by the agent's action, and the agent loses little enough from taking that action, that the principal can pay the agent for taking the action. Let me give you some examples.

The landlord is the principal and the tenant is the agent. The landlord wants the agent to take care of the premises: to keep them clean and not to subject them to too much wear and tear. But the landlord cannot directly observe the tenant, so it may not be clear whether the washing machine broke because the tenant stuffed too many clothes in it or because it malfunctioned. A security deposit minimizes agency costs. The tenant knows that if he trashes the apartment, the landlord will keep his security deposit, so he has an incentive to take care. At the same time, the tenant will usually not be liable if, for example, the entire building is destroyed by fire, or he may be judgment proof in any case. The tenant thus does not bear all the risk of a bad outcome. Like the real estate agent, the tenant has some incentive to take care, but does not bear all the risk of the bad outcome.

A manager of a corporation is an agent of the shareholders. The problem again is that the shareholders cannot directly observe the manager's level of effort. Did sales collapse because the manager did not take important clients out to restaurants often enough, or because of a subtle shift in demand? Did sales skyrocket because the managers spent so much time on the phone or because of the independent efforts of subordinates? Shareholders can give managers the right incentives by paying them solely in stock, so they make money if the company does well, and not otherwise. But

---

8. See Saul Levmore, Commissions and Conflicts in Agency Arrangements: Lawyers, Real Estate Brokers, Under-writers and Other Agents' Rewards, 36 J. Law. & Econ. 503 (1993).

managers will not accept this level of risk. If a recession strikes, and demand for the firm's product dries up, the manager would receive no compensation. So compensation schemes typically include a salary plus stock or stock options.

The insurance company is the principal and the client is the agent. This might sound backwards, but it makes sense. The client's task is to drive his car carefully or recklessly. The insurer benefits if the client drives the car carefully, because this minimizes the chance of accident and payment of insurance. But if the client is fully insured, the client has little incentive to drive carefully. The solution is the deductible: the insurer will not pay the client's full losses, and because the client absorbs some of the loss, he has an incentive to take care. However, it would defeat the purpose of insurance to give the client nothing if he has an accident, although this would give the client the best incentives to take care. You buy insurance precisely to protect yourself against risk.

Your doctor is your agent, and you—the patient—are the principal. You pay your doctor to examine you for illness, and you hope that your doctor puts in the right level of effort. Your lawyer also is your agent, and you—the client—are the principal. Notice that in both cases it is very difficult to monitor the agent. You never really know whether the doctor or lawyer did a good or bad job. Worse, often you don't even know how to evaluate the output: you are not around when your will is executed, so you won't know if there are any mistakes. Concerns about monitoring when the principal is extremely ignorant about the nature of the agent's tasks lead to professionalization. The agents create bodies of experts that supervise them. This is supposed to give the principals confidence that the agents will do a good job. Whether it does or not is another question.

The agency model can be extended outside the employment context. Think about how a politician is the agent of citizens. Or how administrative agencies like the EPA are the agents of Congress (or are they the agents of the President?). Or how judges are agents of Congress. What are the agency problems in this context? Politicians engage in a high level of effort when they implement the interests and values of citizens, and low effort when they accept bribes or respond to the demands of interest groups. Is campaign finance reform the solution to an agency problem? Administrative agencies are supposed to implement statutes under the President's direction, not create regulations that benefit industries or lobbyists. Judges are supposed to enforce laws, not implement their personal or ideological preferences. So these are the agency costs; think about how the political process might minimize them or make them worse.

There is a sense in which every citizen is an agent for every other citizen. When you drive carefully, you are a good agent for other drivers, and when they driver carefully, they are acting as good agents for you. Littering or failing to pay taxes might be considered shirking or low-effort behavior on the part of citizen-agents, the result of high agency costs, that is, the high costs for each citizen of monitoring all other citizens. The police and the courts, then, are an attempt to minimize agency costs.

Let me conclude my discussion of agency relationships by considering the case of restaurants and waiters. The manager of the restaurant is the principal, and the waiters are agents. The waiters' task is to provide good service. If the waiters use a high level of effort, the manager will benefit from increased sales. But waiters find it easier to be rude, or to be slow, than to be prompt and courteous to obnoxious customers. The manager might be able to minimize agency costs by observing some waiters some of the time, but she will generally be busy doing other things.

Waiters earn a lot of money from tips; at the same time they are paid a flat wage by the restaurant. This is exactly the sort of mixed contract that the agency model predicts. The flat wage protects the waiter from slow nights and miserly customers; the tips give the waiter an incentive to do a good job. But there is a twist to this story. Waiters often pool their tips and divide them evenly; other times, the managers require them to pool their tips and divide them evenly. Notice that this increases insurance against bad tippers, but reduces the incentive to provide good service. Part of the reason for pooling from the manager's perspective comes from the multiple agent problem: when waiters depend heavily on tips, they have no incentive to cooperate with each other. This is why a waiter who does not serve your table will sometimes be rude or impatient when you ask him for some help. To enhance cooperation, the manager requires pooling of tips.

But this does not mean that there is no incentive to provide good service. When customers pay with credit cards, they record their tip on a piece of paper—the receipt, of course, which will have the waiter's name or code number—that the manager will be able to see. So the manager will learn about the quality of service provided by different waiters, and the manager can reward good waiters and punish bad waiters by giving better waiters the more popular tables or promoting them or by firing the bad waiters.

IV. Applications in Law

As a private citizen and as a lawyer, you will have to deal with contracts all the time. As a private citizen, you will want to know whether the contracts you enter serve your interests. When you are in the position of agent—say, as an employee of a law firm, or as the lawyer for a client, or as a tenant, or as the purchaser of insurance, or as the renter of a car—your main concern will be about the insurance side of the contract. The other person will want to give you high-powered incentives, and one incentive is to make you pay if something goes wrong. You have to be alert for provisions in the contract that make you responsible for losses. You might be made liable, for example, if you damage the car that you rent; or you might forfeit your insurance coverage if you fail to install smoke detectors; or you might be subject to firing or even criminal prosecution if you fake your billing records while a lawyer at a firm. If you don't like provisions that create high-powered incentives, demand that they be removed or look for another contractual partner.

When you are in the position of principal—say, as the manager of a law firm, or as a landlord, or as a homeowner who pays a contractor to renovate the kitchen, or as an investor in a company—your main concern will be about the incentives side of the contract. You want your agent or agents to work hard, to take care, to do a good job. You will think about bonuses, promotions, commissions, and penalties. The agent will resist, and you will have to compromise.

And as a lawyer, your clients will show you the contracts that they are thinking about entering, and they will ask you for your advice. And you will give them advice that will reflect agency principles, whether you've learned them or not. You will warn them about their responsibilities under the contract, the extent to which they might have to pay; and you will warn them about the incentives that the other person faces under the contract.

Agency principles also help us understand the design of the law. Let me give some examples.

A.   Contract law

Many laws regulate contracts. One relevant cluster of examples consists of laws that regulate the contracts between real estate agents, buyers, and sellers. Typically, real estate agents work for sellers, but sometimes buyers do not realize this, and share confidences with the real estate agent which the agent will duly exploit. A response in some states has been the enactment of laws that require the agent to act as a "dual" agent for the seller and the buyer. One should ask oneself what effect this law will have. It may be unenforceable, because it is hard to tell whether the agent violates the buyer's confidences when she uses that information to propose a price higher than what the seller might otherwise extract. If it does restrict agents' freedom, then it might make sellers more reluctant to hire real estate agents. But the law might also solve a contract problem: the optimal contract would be negotiated ex ante by buyer, seller, and agent; perhaps the law supplies the terms that the parties would agree to if they had the opportunity to negotiate.

When analyzing contract law we often talk in very general terms. We say that the promisor is the person who must perform now; whereas the promisee is the person who paid him a while ago and is now entitled to performance. For example, the promisor is the employee who failed to reach sales goals; the promisee is the employer who expected the promisor to attain these goals. So the promisor is the agent, and the promisee is the principal.

Let me put this in another way. The promisee will often write down in a contract, sometimes in great detail, the promisor's obligations. When the promisor fails to satisfy these obligations, he breaches the contract. The promisee sues for damages. If the court decides that the promisor did not satisfy his obligations, it will award damages. So far so good.

But what should the level of damages be? Here we can use the agency model. Simplifying greatly, we can treat breach as "low effort" and performance as "high effort." If damages are too low—say, 0—the promisor has no incentive to perform. She is like the real estate agent who is paid a flat fee to sell your house. So we predict the promisor to breach when damages are set very low.

Suppose we set the level of damages at some high amount, say, the value to the promisee of performance (expectation damages). Now the promisor has an incentive to perform. She will perform, in fact, as long as the cost of performance is less than the amount of damages. This might seem like a good outcome.

But the agency model helps us see two problems with this analysis. First, if the promisee is risk-averse and the promisor is risk-neutral—and this will be roughly correct in the standard employment relationship—a high level of damages will make contracts unattractive to the promisor. Employees know that there is some chance that they will not be able to avoid breach, because bad luck can never be eliminated. Think of the real estate agent who knows that even if she puts in high effort, there is some chance that she will not be able to sell the house for a high price. Just as she does not want to enter a contract that gives her nothing if she fails to sell a house, she would not want to enter a contract that forces her to pay expectation damages if, because of bad luck, she is unable to perform. Thus, the standard measure of damages—expectation damages—may be too high.

Second, don't forget that sometimes the nominal principal is also an agent. The employer might be an agent in the sense that if he uses a high level of effort, the employee is more likely to be able to perform. For example, maybe the employer is expected to provide the employee with some training. The employer fails to do so, and so the employee finds it too hard to perform. If the failure to train is not technically a breach—say, it's not included in the contract—expectation damages provides the wrong incentives, because they reward the employer who fails to engage in high effort. A low level of damages if the employee breaches would give the employer the optimal incentives to train the employee. But then we see the tension—a low level of damages also reduces the employee's incentives to engage in high effort. A high level of damages, like expectation damages, might give the employee good incentives while giving the employer bad incentives; but a low level of damages, like zero damages, might give the employee bad incentives while giving the employer good incentives.

I have only scratched the surface of a very complex subject. But I hope I have given you a sense of how agency principles shed light on contract doctrines.[9]

B.   Other areas of law

Now I am going to give you a quick tour of some of your other classes.

Tort law. Tort law often matters in contractual relationships. Product liability law makes a manufacturer strictly liable for injuries caused by its products. The manufacturer is agent, the consumer is principle. Vicarious liability rules, the old fellow servant rule, and workers' compensation all govern the relationship between employers and employees. So these laws can be analyzed straightforwardly using agency models. But think also about whether it makes to sense to say that when I drive down the road, I am an agent for pedestrians or other drivers, who are principals; and the other drivers are agents for me? The standard economic models of negligence and strict liability can be cashed out in terms of the tradeoff between optimal incentives and optimal insurance for risk-averse people, on analogy to the agency models.[10]

Property law. Historically, many towns had what were called "commons." (Think of the Boston Commons, for example.) This was common property: generally speaking anyone in the community could forage on the commons or graze his livestock on the commons. Every citizen is an agent for the community. The agency problem is that I might overforage or overgraze my sheep, with the result that there will not be enough left for others. There is a similar problem with fisheries, or for that matter, air, water, and

9. A recent survey of this literature is Steven Shavell, Contracts, 1 The New Palgrave Dictionary of Economics and the Law 436 (Peter Newman ed. 1998).

10. See William Landes & Richard A. Posner, The Economic Structure of Tort Law (1987); Steven Shavell, Economic Analysis of Accident Law (1987).

soil, which can be overused through pollution. To return to the commons, we could give people the right incentives by dividing the commons into private strips of property. Now I will not overforage because I incur all the losses if nothing grows next year. The problem is that if I can forage only from my strip, and if random environmental factors cause my strip to be barren one year while others' are not, then I am out of luck. So private property creates better incentives not to overforage, but at the cost of bad insurance for the risk-averse. By contrast, the commons insures me against variations in the growing patterns on any small piece of it. One compromise is private property, but with some sort of side deal—an insurance contract that gives me the right to forage on your property only when some easily monitored condition—say, a flood— makes mine unusable.[11]

Civil procedure. Is the lawyer an agent of the client, as we said above, or is the lawyer an agent of the court? The client wants the lawyer to do whatever it takes to win her case. The court wants the lawyer to expose the truth, and not to delay, harass the other side, and so on. If the client can get the lawyer to sign a high-power incentive contract—like the contingency fee contract—we can expect the lawyer to serve the client well but the court poorly. This is the sort of lawyer who would knowingly allow his client to commit perjury, would indeed encourage his client to commit perjury. But the court does not want this, and so threatens the lawyer with sanctions if the lawyer goes too far. We can imagine the lawyer as agent of the court. This lawyer might even be paid by the government. But this lawyer would be less concerned with enabling his client to win than with pleasing the court. He would not suborn perjury, but he would not try very hard to seek out hard-to-find evidence that would benefit his client's case.[12]

Corporate law. Corporate managers and directors are agents of shareholders. I mentioned above that corporate employment contracts are designed to minimize agency costs, and so one way the law can minimize agency costs is just by enforcing these contracts. But often contracts are not enough; they may have gaps as a result of transaction costs or information asymmetries. Corporate law, on one view, fills these gaps with default terms. These terms include the general duties of care and loyalty, but also (arguably) such features as limited liability, the derivative suit, voting rules, and rules governing the disclosure of information when a firm issues securities. A vivid example comes from the wave of corporate

11. For a general discussion, see Robert Ellickson, Property in Land, 102 Yale L.J. 1315 (1993).

12. An agency model of lawyering can be found in Geoffrey Miller, Some Agency Problems in Settlement, 16 J. Legal Stud. 189 (1987); see also Levmore, supra at 521–25.

takeovers in the 1980s. Many people objected to takeovers because they often resulted in the loss of jobs and the disruption of local communities. There was much enthusiasm for state laws that interfere with takeover attempts. But the agency model suggests that takeovers are desirable. They can occur only when managers fail to maximize the value of the corporation, for they are motivated by the belief that a better managed company would be worth more. Corporate raiders, despite their unsavory reputations in some quarters, are the solution to an agency problem, and on this view should be celebrated rather than reviled.[13]

The Rest of Law. Once one has mastered the agency model, it is a fine game, especially on long car trips, to apply it to everything in the universe. Let me mention a few other legal topics. In labor law, the union represents the employees; the union is the agent, the employees are principals. Labor law, among other things, constrains unions so that they do not violate the interests of employees. The election rules also try to minimize agency problems by dividing employees into bargaining units on the basis of the employees' interests. In corporate bankruptcy, it is useful to think of the debtor as an agent of the creditors which, because of the debtor's insolvency, become residual claimants. In employment and franchise law, the employment and termination at will default rules are often justified on the theory that the principals (the employer, the franchisor) have no more effective way of deterring the agent from misbehavior than by ending the relationship. In administrative law, the notice and comment provisions of the Administrative Procedure Act are often justified on the theory that they enable regulated parties to alert Congress when agencies deviate from the legislative mandate. In international law there is much concern about whether international institutions, including international arbitrators, have the right incentives to respect the interests of sovereign nations.

An old theory of political organization holds that government is invented to solve an agency problem. Each citizen is an agent of every other citizen, but no citizen has the incentive to use care when, for example, littering or driving. The government is invented to solve this agency problem. The government enacts laws that deter moral hazard, and it punishes people who violate those laws. But this creates a new agency problem. The government consists of people; once these people are given guns, what prevents them from acting contrary to the interest of citizens? One possibility is the Constitution, which is a set of rules that restricts the behavior of

---

13. There is a vast literature on this subject. See, e.g., Frank H. Easterbrook and Daniel R. Fischel, The Economic Structure of Corporate Law (1991); Paul G. Mahoney, Mandatory Disclosure as a Solution to Agency Problems, 62 U. Chi. L. Rev. 1047 (1995).

the government. The Supreme Court enforces the Constitution. But what prevents Supreme Court justices from engaging in moral hazard? The solution to every agency problem creates a new agency problem, or so it might appear.

V.   Conclusion

When you think about the purposes of the law, and why it might or might not make sense, think about whether it seems to be responding to agency relationships. Think about what the agency costs are, and how they can be minimized. I'm not saying that agency relationships are all that there is. They are only a small part. But agency models can help you see connections between different areas of the law, and how different areas of the law respond in similar ways to common problems.

One last agency relationship. Professors are agents of their students. The professor's task is to educate the student, and this can be done well or poorly. Lazy professors, or professors who want to make lots of money or become famous scholars, might engage in low effort, which leaves them time to go on vacation, or consult, or do research. How is the agency problem solved? One solution is reliance on student evaluations. The students, who are the principals, directly monitor the professors. Our salaries could be a simple function of the scores we receive on these evaluations.

Fortunately, there are three problems with this approach. First, we are risk-averse. If I receive no salary this year, because my evaluations sink below a certain level, I will probably look for another job—even if on average my evaluations are very high. A possible response to this problem is to base compensation on a moving average of my evaluations, but then my incentives will not be as sharp. If I do very well in one year, I may slack off the next year.

Second, students often don't realize they have received a good education until long after they have filled out the evaluation. You will not know until you are lawyers. In this way, the teacher relationship is like the doctor/patient or lawyer/client relationships, where the great gulf between the knowledge of the agent and the information of the principal frustrates the use of contracts to provide optimal incentives.

Interestingly, universities have managed to develop a solution to this problem. They receive a good portion of their funding from alumni who make donations. The hope is that alumni, who are now in the position to evaluate their education, will donate a lot if the education was good, and this—through the offices of the dean—will ensure that professors do a good job. Notice that it is not so necessary for elementary and high school education; there we expect parents to be able to monitor the teachers by observing the progress of their children. Agency costs are minimized because parents complain, or remove their children from school, if teachers do a bad job. But in the university setting, the solution is more complex, because students' parents generally don't know enough to be able to evaluate their children's progress.

Third, scholars are supposed to engage in scholarship. If their salaries were solely a function of student evaluations, they would focus entirely on teaching, and do very little scholarship, possibly at the cost of the reputation of the law school, and therefore of the long-term value of the students' diploma. This is the problem that arises when the agent has more than one task, which I discussed above.

The result of these complications is that monitoring and re-warding of professors is quite complex. An intermediate institution, namely the dean, is invented to persuade students and alumni that the faculty does a good job, and also to monitor the faculty and reward those who do well and punish those who do poorly. This is all done, of course, in a genial and subtle manner—with lots of informal pressure, and a lot of work on the front end to screen out professors who are unlikely to produce scholarship or take their teaching seriously. The dean, like all of us, must spend a good part of his time analyzing agency relationships, and figuring out ways to minimize agency costs.

Study Questions:

1. Charities, religious organizations, and some businesses (like hospitals) are "nonprofits." They do not pay taxes, but they also do not have shareholders. Managers draw a salary. What are the agency problems raised by these sorts of institutions? How does the law deal with them?

2. When contracts are vague, courts often find an implied "good faith" or "best efforts" term. For example, a court might interpret a requirements contract to forbid the buyer to demand "too much" or "too little." Is this interpretation reasonable in light of the agency model?

3. Police officers are agents (of whom?). When they misbehave, they can be punished like any other employee: demotion, termination, pay cuts, etc. In what way might the exclusionary rule be understood as a solution to an agency problem? Does it make sense?

4. When two people divorce, a court will often appoint a mediator to resolve disputes over custody and the distribution of property. In what sense is the mediator an agent for both parties? Also compare the use of a mediator to resolve a dispute between two corporations. Typically, the mediator will insist on dealing directly with the CEOs of the corporations rather than with their lawyers. How might the agency model shed light on this practice?

5. Corporate reorganization is a lengthy process, and often the manager of the debtor corporation runs its day-to-day affairs while creditors and other interested parties haggle over the reorganization. As noted in the text, the manager is an agent of the creditor, and this creates agency problems. Sometimes, an independent trustee is appointed to operate the business instead of the manager, especially when fraud or criminal behavior is suspected. From the agency perspective, why wouldn't it make more sense to make appointment of an independent trustee more routine?

INDEX

References are to Pages

AGENCY MODELS
Generally, 225 et seq.
Contractual incentives, 227
Corporation law
    Managers and owners, agency rela-
        tions between, 232
    Takeovers, 239
Dual agents, 236
Insurer and insured, 234
Landlord and tenant, 233
Law professors and students, 241
Partners' relations, 232
Physician and patient, 234
Property law applications, 238
Social norms and, 235
Tort law applications, 238

ANTITRUST
See Monopolies and Restraints of Trade,
    this index

BANKRUPTCY
Capital adequacy regulation and, 74
Creditors' rights and, 191
Equitable subordination rules, 74
Prisoner's Dilemma game, application
    to, 45

BOUNDARIES
See Property Law, this index

CAPITAL SOLVENCY REGULATION
Corporation Law, this index
Securities Regulation, this index

COASE THEOREM
Generally, 99
See also Transaction Costs, this index
Property rights, defining of, 188

COLLECTIVE ACTION PROBLEM
Generally, 179

COMPROMISE AND SETTLEMENT
See Game Theory, this index

COMPUTER SOFTWARE PROTECTION
See Intellectual Property Law, this in-
    dex

CONSUMER LAW
Bankruptcy protection, economic analy-
    sis of, 191
Carrier deregulation and service levels,
    194
Retail price maintenance, 193
Risk misperception by product buyers,
    88
Warranties in monopolized markets, 87

CONTRACT LAW
Agency incentives, 227
Anticipatory breach, 49
Baby selling, 195
Carrots and sticks, contractual, 215
Consequential damages
    Foreseeability of, 60
    Foreseeable damage standard com-
        pared, 62
Damage measures and incentives to per-
    form, 49 et seq., 56
Default rules of, 81
Disclosure regulations, 95
Discontinuities, 218
Economic analysis of law, 189 et seq.
Efficient clauses, 83
Efficient legal restriction on freedom of
    contract, 82
Expectation damages
    Common law approach generally, 50
    Consequential damages compared, 61
    Incentives to breach and, 53
    Overcompensation, 51
    Reliance damages compared, 58
    Specific performance and, 64
Externalities, contract terms creating,
    82

245

CONTRACT LAW—Cont'd
Freedom of contract, 81 et seq.
Game Theory, this index
Imperfect information problems, 88 et seq.
Implied vs express contrary agreement of parties, 81
Incentives to perform
    Breach and expectation damages, 53
    Reliance damages and, 58
    Social costs, 55
Inefficient terms and monopolistic practices, 85
Insurance contracts, agency model of, 234
Intellectual property, contractual protection of rights in, 134
Liquidated damages
    generally, 64
    Monopolistic practices and, 86n
Lost profits, 60
Market failure and freedom of contract, 81 et seq.
Penalty damages, 216
Punitive damages, 64
Reliance damages
    generally, 57
    Expectation damages compared, 58
    Incentives to perform, 58
Repossession provisions, efficient and inefficient, 92
Rescuer liability, analysis of, 194
Restitution, 64
Risk misperception by product buyers, 88
Rules and bargains around them, 203
Social costs
    Incentives to perform and, 55
    Transactions costs and, 59
Surrogate motherhood contracts, 195
Third parties, contract terms affecting, 82
Transaction costs
    Damage measures and, 59
    Opting out and, 62
Usury prohibitions, 100
Values and consequences, 189 et seq.
Warranties in monopolized markets, 87

COPYRIGHTS
See Intellectual Property Law, this index

CORPORATION LAW
Agency costs, 66
Agency models
    Relationships between managers and owners, 232

CORPORATION LAW—Cont'd
Agency models—Cont'd
    Takeovers, 239
Bankruptcy and capital adequacy, 74
Capital solvency regulation, 65 et seq.
Command-and-control regulation, 69
Conflicting interests of managers and owners, 66
Costs of capital regulation, 78
Debt holders vs equity owners, interests of
    generally, 66
    Capital regulation, 68
Double liability systems, 76
European regulatory systems, 73
Ex ante and ex post regulation, 70
Financial firms, capital adequacy regulation of, 76 et seq.
Insolvency protection through capital regulation, 68
Limited liability
    Arguments against, 75
    Ex post regulation, 70
    Tort liabilities, 75
    Veil piercing, 74
Managerial abuse, 66
Modigliani–Miller irrelevance hypothesis of corporate value, 67
Multiple liability systems, 75
Par value system of regulation
    generally, 71
    Failure of, 73
Piercing the veil doctrine as capital regulation system, 74
Problems of capital regulation, 78
Risk attitudes of debt holders and equity owners, 67
Takeovers, agency model of, 239
Tort liabilities and limited liability of shareholders, 75

CREDITORS' RIGHTS
Bankruptcy protection, economic analysis of, 191

CRIMINAL LAW
Baby selling, 195
Behavioral effects of laws, 172
Discontinuities, 219
Preferences and social norms, 139
Propaganda and social norms, 145
Roles, redefining by law, 148
Seatbelt laws, 206
Social norms
    Altering, appropriateness of, 140
    Alternatives to mandatory prohibitions, 167
    Changing through government action, 161 et seq.
Values and consequences, 189 et seq.

DEMOCRACY
See Legislation and Legislative Processes, this index

EAVESDROPPING
Property rights and privacy rights, 181

ECONOMETRICS
See Regression Analysis, this index

EMPLOYMENT RELATIONSHIP
Agency problems, 225 et seq.
At will employment, 219
Carrots and sticks, contractual, 215
ERISA, economic analysis of, 195

FEDERALISM
Capital adequacy regulation and, 70, 77

FINANCIAL FIRMS
Capital adequacy regulation of, 76 et seq.

GAME THEORY
Generally, 29 et seq.
Backwards induction, 41
Coordination games, 40, 43
Decision trees, 41
Dominant strategies, 32
Extensive form games, 39
Forward induction, 44n
Iterated dominance, 36
Nash equilibria, 40
Predicting behavior, 36
Prisoner's dilemma
    Embedded, 43
    Norm choices and, 166
    Simple, 31
Rational behavior assumptions, 39
Strictly dominant strategies, 35
Tournament theory, 216
Ultimatum game
    generally, 135
    Shame and, 160

INSOLVENCY
See Corporation Law, this index

INSURANCE LAW
Agency model of contracts of insurance, 234
Capital adequacy regulation, 76 et seq.

INTELLECTUAL PROPERTY LAW
Generally, 113 et seq.
Access to innovations and further innovation, 115
Algorithms, patentability, 123
Appropriability problem, 114
Audio recording, 118
Biotechnology protection
    generally, 120
    DNA sequences, 130

INTELLECTUAL PROPERTY LAW
—Cont'd
Biotechnology protection—Cont'd
    Patentability, 124
    Products, biotech, 126
    Utility requirement for patentability, 130 et seq.
Cable television competition, 118
Contractual protection of rights in, 134
DNA sequences
    generally, 120
    Patent protection, 130
Economic foundations of, 114 et seq.
Efficient copyright protection legislation, 134
Fair use, 134
Idea/expression distinction, 121
Incentive/access balance, 116
Nature, products of, 119
Protecting new technologies, 116
Public goods problem, 114
Satellite transmission, 118
Software, form of protection of
    generally, 114
    Algorithms, 123
    Copyright protection, 120
    Literary works protection, 117
    Patent law protection, 119, 122
Utility, patentable, and biotechnology research, 130 et seq.

LANDLORD AND TENANT
Agency model of relationship between, 233

LEGISLATION AND LEGISLATIVE PROCESSES
Generally, 101 et seq.
Agency model of relationship between legislators and regulators, 234
Behavioral effects of laws, 172
Bicameralism, 112
Changing social norms, 161 et seq.
Copyright, efficient protection legislation, 134
ERISA, economic analysis of, 195
Expressive function of law, 140, 164, 170
Government action and social norms, 161 et seq.
Intent, legislative, 112
Interest groups, 104
Market constraints and vote trading, 105
Market theory of electoral process, 101
Pork, 103
Preferences, cycles of, 108
Roles, redefining by law, 148
Social norms, changing through government action, 161 et seq.

LEGISLATION AND LEGISLATIVE PRO-CESSES—Cont'd
Vote trading, electoral market constraint and, 105

MARKETS
See Contract Law, this index

MONOPOLIES AND RESTRAINTS OF TRADE
Cable television competition, 118
Cartel practices, 193
Economic analysis of law, 189 et seq.
Inefficient contract terms and monopolistic practices, 85
Price and non price competition, 194
Pricesetters and pricetakers, 30
Retail price maintenance, 193
Values and consequences, 189 et seq.
Warranties in monopolized markets, 87

NEGLIGENCE
See Tort Law, this index

NORMS
See Social Norms, this index

PARETO IMPROVEMENTS
Collective action, 165
Private property and, 180
Social norms and, 145n

PARTNERSHIP
Agency relations between partners, 232

PATENTS
See Intellectual Property Law, this index

PENALTIES
See also Criminal Law, this index
Carrots and torts, 203 et seq.

POSITIVE ANALYSIS
Generally, 190

PRIVACY RIGHTS
Property rights and, 181

PRODUCTS LIABILITY
Risk misperception by product buyers, 88

PROPERTY LAW
Agency models, 238
Boundaries
  Costs and benefits, 177
  Highways on, 178
  Live and let live, rule of, 179
  Relaxation of boundary rules, 177
  Strong boundaries and tort principles, 179

PROPERTY LAW—Cont'd
Boundaries—Cont'd
  Temporal, 185
  Waste and temporal boundaries, 185
Coase Theorem and property rights, 188
Collective action problem, 179
Common areas
  generally, 176
  Agency model of behavior with respect to, 238
Condemnation vs landmark status designation, 199
Consensual commons, 178
Easements of lateral support, 180
Fences, 175
Highways, takings of private property for, 178
Landmark status designations, property rights and, 199
Lateral support easements, 180
Nuisances
  Nontrespassory invasion, 183
  Reciprocal nuisances, 179
  Social costs, 182
Privacy rights and property rights, 181
Social costs, nuisances and, 182
Strong boundaries and tort principles, 179
Temporal boundaries, 185
Transaction costs and property rights, 175 et seq.
Trespass and nuisance, 183
Values and consequences, 189 et seq.
Waste and temporal boundaries, 185

PUBLIC CHOICE
See Legislation and Legislative Processes, this index

RATIONALITY
Decision making and, 192
Essential assumption of, 191

REGRESSION ANALYSIS
Generally, 1 et seq.
Bell curve distributions, 14
Burden of proof, 26
Civil rights studies of wage discrimination, 10 et seq.
Collinear variables, 23
Complex relationships, 3n
Computerized programs, 17
Consistent estimators, 9
Data mining, 27
Dependent or endogenous variable defined, 4
Dummy variables, 11
Earnings model
  generally, 2 et seq.

REGRESSION ANALYSIS—Cont'd
Earnings model—Cont'd
  Discriminatory wage practices, proof of, 10 et seq.
Econometrics defined, 1
Error types, 18
Errors in variables, 22
Estimated error, 5
Estimators, 8
Explanatory or exogenous variables generally, 4
  Multiple regression analysis of large numbers of, 7
Extraneous variables, 22
Gender rights studies of wage discrimination, 10 et seq.
Generalized least squares, 10
Goodness of fit, 19 et seq.
Linear estimators, 10
Linearity of relationships, 4
Measurement error and noise factors, 22
Minimum SSE criterion
  Definition, 6
  Properties of, 8
Multicollinearity, 23 et seq.
Multiple regression, 6 et seq.
Noise factors
  Assumptive values, 5
  Definition, 4
  Measurement error and, 22
  Measurement problems, 13
  Randomness of noise term, 8
Nonlinear relationships, 3n, 4
Normal distribution, 14
Null hypothesis, 14
Omitted variable problems, 20 et seq.
Omitted variables bias
  Definition, 2
  Multiple regression and, 6
One- and two-tailed tests, 15 et seq.
Parameters
  Estimates, 4
  Statistically significant parameters, 27
  Problems of, 20 et seq.
Proxies for imprecisely measurable variables, 26
Scatter diagrams, 3
Standard error, 14
Statistical inferences, 14
Statistical significance assessments, 1
Statistically significant parameters, 27
T-distributions
  generally, 14
  Standard tables, 17n
Total variation measurements, 19

REGRESSION ANALYSIS—Cont'd
T-distributions—Cont'd
Type I and type II errors, 18
Unbiased estimators, 8
Unobservable variables, 22n
Unstable relationships between variables, 3n
Variance defined, 9n
Weight of evidence and regression studies, 27

REGULATORY LAW
Generally, 203 et seq.
Agency model of relationship between legislators and regulators, 234
Bargaining around rules, 203
Capital solvency regulation, 65 et seq.
Child raising norms, incentives to promote, 210
Deregulation, 194
Disclosure regulations and efficient markets, 95
Freedom of contract and, 81 et seq.
Incentives, positive and negative, 203 et seq.
Landmark status designations, property rights and, 199
Market regulation and freedom of contract, 81 et seq.
Seatbelt laws, 206
Secondary effects of regulation, 210
Second-level costs, 208
Unintended consequences, 210
Usury prohibitions and freedom of contract, 100

RESTRAINTS OF TRADE
See Monopolies and Restraints of Trade, this index

REWARDS
Carrots and torts, 203 et seq.

RISK
Buyers, misperception of product risks by, 88
Corporate debt holders and equity owners, attitudes of towards risk, 67
Financial firms, capital adequacy regulation of, 76
Social norms and, 137

ROLES
See Social Norms, this index

SALES
See Contract Law, this index

SECURITIES REGULATION
Broker-dealers, capital adequacy regulation of, 76
Capital solvency regulation, 65 et seq.
Command-and-control regulation, 69
Debt holders vs equity owners, protection of interests of, 68
Ex ante and ex post regulation, 70
Federal vs state regulatory regimes, 70
Federalism, regulatory, 77
Institutional investors, effect of, 80
Modigliani–Miller irrelevance hypothesis of corporate value, 67
Par value system of regulation
    generally, 71
    Failure of, 73
Watered stock and par value system of regulation, 72

SOCIAL COSTS
Incentives to perform contracts and, 55
Nuisance law and, 182
Transactions costs and, 59

SOCIAL NORMS
Generally, 135 et seq.
Agency model of, 235
Altering norms, appropriateness of, 140
Altruism and, 160
Ascriptive roles, 151
Autonomy and, 167 et seq.
Bandwagons, norm
    generally, 140
    Divisions in self and, 153
    Sanctions and, 153
    Tipping point, 142
Behavior influencing, 141
Behavioral effects of laws, 172
Beliefs and, 152
Cascades, norm
    generally, 140
    Definition, 142
Caste societies, 168
Child raising norms, incentives to promote, 210
Choices, preferences as, 154 et seq.
Codified, 144
Collective action problems, resolution of, 145, 165
Compliance standards, 153
Conduct, expressive, 150
Conformists and nonconformists, 145
Constraining qualities of, 145
Contested norms, 146
Criminal law, social norms as alternative to, 167
Criminal laws, changing norms through, 164
Cross-cultural understanding and, 145n

SOCIAL NORMS—Cont'd
Definition, 143
Despised norms, compliance with, 153
Disintegrating, effect of, 145
Eavesdropping, 181
Education, changing through, 163
Enforcement, 144
Entrepreneurs, norm
    Definition, 140
    Political actors as, 153
Expressive conduct, 150
Expressive functions of laws, 170
Extremeness aversion, 155
Facilitative qualities of, 145
Flouting, 145
Freedom and roles, 147
Freedom reducing, 144
Free-riding and, 160
Government action and, 161 et seq.
Law, redefining roles by, 148
Littering behavior, 135
Majority behaviors and beliefs, 153
Metapreferences, 157
Normative analysis, 190
Pareto improvements
    generally, 145n
    Collective action, 165
Paternalism and, 162
Perfectionism and, 162
Persuasion, changing through, 163
Political actors as norm entrepreneurs, 153
Preferences
    generally, 139
    Choices and, 154 et seq.
    Definition, 142
Prisoner's dilemma theory, 166
Propaganda and, 145
Rationality and
    generally, 139
    Relation between, 161
Reputational benefit, 144
Risk-averse and risk-inclined behavior, 137
Role-specific norms, 147
Sanctions
    Enforcement through, 144
    Norm bandwagons effected by, 153
Seatbelt laws, 206
Shame and reaction to, 159
Society, norm requirements of, 167
Subculture norms, 145
Subsidies of behavior, norms as
    generally, 141
    Changing, 164
Surrogate motherhood contracts, 195

SOCIAL NORMS—Cont'd

Taxes on behavior, norms as
    generally, 141
    Changing, 164
Teenagers and norm rejection, 146
Testing norms, 162
Tipping point and norm bandwagons,
    142
Tools for changing, 163
Ultimatum game, shame and responses
    to, 160
Willingness to pay and willingness to
    accept, 158 et seq.

SOFTWARE PROTECTION

See Intellectual Property Law, this in-
    dex

STATISTICS

See Regression Analysis, this index

STATUTES

See Legislation and Legislative Process-
    es, this index

STRATEGY

See Game Theory, this index

STRICT LIABILITY

See Tort Law, this index

TORT LAW

Agency models, 238
Bargaining around rules, 203
Carrots and torts, 203 et seq.
Corporate torts and limited liability of
    shareholders, 75
Discontinuities, 219
Due care and liability

TORT LAW—Cont'd

Due care and liability—Cont'd
    Game theory analysis, 33 et seq.
    Hand formula, 192
Hand negligence formula, 192
Incentives, positive and negative, 203 et
    seq.
Liability and due care
    Game theory analysis, 33 et seq.
    Hand formula, 192
Negligence and contributory negligence,
    37
Nuisance, 179
Positive and negative incentives, 203 et
    seq.
Privacy rights and trespass law, 181
Rescuers' actions, 194
Strict liability, Hand formula analysis of,
    192
Tort principles, strong boundaries and,
    179
Trespass, 179
Values and consequences, 189 et seq.

TRANSACTION COSTS

See also Coase Theorem, this index
Contract default rules, 62
Contract law damage measures and, 59
Property rights and, 175 et seq., 188
Regulatory carrot/stick approaches, 206
Rescuer liability, analysis of, 194

TRUSTS

Spendthrift trusts, economic analysis of,
    191

WARRANTIES

Risk misperception by product buyers,
    88